MW01539153

Selective Mutism In Children And Teenagers

Scarlett R. Harris

All rights reserved. Copyright © 2023 Scarlett R. Harris

COPYRIGHT © 2023 Scarlett R. Harris

All rights reserved.

No part of this book must be reproduced, stored in a retrieval system, or shared by any means, electronic, mechanical, photocopying, recording, or otherwise, without written permission from the publisher.

Every precaution has been taken in the preparation of this book; still the publisher and author assume no responsibility for errors or omissions. Nor do they assume any liability for damages resulting from the use of the information contained herein.

Legal Notice:

This book is copyright protected and is only meant for your individual use. You are not allowed to amend, distribute, sell, use, quote or paraphrase any of its part without the written consent of the author or publisher.

Introduction

This is a comprehensive resource designed to provide a thorough understanding of selective mutism and effective strategies for its treatment. This guide is a valuable tool for parents, teachers, and therapists seeking to support children struggling with selective mutism. Through a detailed exploration of various aspects of the condition and its treatment, the guide equips readers with practical interventions and techniques.

The guide starts by introducing the concept of selective mutism, outlining its diagnostic criteria according to the DSM V. It delves into the different levels and potential causes of selective mutism, helping readers gain insights into the factors that contribute to this condition. It also examines the common characteristics exhibited by children with selective mutism, including social anxiety symptoms, avoidance behavior, reinforced anxiety, shyness, language difficulties, and other associated symptoms.

A significant portion of the guide is dedicated to providing a holistic treatment approach, emphasizing collaboration among parents, teachers, and therapists. The guide presents an ecosystems approach, recognizing the interconnectedness of home and school environments in a child's life. It outlines the roles and interventions of each stakeholder in the child's support system, ensuring a cohesive and comprehensive treatment plan.

The guide offers separate manuals for parents, teachers, and therapists, tailored to their respective roles in the child's treatment journey. These manuals include detailed content, interventions, strategies, and techniques that address the challenges of selective mutism in different settings. From home-based sessions to school-based interventions, the guide provides step-by-step guidance on creating a supportive environment and helping children overcome their anxiety.

Throughout the therapist's manuals, the guide outlines the stages of therapy, incorporating behavioral, cognitive-behavioral, and psychoeducational tools. It provides insights into understanding and addressing the anxiety that underlies selective mutism, using techniques like cognitive restructuring and relaxation techniques.

Overall, this book is a comprehensive and structured resource that equips readers with the knowledge and tools to effectively address selective mutism in children. With its focus on collaboration and holistic treatment, the guide aims to help children find their voices and thrive in both home and school environments.

Contents

What is Selective Mutism?

Selective mutism (SM) is a social anxiety disorder in which children and young people consistently fail to speak in select situations despite their ability to understand and use language. Children with SM usually speak to family members at home but do not speak in kindergarten or school. The speech patterns of each child with SM vary along a continuum of severity—from children who speak to everyone outside school and to select peers in school, to children who are unable to speak to anyone in school, including peers and staff. Some will not speak to anyone outside their home or only to certain family members inside their home, and rarely some do not speak to nuclear family members inside the home. Often there is a marked contrast between the outgoing and communicative child at home and the inhibited, introverted functioning at school.

When another condition exists that accounts better for the failure to speak, such as pervasive developmental disorder, retardation, psychosis, or a lack of language skills, then the child is not considered to have SM. However, one can have SM together with another condition, such as autism. In these cases, the SM should be treated in order to optimize the child's social interaction.

There are additional traits that research has found to be associated with SM; again, each child has a unique set of characteristics. Research studies have found that over 90% of children with SM suffer from social anxiety, and 30–70% have some language or speech impairment. Other associated conditions could include shyness and hypersensitivity, oppositional behavior, stubbornness and perfectionism, neuro-developmental disorder or delay (often auditory processing delay), and learning disabilities.

There is often a genetic component of shyness or a history of SM in one of the child's parents or siblings. In addition, bilingualism, immigration and disconnectedness from the cultural milieu of the outside society are sometimes found in the families of children with SM.

No link has been found between intelligence and SM, and no connection has been found in the large research studies between traumatic events and SM. For a sensitive, anxious child, seemingly everyday events may be experienced as traumatic, such as being shouted at by a teacher, being embarrassed in front of a class, or being mocked by peers for a mispronunciation.

Most research has found that the incidence of SM is around 0.7% or seven children in every one thousand, and it has been found to be three times that number in children from bilingual homes. It is most prevalent between the ages of four and eight;onset usually occurs when the child first enters an educational framework in which speech is expected, but sometimes onset is gradual—the child's speech output diminishes until he eventually stops speaking.

DSM V Diagnostic Criteria
(American Psychiatric Association)

Selective Mutism (formerly Elective Mutism)

A. Consistent failure to speak in specific social situations (in which there is an expectation for speaking, e.g. at school) despite speaking in other situations.

B. The disturbance interferes with educational or occupational achievement or with social communication.

C. The duration of the disturbance is at least one month (not limited to the first month of school).

D. The failure to speak is not due to a lack of knowledge of, or comfort with, the spoken language required in the social situation.

E. The disturbance is not better accounted for by a Communication Disorder (e.g. stuttering) and does not occur exclusively during the course of a Pervasive Developmental Disorder, Schizophrenia, or other Psychotic Disorder.

Levels of Selective Mutism

The degree of severity of selective mutism varies from child to child. At one end of the continuum is a child who speaks to no one outside his closest family and even fails to speak to some immediate family members; at the other end may be a child who speaks to everyone —adults and peers—except for his teacher in school. The following division of four levels of SM can be broken down into numerous subdivisions.Furthermore,the same child functions differently in different contexts. The child with the most severe SM in kindergarten may have absolutely normal behavior at home and at his grandparents', whereas a child with mild SM in school may also have mild SM in the presence of any non–nuclear family member. Thus these categorizations are not absolute within the functioning of any real child.

1. The most severe level is of total **non-communication** in the places where the child fails to speak. He barely uses nonverbal communication such as nodding. He may have hardly any facial expression, as though he wears a mask.

He may be "frozen" in his body gestures, so that he fails to move with spontaneity and may even have to be physically moved from the standing to sitting position by a teacher or to have a spoon placed in his hand before he begins to eat. These children are frequently misdiagnosed in their kindergarten as autistic, and staff are often amazed when the parents or therapist report regular age and stage appropriate behavior at home.

2. **Nonverbal communication:** The child communicates nonverbally in the place in which his SM is manifest. He may both respond and initiate nonverbally, or it may be hard for him to initiate. He may use gestures such as nodding yes and no and pointing; use facial expressions such as smiling and frowning; he may communicate via recordings of his voice on iPads or computers; whisper to a chosen spokesperson, peer, or a family member who relays the message. The child at this level may participate to a greater or lesser degree in kindergarten or school; some children with SM who communicate nonverbally do absolutely everything in school or kindergarten except speak. They may function well socially and perform in school choirs (without emitting a sound!). Others may be reticent and rarely participate in school activities.

3. **Whispering and emitting sounds:** The child may be able to emit sounds, such as animal sounds, clicking with his tongue, whistling, or pronouncing consonants such as "t" or "s." The child fails to emit words at an appropriate volume, but may whisper.

4. **Verbal communication:** The child says words at an audible volume. He may still be reticent, and progress may be gradual—first speaking to select staff or peers and

slowly generalizing to more people. Initial verbalizations may be reading from cards, indirect speech, or only select words such as yes and no. Some children, once they break the verbal barrier, speak freely to everyone, as though a dam has been burst.

Causes of Selective Mutism

Selective mutism is caused by the interaction between the nature of the child and external factors—nature and nurture. One can conceptualize this as various factors fitting into one of three groups: predisposing factors, triggers, and maintaining factors.

Predisposing factors include elements of the child's psychological and physiological makeup that cause him to be vulnerable to selective mutism. This could include an anxious or shy nature, stubbornness and perfectionism, or a family history of shyness. Many children with SM have some type of speech difficulty, including lacking confidence in their expressive language due to bilingualism.

When there is a combination of predisposing factors that heighten the child's vulnerability to SM, along with triggers—events such as kindergarten admission or a geographical move which are challenging or unsettling for the child—the scales can tip and bring about the onset of SM.

Causes of SM: Predisposing and Maintaining Factors, Triggers (Adapted from Shipon-Blum 2007)

Predisposing factors:

- Child's anxiety, shyness, timidity, hyper-sensitivity
- Family history of shyness, anxiety, or selective mutism—can include anxious parents, anxious behavior modeling by parents
- Speech impairment of child—usually expressive language
- Bilingualism and disconnectedness from the predominant culture
- Neuro-developmental disorder or delay, often auditory processing disorder

Triggers:

- School or kindergarten admission
- Frequent geographical moves
- Family moving to area with different spoken language
- Negative reactions to child talking—bullying, shouting, mocking etc.

Maintaining factors:

- Social isolation of families
- Misdiagnosis (oppositional behavior, autism, retardation)
- Lack of early and appropriate intervention
- Lack of understanding by teachers, families, psychologists
- Reinforcement by increased attention or affection
- Heightened anxiety levels caused by pressure to speak
- Ability to convey messages nonverbally
- Lack of belief in ability to overcome SM

Maintaining factors facilitate the entrenchment of the condition—potentially slowing the child's recovery from selective mutism. For example, if SM is misdiagnosed in school as oppositional behavior, and is therefore not afforded appropriate treatment, or if there is great pressure on the child to speak which heightens his anxiety levels and paradoxically makes it harder for him to speak, then the duration of the SM may be lengthened.

It should be noted that the table above includes a broad list of possible partial causes of SM; no one child will have more than several of the causes, and many will have no more than a couple of them. When assessing or treating a child with SM it is important not to attempt to project on the child all that has been found in research to have some association with SM, and thus to fabricate a clinical picture far more severe than the actual traits of the child who stands before you. Failing to see the mental health and personality assets along with the difficulties of the child with SM can lead to a downward spiral wherein parents feel that their child is misunderstood, which may in turn generate a defensive parental stance. Furthermore, discerning and building on the strengths of the child with SM is vital both for the child's self-esteem and for his fortitude in overcoming SM.

Let's illustrate the interaction between the **predisposing** factors and **triggers** and the consequent **maintaining** factors with five year old Don, whom we introduced at the beginning of the book.

*Don was genetically **predisposed** to be a shy and anxious child; his parents and siblings were also prone to timidity and worry. He came from a Spanish-speaking home, and when he started preschool, he spoke poor English. This, together with his perfectionism, was a hurdle to jump when speaking in kindergarten—he was painfully* aware of his English-language deficiency, and this heightened his social anxiety when speech was required. His family maintained an insular social circle of Spanish-speaking friends and rarely stepped into the local English-speaking society. These were predisposing factors effecting Don when he entered his first English-speaking kindergarten at the age of four. The **trigger** of entering kindergarten, having to function within a large and boisterous social group in a language he barely knew, together with his predisposing factors of shyness, anxiety, and perfectionism, and with his family setting and functioning, may account for his silent avoidance of speech on his first day at kindergarten.

How was his **SM maintained?** A viscous cycle called reinforced anxiety was set in motion—Don's silence in settings in which he was unsure of himself or when he had to speak in English lowered his anxiety levels. This is illustrated and explained shortly. In addition, his parents did not venture out into English-speaking circles so that Don was hardly exposed to English within the secure setting of his home with his parents. He absorbed from his parents' avoidance of English that there was something dangerous or at best undesirable about speaking English to strangers. While his disorder was diagnosed as SM, his obvious intelligence and competence in the academic kindergarten tasks disinclined his parents from seeking help early on. He benefited from much maternal attention due to his SM—his sensitive mother empathized with his suffering in kindergarten and showered him with playfulness and love on his daily return home.

Let's further explore the causes of SM, and the possible interplay between distinct elements: **Predisposing factors** include the traits with which the child is born - such as his level of sensitivity, shyness, and anxiety, which develop further as a result of his interaction with his environment. Thus a child who is born with a tendency to be anxious may observe one of his parents' insecure social communication with strangers, and this may increase his guardedness with people beyond the confines of his immediate family. A child who comes from a bilingual family and has a tendency toward perfectionism may be daunted by the task of speaking in a language in which he feels uncertain, and is unsure that he will be able to speak sufficiently well to satisfy his self-critical standards. A child with neurodevelopmental difficulties, such as slower than usual auditory processing, together with an anxious nature, may encounter difficulty on both fronts when asked a question in kindergarten, and may refrain from responding. Below we discuss in more detail how shyness, anxiety, and other traits associated with SM including perfectionism and neurodevelopmental delays may intersect with SM.

Triggers are environmental situations that together with the constellation of traits and experiences that the child has accrued up until that point are sufficient to induce selective mutism. The most common trigger is entering an educational framework, which is daunting and full of challenges for any child – including establishing relationships with authority figures; developing new friendships and managing peer relationships with all sorts of children; mastering cognitive and motor skills; abiding by rules; and managing promises of rewards and fear of punishments implicit in kindergarten or school. For a child who may have a combination of shyness and insecurity in the spoken language, the demands of entering kindergarten may generate a defense mechanism of not responding, thus distancing himself from the threatening situation, and giving himself a method (albeit dysfunctional) of control. Other triggers may be geographical moves, which involve adjusting to not only a new school setting, but also new peer relationships and physical surroundings, together with the heartbreak of leaving developed social ties and familiar environments. When a new language is thrown into the stew, which perhaps exacerbates some objective language difficulty, the sum total may be beyond the ability of the child to adaptively contend with.

Maintaining factors, as illustrated by Don's case, are often the most natural way a caring parent will attempt to sooth and protect her child. This could include an abundance of attention, a relaxation of rules, or sometimes allowing a child to extract himself from the anxiety provoking situation and stay at home. The parents' speedy removal of the child from the anxiety provoking situation may indeed ease his discomfort, yet it also prevents the development of coping by disabling the response that is vital in overcoming anxiety – **habituation**. When a child is immediately rescued from any situation requiring speech, he cannot habituate to it, nor understand that he can tolerate the discomfort involved. More about this soon in the mechanics of "reinforced anxiety."

An unfortunate maintaining factor is often the misdiagnosis and failure to treat SM. School staff and mental health professionals alike who are unfamiliar with SM may think that the child will "decide" to speak imminently, failing to realize that he is not voluntarily withholding speech. Others may feel that that child is oppositional or that the abstention is normal shyness and doesn't require intervention. Children with SM can be overlooked as they usually are not disruptive to the class, and may be perceived as blessedly silent and accommodating. This is in contrast to acting out children who may make others perceive their need for help through their disruptive behavior. Even when correctly diagnosed and understood,children with SM are frequently left without treatment as they appear to have found a modus vivendi which may include attending school, some social interaction, and academic achievement. The caregivers and educators may not realize how on the one hand, the child is suffering as a result of his inability to speak, and on the other, development on at least certain fronts is curtailed by his SM – be it social skills, academic achievements and appropriate placement, or self-confidence and feelings of competence. Last but by no means least, there may be a lack of understanding regarding how effectively SM can usually be improved and overcome with therapy or parents' and teachers' interventions. Early intervention is usually effective and can circumvent suffering and enable healthy development.

Characteristics of Children with SM

Research has pinpointed certain characteristics that have been found to be associated with SM. These include social anxiety, perfectionism, language issues, and neurodevelopmental delays. Here we will describe the most commonly found traits.

Social-Anxiety Symptoms

The trait most commonly associated with SM is social anxiety— found in over 90 percent of children with SM (Black and Uhde 1995). These children may be shy when meeting new people and anxious when in a crowd of people; they may dislike being in the spotlight and, augmented by their trait of perfectionism, be afraid of responding inadequately. Anxiety can also be associated with eating in public or going to the bathroom outside the home. Anxiety can cause psychosomatic physical symptoms such as stomachaches and headaches. It is also behind the frozen demeanor of the child with severe SM, who appears to have an expressionless mask on his or her face as well as stiff and abrupt movements. This is often incorrectly diagnosed as due to gross motor problems, when the root may be anxiety. In these cases, when the anxiety is alleviated, the motor problems often miraculously disappear! Some older children with SM seem to be anxiety-free—they appear to interact socially with aplomb, yet the anxiety may be a relic from the time when the SM became entrenched; over the years the child may have gained confidence and become less anxious, but the lack of speech has remained.

In addition to the lack of speech, many children with SM display timidity in their social communication, some selectively in kindergarten, and others in many settings. They may avoid eye contact, respond but not initiate contact, and feel unsure as to how to maintain social interaction. When such children do not receive help early on, social skills deficits may accrue.

Avoidance behavior

How is speech avoidance acquired, and how does it become entrenched? How does the mechanism of anxiety work to establish the entrenched behavior of not speaking to certain people or in specific settings, and how can that anxiety be extinguished?

Let's take a look at how SM becomes entrenched: A child who has a propensity to anxiety may enter kindergarten for the first time at the age of three. He may be bewildered and flustered by the multitude of children and perturbed by the separation from his mother. He might be vicariously scared by witnessing the teacher shouting at another child who has misbehaved. He is then approached by the same teacher and is in a state of high anxiety. He is asked a question, is unsure of himself (perhaps there is some linguistic difficulty thrown into the pot), and is apprehensive of the teacher's reaction. He abstains from responding and consequently feels less anxious. He comes to associate non-speech with low anxiety. So the next time he is approached and spoken to, he will refrain from answering; his anxiety level will plummet, and this will cause his silent response to be reinforced. This is schematized below.

Reinforced Anxiety

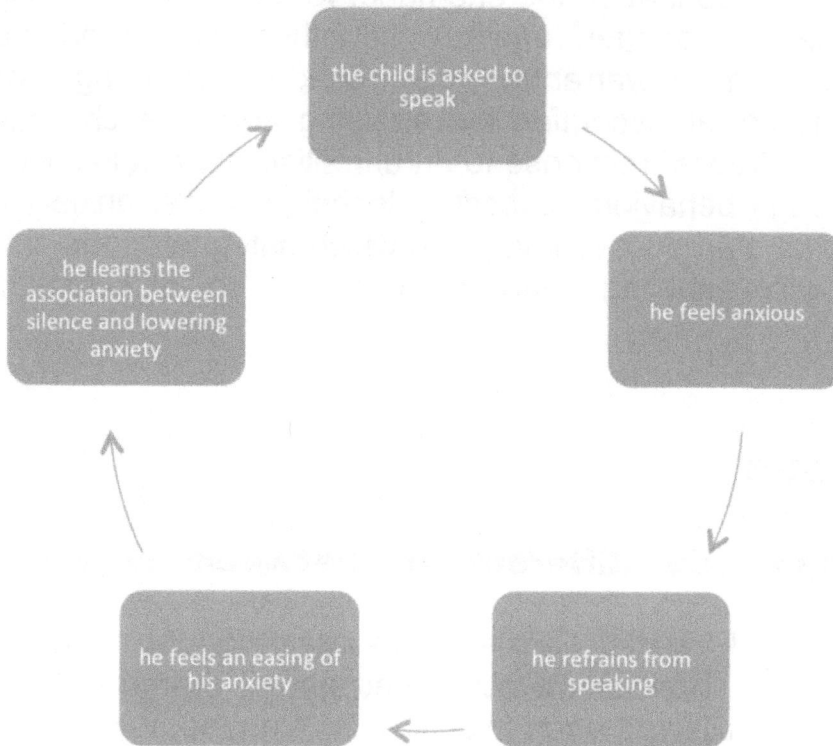

```
                    ┌──────────────────┐
                    │  the child is    │
                    │  asked to speak  │
                    └──────────────────┘
   ┌─────────────────┐               ┌──────────────────┐
   │ he learns the   │               │ he feels anxious │
   │ association     │               │                  │
   │ between silence │               └──────────────────┘
   │ and lowering    │
   │ anxiety         │               ┌──────────────────┐
   └─────────────────┘               │ he refrains from │
   ┌─────────────────┐               │ speaking         │
   │ he feels an     │               └──────────────────┘
   │ easing of his   │
   │ anxiety         │
   └─────────────────┘
```

This is the cycle that has to be interrupted in therapy or by teachers' or parents' intervention. In chapter 8 on cognitive-behavioral techniques, we present an alternative, adaptive cycle of lowering anxiety and enabling speech.

Anxiety is a necessary and positive part of our feelings. It safeguards us in the face of perceived danger; if we see a car fast approaching us, our fear will ready our sympathetic nervous system, giving us a burst of energy, increasing the blood supply, and preparing our muscles for action. The "fight or flight or freeze" response is activated—in this case a "flight" response would be to jump out of the way of the advancing car. Regulation of the level of anxiety is vital so that on the one hand, we do not expose ourselves to unnecessary danger, and on the other, we do not paralyze ourselves from unwarranted fear. Children suffering from SM respond to social discomfort by refraining from speech. This is an unadaptive "freeze" response to an unrealistic fear. It is important to learn through behavioral exposure techniques that anxiety can be regulated at a productive level, one which safeguards the child from danger while enabling adaptive, normative social communication responses.

Shyness

How can one differentiate between shyness and anxiety?

Shyness and social anxiety disorder (SAD) share many characteristics. How can a concerned parent discern between the two? Social anxiety is often mistaken for extreme shyness, and the vast majority of people suffering from social anxiety do not receive treatment, which is lamentable, as therapy is often effective. The symptoms that distinguish shyness from social anxiety are the intensity of the fear, the degree of avoidance, and the impairment of functioning that it causes in a person's life. People with social anxiety don't feel nervous before going to a party in the same way a shy person might. They may worry about the party for days beforehand, lose sleep due to anxiety, and have strong physiological symptoms of anxiety during the feared situation such as increased heartbeat, sweating, or trembling. The person usually realizes that his fears are irrational and that they are beyond his control. Sometimes children who suffer from SAD may not develop appropriate social behaviors and, as they grow with the disorder, the social fears may be a part of their way of life in which avoidance is a prominent defense mechanism. Sufferers may be socially isolated, and later on in life, there may be a tendency to depression.

What is the difference between shyness and introversion?
Being shy and being introverted aren't the same thing, although they may look similar. An introvert enjoys time alone and gets emotionally drained after spending a lot of time with others. A shy person doesn't necessarily want to be alone but is afraid to interact with others.

Consider two children in the same classroom, one introverted and one shy. The teacher is organizing an activity for all the children in the room. The introverted child wants to remain at her desk and read a book because that is what she prefers to do. The shy child wants to join the other children but remains at her desk because she is afraid to join them.

Children can be helped to overcome their shyness so that they can engage in activities they are attracted to, but introversion is a fixed characteristic like hair color or height. Not all introverts are shy— many are not; an introvert will have lower requirements for social activities and stimulation than an extrovert.

While therapy can help the shy person, trying to encourage an introvert to be an outgoing extrovert can be stressful and upsetting because it is attempting to alter a basic trait. Introverts can learn coping strategies to help them deal with social situations, but they will always be introverts. There are many positive traits associated with introversion, such as a rich inner world, introspection, and independence of thought. It is important that teachers and parents respect the introverted child's tendencies, appreciate her strengths, and do not try to turn her into someone she isn't. (Note the fixture in any introvert's report card "Must participate more in class!") Susan Cain's excellent book *Quiet* extols the virtues of the introvert.

Don, who we described above, has both the social anxiety inherent in SM, and he is an introvert. While he enjoys social activities, he spends much of his time playing solitary games; the optimal amount of social stimulation he requires is much lower than that of his extroverted sister, who is happiest when surrounded by friends and family. For Don, the aim of therapy should be to enable him to speak at will, not to ensure that he is constantly chatting and interacting socially, which goes against his introverted nature.

Language difficulties, bilingualism

Not surprisingly, language and SM are intimately connected—this is the symptom through which the child's social anxiety is expressed. Research studies have reported that between 30 and 70 percent of children with SM have language difficulties. An anxious child who is unsure about how well he can express himself, or is perhaps concerned that others will mock his pronunciation, may develop SM. It is important to note that many children with SM have no language difficulties.

Bilingual children have higher language acquisition demands than most children. Acquiring a second language sequentially normally takes between three and six years, during which time functioning in a language in which the child is not fully proficient may affect his self-esteem.

In our research (Elizur and Perednik 2003) we found that the incidence of SM for bilingual children was three times that of children who spoke only one language. The combination of several vulnerabilities—innate, learned, and situational—could together amount to sufficient stress to cause SM. For example, consider a child who has a tendency to anxiety, is unsure about expressing himself in a second language and perhaps feels insecure when outside the confines of the insular immigrant subculture within which his family lives. This constellation of causal factors, together with anxiety provoking triggers such as entering kindergarten, may be sufficient to facilitate SM.

Parents should pay attention to the language skills their child displays in her mother tongue in order to distinguish between difficulties inherent in bilingual language acquisition and objective language difficulties—which will usually be manifest in both languages.

Developmental disorder/delay

Research studies have found that up to 70 percent of children with SM have some developmental delay in addition to anxiety. As with bilingualism, the combination of stressors—innate, learned, and situational—may amount to a load sufficient to trigger SM. Delays may include fine and gross motor development, speech delays, emotional and social difficulties, and cognitive delays.

Auditory processing

Recent research (Bar-Haim et al. 2004) suggests that some children with selective mutism experience difficulty speaking while simultaneously processing incoming sounds. These children may gradually learn to restrict talking to the minimum in situations that require complex auditory processing.

Sensory Integration Dysfunction (DSI)

Sensory integration (also called sensory processing) refers to the way the nervous system receives messages from the senses and turns them into appropriate motor and behavioral responses. A person with DSI finds it difficult to process and act upon information received through the senses. Children who have sensory integration difficulties may feel sensation too strongly. As a result, they may have "freeze" responses to sensation, a condition called "sensory defensiveness." In the classroom or kindergarten setting, there are many people and much loud noise, which may cause sensory overload and distress, which together with the child's anxious nature causes him to freeze and be unable to speak. Neuroscientist A. Ayres described DSI as a neurological "traffic jam" that prevents certain parts of the brain from receiving the information needed to interpret sensory information in order to act on it—for example, to process a question from a kindergarten teacher and to respond verbally.

Perfectionism

Perfectionism often goes together with anxiety disorders, in that the anxious person may be concerned about impeccable functioning, as a result of which he or she is stressed about or refrains from doing a given task. One of the causes of SM is often the child's fear as to whether he'll be able to express himself adequately, whether his pronunciation is passable, and whether he knows the answer.

Slow-to-warm-up personality

This personality type is associated with anxiety and is often found in children with SM; it manifests as a lack of flexibility when adjusting to new situations and people and a relatively long "warming up" period before feeling confident and relaxed in a new setting. Thomas and Chess (1992) found that a cluster of traits make up this personality type, including low activity level, low adaptability, and low intensity of mood. These children show mildly negative responses when exposed to new situations but slowly become accustomed to them with repeated exposure. Children can be helped by being prepared in advance for new situations, by receiving support and encouragement during this adaptation period, and by being allowed the time to adjust and to warm up, which may be significantly longer than the norm.

Other Common Symptoms

Other anxiety disorders

All anxiety conditions have high comorbidity rates with other anxiety disorders. The anxious disposition that underlies SM may also cause separation anxiety, obsessive compulsive disorders, phobias, or other fears. One of the concerns in failing to treat SM is that it may eventually generalize to additional disorders such as agoraphobia or generalized anxiety disorder. However, it should be noted that many children with SM do not suffer from any other anxiety disorder.

Low frustration tolerance

Here again is the question of the chicken or the egg. Children who have restrained themselves during the entire school day may return home with a short fuse, letting out their frustration in the setting in which they speak freely.

Oppositional disorder

While it is often cited in the literature, oppositional behavior is more a byproduct than a cause or element of SM. The child who doesn't speak is rarely opposing anyone; rather she is paralyzed by fear. If it were oppositional, it would be the child's decision to speak or to be silent depending on whether she will lose or gain from speaking. A child suffering from selective mutism, like a phobia, is unable to speak, even though frequently she would give the world to be able to talk. While a child with SM may have oppositional traits, these are usually not causal rather comorbid.

Diathesis-Stress Model

In our research, we focused on bilingualism and SM, formulating a diathesis-stress model that elucidates how SM is caused (Elizur and Perednik 2003). "Diathesis" means "vulnerability or disposition." The theory proposes that each child's unique vulnerability interacts with stressors from the child's life experiences, causing selective mutism. The child's vulnerability can be made up of genetic, inborn traits, such as a tendency to anxiety; cognitive styles, or the child's way of thinking about what he experiences; and situational factors such as geographical moves. This predisposition interacts with events that are challenging for the child and activate his stress response. When the combination of the vulnerability and the stress overstep the child's toleration threshold, a maladaptive response can occur—in our case, the inability to respond verbally.

Protective factors are strengths that the child possesses, such as a gregarious nature or finely honed social skills, which may cushion him from the stressors and their interaction with his vulnerabilities.

This is a multi-causal developmental model, meaning that for any child, the combination of vulnerabilities and life experiences are unique to her and can be made up of a variety of constellations of the causes, stressors, and triggers we discuss in this chapter.

We found in our research some interesting constellations that are subtypes of SM. The bilingual children tended to have fewer comorbid symptoms such as developmental delays; it seemed that the burden of bilingualism together with an anxious disposition were often sufficient to trigger SM. On the other hand, the children in our study who were not bilingual tended to have more comorbid symptoms such as social-skills delays or learning disabilities.

In my clinical work with bilingual children, it seems likely that for many of them, had they not had the geographical moves and the need to cope with cultural incongruities and multiple languages, they may not have developed SM. In contrast,children without language difficulties or bilingualism have other factors that make up their individual constellation of traits and causes that brought about their SM.

We have seen that there is much diversity regarding the manifestation and causes of SM. Each child has a unique constellation of traits, which nearly always includes an anxious disposition and frequently includes language issues. These interact with situational stressors and life experiences to determine whether the child will develop SM. These multiple patterns of etiology and traits make it invaluable to assess each child's difficulties and strengths before embarking on therapy or intervention so that a suitable remedy for the respective causes of each child will be found in the makeup of his or her treatment.

Three-Way Integrative Treatment: Parents, Teachers, and Therapists

Treating SM in the Home and School: An Ecosystems Approach

Therapy at Home and in School

Expanding the Child's Comfort Zone

Three Points of View: Parents', Teacher's, Therapist's

Assessment

Three-Way Integrative Treatment: Parents, Teachers, and Therapists

Before moving on to the bulk of the book, which will be about how to treat SM, let's look at the three-way intervention we advocate involving the teacher, parents, and therapist. Here we will view the perspectives of the child, the parents, and the teachers and consider where interventions may take place most effectively.

Treating SM in the Home and School An Ecosystems Approach

Since SM is a condition that manifests in select settings, it is usually effective to treat the child in the place in which the symptom is most pronounced. A basic tenet of behavioral therapy is that at least part of the exposure to the feared stimuli takes place in the setting in which it occurs. In the case of SM, this is usually in the school or kindergarten, as well as in additional places such as grandparents' homes, doctor's offices, and so on. Families and teachers of children with SM should take an active part in implementing the therapy. Shortly we will describe how this multiple-location intervention may unfold.

Our ideal intervention would involve convening the triumvirate of people who are most significant in the child's attempt to battle SM—his parents, teachers, and therapist. Together they can construct an intervention plan that will include measures to help the child speak and improve his social communication in the places or with the people with whom it is currently impaired. The first joint step is to assess the child, to determine that she indeed has SM, and to estimate her strengths and difficulties.

Therapy at Home and in School

Therapy at home

We advocate, whenever possible, beginning the intervention with several home sessions. Traditional therapy as we know it takes place in a therapist's clinic. This may be appropriate for therapy with adults who are able to comprehend and retain insights achieved in therapy and to apply that understanding in their daily lives. It may be adequate for certain types of psychodynamic therapy for children, such as play therapy, in which the theory is that the corrective or insightful experience in therapy will mold the child's psyche and improve his way of seeing and interacting with the world. However, in behavioral therapy or cognitive behavioral therapy, the clinic setting has severe shortcomings.

Firstly, an inhibited child may take months or years to develop the open relationship with the therapist that is required in order for healing to take place. Many children come to our clinic for help after months or years of psychodynamic therapy,during which entire time they spoke to the therapist in a laconic whisper at best. When starting therapy with home sessions using our method, the child will usually speak to the therapist freely on average within four sessions.

Secondly, by establishing a warm relationship with the child initially in her home, you are circumventing the artificial setting of the clinic, giving the child the message that this therapeutic relationship is about her real life. The therapist will be able to see the abilities, tendencies, and traits of the child; her place in her family; and her family's characteristics and consequently plug all these strengths into the therapeutic process.

Thirdly, this professional/social alliance between family, therapist, and teacher is egalitarian—all parties have specialized knowledge that will be interchanged and pooled in a joint attempt to help the child. Usually a home visit exposes the positive sides of the families, whereas meeting an anxious family in a sterile clinic setting can bring out the most defensive, reticent modes of interacting—on both sides. As explained later on, the home sessions are planned by the therapist with the parents and then are led jointly. This cements the professional relationship between the parents and therapist, who share responsibility for the intervention's success.

Fourthly, the therapist is aligning herself with the family by inserting herself in to the home within the group of people with whom the child interacts socially with the greatest ease. By later transferring the therapy to the school, she is blurring the distinction that the child has constructed between how he relates to people within and outside of the home.

Therapy at school
How can one include the third corner of the triumvirate—teachers? They are vital players in this saga, as it is in their territory that the SM is usually most pronounced. It is best when they are involved from the start in four main ways: assessing the child's condition, planning the interventions, participating in home- and/or school-based sessions, and specific teachers' interventions. While this sounds like too much to ask of a teacher of a bustling, demanding class, it is usually a truly well-spent investment of time and effort—often a relatively contained teacher's intervention can circumvent months or years of attempting to help a child with SM. In this way a teacher can make a huge difference in the life of his student.

Teachers are vital to the assessment and planning stages; they have much information to offer regarding the child's school functioning, and their involvement in the planning ensures that two objectives are being met:they will be able to assist with the logistics of therapy within the school, and they may begin their own interventions early on, designed to foster growth and progress.

The aim is to start the therapy in the child's home, establishing a relaxed, verbal, playful relationship with him there, and then to move it to the school or kindergarten, transferring the relationship to the place in which the SM is strongest, enabling the child to speak therein. The relationship with the therapist is a kind of transitional object that brings a piece of home to the school. Once he is speaking to the therapist in school (the therapist can also be the teacher or parent, as we will see later), the aim will be to generalize speech to as many people and places as possible within the school or kindergarten. On the one hand, it is common sense and straightforward; on the other hand, it is based on behavioral premises and requires determination, consistency, warmth, empathy, and knowledge to ensure success.

Expanding the Child's Comfort Zone

Progress is achieved through successive, graduated steps; each step will ease the child toward the edge of his comfort zone, taking him closer to speech.

"Life begins at the end of your comfort zone."

"If you want something you never had, you've got to do something you've never done."

There is wisdom to be found on fridge magnets!

A comfort zone (CZ) is the area within which we feel relatively anxiety-free or in which anxiety remains tolerable. People lead most of their lives within their self-circumscribed comfort zone, where they feel quite unthreatened and in control. In order to grow and expand your behavioral repertoire, you may have to step to the periphery of your comfort zone and beyond. In the treatment of anxiety and SM, the trick is to work at the edge of the child's comfort zone, gradually expanding its boundaries.

How can a therapist or teacher know where the confines of the child's comfort zone lie? There are a few ways to know—firstly, empathy and intuition, estimating what the child is able to do without putting his anxiety on overload. Intuition involves trying to cognitively understand the child's ability to grow based on your knowledge and experience of him, and empathy is feeling how the child is emotionally at any given point in therapy. Herein lies the therapist's craft:the ability to understand, feel, and connect with another person in order to facilitate healing.

A second way of mapping the borders of a child's CZ is trial and error—each successive step is built based on the therapist's understanding of the child. If a step is attempted in therapy that is insurmountable for the child, that implies that it strayed too far beyond the edge of the child's comfort zone. In the following chapters, we will explain how to construct interventions in which the child's CZ is gradually expanded until speech and improved social communication enter into its confines!

Three Points of View: Parents', Teacher's, Therapist's

Let's take a look at the parents', therapist's, kindergarten teacher's, and Don's feelings at the onset of therapy. Don's parents, having become aware that his SM was not waning, were deeply concerned about his school placement one year from now. They were well read on the subject and wanted to pull out all the stops to help Don improve. They had been shocked at the end of the previous year's kindergarten party when they saw Don retreat inside his shell, frozen in his expression and unmovable on his mother's lap. This was in stark contrast with the other excited and boisterous children gleefully performing for their parents. Knowing how Don behaves so normally at home, they were critical of the kindergarten, wondering how he could be so communicative at home yet so withdrawn in kindergarten. It seemed to be an indictment of what the staff was, or was refraining from, doing.

During the initial meeting in the kindergarten with the therapist and parents, the teacher expressed concern about whether she could invest the time and effort we were suggesting, uncertain that her kindergarten had the resources required for Don to improve and skeptical about whether he could progress in a regular framework, thinking aloud that a special-education framework may be appropriate. On the other hand, while she saw that Don was non-communicative in kindergarten, she was not convinced that he was suffering or that she was obliged to help him, since he went through the motions of participating in the kindergarten learning activities and did not cause any disruption to other children or staff. His above-average intelligence and fine motor skills further created the impression that he was gaining all he needed academically and that perhaps this present state of affairs could continue. The combination of unwillingness to help, uncertainty that this was the required framework, and the contradictory thought that he could continue as he was for a while longer, was distressing for the parents to hear. She further insinuated that Don's parents were being both overprotective and over-demanding and that perhaps this was causing Don's problems. It looked like the meeting would end either in a parting of ways or with severe differences of opinion regarding how Don was feeling and what needed to be done.

One of the jobs of the therapist is to be a mediator between the sides, facilitating mutual understanding and cooperation. In an attempt to have all sides start the intervention from a place of understanding about what SM is and how it can be treated, I elucidated both what is known about SM and my clinical experience of what therapy involves, including how it is usually very effective, and I described how uplifting it can be for families and teachers. I also expressed genuine, deep appreciation for the parents' care and concern and for the teacher's understanding and professionalism. Both the clarification of what the teacher could do—stressing that it would be her decision regarding what she felt able to take upon herself—and giving her the respect of potentially being a significant agent of change in Don's life, changed her attitude dramatically. She was willing to try to help, and she would certainly enable kindergarten-based therapy sessions and involving the parents in the therapy. She was still cautious regarding how demanding the interventions I suggested that she attempt would be; the jury was still out on that. The parents were thrilled at her more hopeful outlook and greater willingness to help.

We discussed both the long-term general plan and what we would jointly be aiming for in the immediate future, as well as what each party would do to further treatment: Don's parents were to invite friends home and supervise the playdates, ensuring that a good time *was had. The structure of the playdates was to be as follows: As soon as the friends arrived, the mother would play a video of Don speaking with his siblings so that his voice would be heard by his friends; then they would play games that required a minimal amount of speech, in the hope that Don would speak to several classmates at home. The kindergarten teacher was to visit Don at home and would immediately be shown a video in which he spoke, hearing his voice for the first time! After that there was a chance that he would talk to her, and, failing that, they would have a pleasant and communicative hour in his home, seeing his bedroom, his toys, and family. The therapist would begin home visits in order to establish a comfortable, verbal, communicative relationship with Don before moving the therapy to the kindergarten. She would begin being inconspicuous and gradually approach him, eventually talking to him. This process is explained in detail in <u>chapter 6</u>, "the Therapist's Manual."*

What was Don feeling prior to the onset of therapy? From what I can surmise from conversations I had later on with Don as well as by observing him, Don felt unhappy in kindergarten, expending much energy on refraining from responding—not talking or emitting sounds, not revealing emotions through facial gestures, taking up as little space and attention as possible. He dreaded the moment that arrived daily when he had to leave his parents at the gate of the kindergarten, his facial expression becoming vacuous and stiff, and his joy of life leaving him for the morning. In short, he was not the natural Don he was at home—bubbly and chatty, full of curiosity and comments on everything that happened. In kindergarten he became cautious, quiet, and still. Though he was admired by other children for his intelligence and drawing ability, he was sidelined socially and could only watch the other children playing and interacting. He enjoyed doing his worksheets and drawings, yet there was always the burden of containing himself, not responding, and holding back.

While cognizant of his intelligence and skills, he was painfully aware that he was unable to speak or play in kindergarten, and he was different and less able in many ways than other children. The first time we met in the kindergarten, in a tiny storage room that served as the therapy room, he told me, "I can't speak to anyone else here; maybe in another year I will."

Assessment

It is important to have an accurate appraisal of the baseline functioning of the child who has SM at the inception of therapy—this includes his functioning at home, at school, and in other settings. A good starting place for initial assessment is a joint interview with the parents, teacher, and therapist. Unless it can be done discreetly, direct observation of the child with SM by the therapist is not recommended at this time since it is preferable to begin the initial home sessions without having been previously noticed by the child in kindergarten or school.

In the assessment interview, it is important to note the following:

From the parents:

- Speaking habits—in which places and to whom the child speaks. See Appendix 1: "Speaking Checklist" for easy documentation
- Etiology of child's speech and social communication
- Child's temperament and characteristics—may be shy, slow to warm, perfectionist, stubborn, persistent, or oppositional
- Child's social functioning—with peers, adults, family members, strangers

- General background of child—pregnancy, birth, early development, feeding, sleeping, toilet training
- Child's current language competence
- Bilingualism, language spoken at home
- Child's anxiety levels in different contexts
- Education history—age child began nursery, kindergarten, school; his functioning in each framework; learning and cognitive abilities and difficulties; social functioning; fine and gross motor skills
- Family interactions with siblings, parents, wider family
- Attachment to and separation from parents
- Family history of anxiety, SM, shyness, and hypersensitivity
- Social/cultural isolation of family, geographical moves
- Child's interests and hobbies, youth groups, after-school classes
- Other difficulties, concerns
- How parents cope with the SM
- Change in SM over time
- Help and treatment received until now

From the teacher:

- Child's speech patterns in school—to whom and in which contexts he speaks and communicates
- Estimation of child's cognitive and learning abilities (may prove to be inaccurate if the child fails to talk to the teacher)
- Estimation of child's fine and gross motor skills
- Participation in school activities
- Separation issues
- Relationship between teacher and child
- Connection between teacher and child's family
- School bathroom habits
- School eating habits

- Social behavior with peers in class and recess
- Interaction with staff
- Child's attention level
- How the teacher manages the SM
- Intervention within the school
- Any change in SM over time
- Other difficulties or concerns
- Child's strengths and interests

There are several questionnaires that are used to diagnose SM, which can be helpful but do not take the place of gathering information by talking with parents and teachers.

"The Selective Mutism Questionnaire" (SMQ) is a seventeen-item questionnaire that was composed and tested by Bergman et al. (2008) and includes the following items:

SMQ Factors
Factor 1: School
Speaks to most peers at school
Speaks to selected peers at school
Answers teacher
Asks teacher questions
Speaks to most teachers
Speaks in groups of peers

Factor 2: Home/Family
Speaks to family at home when others present
Speaks to family in unfamiliar places
Speaks to extended family
Speaks on phone to parents, siblings
Speaks to familiar family friends (adults)
Speaks to babysitter

Factor 3: Public/Social
Speaks to unfamiliar peers
Speaks with unfamiliar family friends (adults)
Speaks with doctor and/or dentist
Speaks to store clerks or waiters
Speaks in clubs or teams outside of school

Recordings and home visits
Two excellent tools that can shed light on the functioning of children with SM who are unlikely to show their optimum functioning when tested for SM are as follows:

Audio or video recordings made at home by the parents when the child is most at ease, to be played to the therapist or teacher in order to discern the child's language and communication skills when not impeded by his SM. It is vital to be aware of the child's optimum home functioning in order to ascertain where to aim for in his social communication and speech at school.

A home visit in which the person carrying out the assessment does not interact in any way with the child with SM but rather tries to be as unobtrusive as possible in order to hear and inconspicuously observe the child in her natural habitat. This will only work if the child will speak in the presence of a stranger at home, even if that stranger does not interact with her at all.

Once the assessment has been carried out and interventions have begun, it is crucial to stop and reassess at regular intervals what progress has been made and which areas are resistant to change.

The following chapters will guide interventions for each of the members of the triumvirate of therapeutic agents of change—parents, therapists (two sections,

one for younger children and one for teens), and teachers. In forging this pact in order to help the child overcome his SM, it is important for each person to appreciate the understanding and resources of his or her colleagues so that these may be pooled and channeled toward growth. This is no small feat to attempt, as each comes from a vantage point of his or her experience, outlook, and priorities.

Parents' Manual

still waters run deep

Contents of Parents' Manual

8. Modeling
9. Increasing independence: enabling/protecting
10. Parenting a shy or socially anxious child
11. How to select a school
12. Choosing a therapist
13. Selective mutism in older children
14. Language issues in bilingual families
15. Transitions
16. Keeping an open mind and a watchful eye

Cognitive-Behavioral Worksheets

Introduction to Parents' Manual

In all probability, you are reading this manual because your child or someone you care for fails to talk in select settings. This manual is a part of a comprehensive treatment program, which includes manuals for parents, teachers, and therapists. Ideally, your child will be assisted to gradually learn to speak normally in all situations by these three sectors. For each one of these people, their task is separate and interconnected, with the joint goal of helping your child to communicate socially in a regular way.

You, as the parent, know your child the best! The teacher and therapist need your guidance as to your understanding of your child, his thoughts and feelings, and his functioning at home and in the world at large. Your collaboration is vital through all stages of the treatment, from assessment, understanding your child's background, the treatment stages, to maintaining your child's progress in the future. As a parent, your concern for your child's welfare is paramount; to this end you have the role of working as a team with the therapist and teacher in the framework of this three-way intervention, with distinct tasks that will be outlined in this manual. It is most conducive to success when a respectful, open, and communicative relationship exists between parents, teacher, and therapist so that each corner of this triumvirate can contribute his expertise while simultaneously gaining and adjusting his understanding by the insights of his colleagues in this enterprise.

This treatment program is based on several principles, which will become clear on an operative level as you read the manual. It aims to build bridges between the diverse settings in which your child lives, enabling him to move seamlessly between contexts. In other words, it aims to understand what allows him to speak at home and to try to incorporate those elements at school so that he will feel more comfortable there. At the same time, some factors at school may be conducive to assertiveness and independence, and the parents may wish to incorporate these factors at some level at home. This outlook is reflected in the locations of the therapy—at home and at school.

In addition, the treatment plan incorporates what is widely accepted today about treating selective mutism:that behavioral methods with cognitive components are thought to be most effective for SM, that it is usually anxiety-based, and that the family and school should be intimately involved in any course of treatment. This program has been developed out of the clinical experience of treating hundreds of children with SM.

The most comprehensive treatment would include having a therapist, teacher, and parents work together, each with their interventions designed to complement each other, with the outcome being a powerful push forward toward speech. However, reality often intrudes in the shape of a less-than-cooperative teacher, overworked or overwhelmed parents, difficulty finding a therapist who specializes in SM, or financial restraints that preclude enlisting a therapist's help. In such situations, whichever resources are available can be harnessed in order to help your child. Many devoted parents have teamed up with teachers and, using this method, have helped their child to overcome SM without the involvement of a therapist.

These treatment manuals are designed in a way so that when time is tight, each may be read and its treatment plan implemented without the necessity of reading the other manuals. Whenever time allows, reading all the manuals is advised—it will give you a full picture of the suggested treatment strategies. It is also advised to read the opening chapters about the causes and characteristics of SM and about the integrative approach where parents, teachers, and therapists work together to help the child to overcome his SM.

How Selective Mutism Can Affect Your Child and Family

While each child and all families are unique and respond to SM in their own way, certain feelings and reactions are common. One thing is almost always the case with a child who is not speaking (usually) in kindergarten or school: a child with SM suffers! He cannot be himself—the more spontaneous,communicative child he is in other contexts. He must expend effort to ensure that his radar informing him of who is in his proximity is always on, and control himself so that when his private space is encroached or when he is in a setting in which he does not speak, he stays quiet. High and constant energy expenditure is required to maintain this awareness and control. This in itself is distressing, however effortless the child with SM appears to make it.

The lack of verbal communication causes the child to miss out on social and learning experiences which would further his development. A child who cannot say what he wants will frequently be included in activities he wishes to avoid and conversely will be excluded from experiences he desperately wants to have. This is a recipe for frustration. This frustration is often taken out on his family when he returns home and can finally express himself. Sometimes the frustration expresses itself in school, as the child makes his presence felt with his hands, not his voice.

When a child with SM is unfortunate enough to be in a context in which he is misunderstood and considered to be unintelligent, unable to communicate, or oppositional, he may be inappropriately labeled and consequently placed in an unsuitable learning environment. This generally exacerbates the child's difficulties.

Parents confronted with a child who fails to speak in school frequently go through a period of heightened anxiety themselves. The parents' concern for their child and their grappling with schools and possible interventions, as well as their long-term projections and postulations regarding future implications for their beloved child, can be overwhelming. To make matters worse, the parents' posturing to get appropriate intervention for their child can be misconstrued as over protectiveness and identified by the school as the cause, not the effect, of the child's SM.

For all these reasons (and many more), early intervention is vital. What's more, it usually works! Response to intervention using behavioral therapy for children with SM has been found to be highly effective. In addition, the following treatment plan is generally experienced by the child as an enjoyable, satisfying experience; once children break the barriers and speak, they usually experience a surge of self-confidence.

How to Talk to Your Child about Selective Mutism

Selective mutism is usually anxiety-based and that must be borne in mind when talking to your child. **One of the aims of discussing speech difficulties with your child is to lower his anxiety levels**. However you choose to express it semantically, the message should be: "We love you exactly as you are. Right now you can't speak in some situations or to some people, but we know that soon you will overcome it and be able to speak." In other words, you are telling your child three things:

1. **You are not anxious about his SM.**
2. **You accept him as he is.**
3. **You have total confidence that he will overcome his SM soon.**

Other family members (siblings, grandparents, etc.) should adopt a similar stance. This bolsters the child's confidence that he has the strength and courage to speak, and your apparent lack of worry will do wonders for lowering his anxiety level. Paradoxically, the more he feels your concern and is pressured to speak, the harder it may be for him to talk, as his anxiety level will rise. Lowering his anxiety level regarding speech is usually prerequisite for enabling speech.

Constant checking as to whether he spoke in kindergarten or school and to whom, transmits to him your anxiety and makes him more anxious. Similarly, prizes offered for speech, or punishments for non-speech are contraindicated—they too may increase your child's anxiety level.

You do not need to try to increase your child's motivation to speak. As explained in the previous section, SM causes suffering and frustration in children, and every child with SM that I have encountered desperately wants to speak.

Another productive message to convey to your child is the normalization of SM. He can be told that many children find it hard to speak in school, are wonderful children, and overcome their SM in time. This is often a relief for a child who may see himself as different or problematic. During therapy, the child can be told that many children have been helped by sessions such as those he is having in school. This should not be said at the beginning of therapy, but rather after it has gotten underway and it is clear to the child that its aim is social communication.

After these two messages have been conveyed to your child, do not engage him in ongoing discussion about SM unless he initiates it. Your frequent discussion of SM may cause him to feel more pressure to speak and in fact make it harder for him to progress.

How to Treat Selective Mutism

It is widely accepted today that the aim of treatment for SM should be to help the child to speak in all his daily environments to all people. Behavioral treatment with cognitive components is generally considered to be the most effective way to remove the symptoms of selective mutism. SM is usually anxiety-based and any treatment plan must take this into consideration. It is most conducive to rapid recovery when the family and school are intimately involved in any course of treatment. In order for this to happen, it is vital to establish an open, communicative, and mutually respectful relationship between the teacher, the parents, and the therapist.

This guide is presented as a comprehensive treatment plan for therapist, parents, and teachers—each with their own tasks but working in conjunction with one another. This is in an ideal situation where there are the resources and the will to tackle SM from all three directions. However, if a full-scale intervention is not possible, or it is thought that it is not called for, then this treatment plan offers a variety of ideas, interventions, and activities that can be implemented by the teacher, parent, or therapist alone, without the full-scale program. In many cases, a partial implementation of the program can bring desirable results and is often sufficient to help the child to overcome selective mutism.

Overview of Therapy

The therapy outlined before you is a behavioral plan that aims to **remove the symptom of failure to speak** in certain settings. I believe that especially with young children, symptom removal is paramount, because the symptom can affect the child's social, language, and learning development, as well as exerting a powerful influence on how the child feels about himself—his self-confidence, his social self-image, and his view of himself as "normal." In addition to this aim of facilitating speech, during the assessment stage other issues may be found that can be addressed within this therapy—for example, independence, assertiveness, and anxiety within the family. These may be incorporated as aims within the therapy, as part of the parents', teacher's, and therapist's interventions.

In some cases, children with SM have additional issues other than difficulty speaking in select places or to certain people. Some have speech impediments, and others may have additional anxiety conditions which may require specific treatment beyond the scope of this plan. Once the failure to speak is remedied, the child will be more able to participate in the requisite treatment for other difficulties should they exist.

When a child successfully overcomes SM, this in itself has a powerful self-affirming effect. The child learns that he has the courage to overcome difficulties, and this can have a ripple effect on further problems the child may have, especially anxiety-related issues.

Prior to the start of treatment, the therapist should meet with the parents and teacher in order to assess the child's speech patterns, his strengths and difficulties, and other factors relating to SM. After the assessment is completed, therapy sessions with the child may begin while guidance will be given simultaneously to the teacher and the parents. The therapist will explain the therapy outline to the parents and will give ongoing updates regarding progress once therapy has started. Three-way meetings involving the therapist, school staff, and parents should be held at regular intervals.

Here follows a summary of the therapist's sessions with the child, then the teacher's interventions will be outlined, and then I will focus on what you as a parent can do to help your child overcome selective mutism.

The Stages of Therapy: Home-Based, School-Based

A primary aim of the therapy is to build on the child's optimum functioning, which is usually at the home, facilitating similar behavior in other surroundings. As such, the **therapy begins, whenever possible, at home**. The aim of these home sessions is to reach the stage wherein the child speaks directly and comfortably to the therapist.

In the initial (usually between two and six) sessions in the child's home, the therapist engages in minimal small talk with the parent, trying to be unobtrusive to the child. The initial aim is that the child speaks in the presence of the therapist. Gradually over the course of the home sessions, the therapist plays with the child and other family members and finally directs speech to the child and plays with him alone. By the end of the home sessions' stage of the program, the child should be speaking directly with the therapist.

In the final home session, the therapist explains to the child that she works with children in schools, and that she intends to have sessions with the child in school in the coming weeks. In these sessions she will play with the child, sometimes together with other children, and hopefully help him to feel comfortable and enjoy school. (With older children a more cognitive-behavioral method is used, including open discussion about the difficulty speaking and joint planning of goals as outlined in chapter 8, the Therapist's Manual for Teens and Preteens. With children up to around third grade, a more behavioral approach is usually recommended.)

Once the child speaks to the therapist in the home, the **therapy is moved to the school**. Therapy then takes place one to three times a week in a designated room in the school. Initially, the aim of the sessions is that the child speaks to the therapist in the therapy room in school; activities include games conducive to speech, listening to recordings of the child from home, and arts and crafts. The activities included in these sessions are adapted in accordance with the child's preferences.

Usually this transfer of location goes smoothly, and the child continues to speak to the therapist in the school therapy room. Occasionally, the child is reticent to speak in the new school setting. If this is the case, the therapist employs a variety of tools to facilitate speech. This could include recording the child at home and playing the recording in the school sessions, and inviting the parents or a sibling to participate in the initial school sessions. There are also behavioral tools that can be used, such as the "sliding in" technique, a form of stimulus shaping developed by Johnson and Wintgens (2001). Here the parent is alone with the child in the schoolroom, and the child speaks to him or her. Then a game is played involving rote speech and some physical activity—for example, the parent and child throw a ball between them and each time the thrower says a number. In small but sure stages, the therapist gradually comes within hearing range of the game, eventually enters the room, and finally participates in the game. All these techniques and strategies are explained fully in <u>chapter 6</u>, the Therapist's Manual.

Once the child is speaking comfortably to the therapist in school, **the generalization stage** takes place. Here the aim is **to broaden the child's speaking habits** to include as many people as possible—initially within the therapy room at school. The therapist invites classmates and staff to join in the sessions in small steps, employing a variety of behavioral techniques when necessary.

Once the child is speaking to several people in the therapy room, the next stage is to broaden the range of settings in which the child speaks. In order to achieve this the sessions are moved either to an open space in the school, such as a hall or play area, or to a corner in the classroom itself. Here, using the same methods of playing, recording, and other activities used up to now, the child is enabled to speak in the classroom setting. Usually, as the child progresses in therapy, spontaneous progress is seen simultaneously in other settings. For example, when the child starts speaking in the sessions to a number of children, it is likely that he will speak to some of these children in recess, or perhaps quietly in the classroom.

Teacher's Interventions

The beauty of this program is its comprehensiveness. It is designed to assist the child in the main settings of his life with a three-pronged intervention: parents, teachers, and therapist who simultaneously strive to assist the child to overcome his difficulty. When all three sectors act in coordination, the effect is powerful. While the therapy is ongoing, both the parents and the teacher will be carrying out their own interventions aimed at helping the child to speak.

The teacher may assess the child's functioning at school, and consider how to help him in five areas:

1. Encouraging a communicative relationship between the teacher and child, initially nonverbal, ultimately verbal
2. Lowering the child's anxiety level in school
3. Helping him interact socially with other children
4. Building his independence, assertiveness, and self-esteem in school, and not exempting him from activities because of the SM
5. Blurring the differentiation the child has made between home and school functioning

The teachers' interventions are fully described in the Teacher's Manual. Here I will give a few examples to illustrate the above points.

Sometimes, when a child fails to speak, the educational staff feel that they do not have the ability to develop a communicative relationship with the child. In this program teachers are encouraged and guided so that they build a warm, supportive, communicative, nonverbal relationship, which is a precursor of verbal contact between child and teacher. The teacher may be guided in developing a structured behavior shaping plan for her to implement within the framework of the warm reciprocal relationship she will have developed with the child. This requires a few minutes daily on the part of the teacher, and is usually most effective when accompanied by guidance and coaching following each teacher-child session (even by phone, a few minutes a day) by the therapist.

This social contact with the teacher plays a fundamental role in easing the anxiety level of the child, as now the child can express to the teacher issues that may be upsetting him, such as bullying, social pressures, and academic concerns. He may request changes that could make him more comfortable at school, such as sitting next to a friend. Another vital key to lowering the child's anxiety level in school is that the staff does not put undue pressure on the child to speak.

The teacher can encourage social interaction with peers by placing the child in small groups of children who seem a good match for him and whom he likes. He might be given a special position or lead a project in an area he likes and is good at.

Finally,contact between the home and school is vital,including home visits, utilizing the parents' understanding of the child, and thinking together with the parents and therapist about elements that could make the child feel more at home in school.

The importance of the teacher's fluid contact with the parents and therapist is a cornerstone of success; each of the three active parties in the treatment must mutually fine-tune the other parties' interventions, communicating progress and setbacks as well as appraisals of what more can be done. This can take place in prearranged meetings at set intervals and be supplemented by weekly phone conversations. When the significant adults in all of the main contexts in the child's life are working together toward a common aim, the effect is powerful; the whole is far more potent than the sum total of its parts.

Parents' Interventions and Tasks

I have seen many concerned and able parents carry out structured treatment plans that have cured or significantly eased their child's selective mutism. Here follow interventions specific to the parents, which may be carried out in conjunction with the therapist and/or teacher.

1. Assessment

The first three points are relevant when a therapist is implementing a treatment plan. Prior to the start of treatment, a comprehensive assessment is made, in which the therapist collates information from the home and school in order to estimate the level of functioning and the emotional state of the child, as well as his strengths and abilities and any additional difficulties. This process is important in order to tailor the therapy to your child. The parents, as the greatest experts on their child, are indispensable contributors to the evaluation.

2. Home therapy sessions

Once the initial therapy sessions begin in the home, the parents facilitate and conduct them together with the therapist. They plan who is to be present, they set the time and place of the sessions, and they ensure that the activities in these sessions are enjoyable and appropriate. Parents must provide recording devices, which are to be used in the home sessions and in between meetings, as well as in the school-based therapy sessions. In short, parents work together with the therapist to ensure the success of the home sessions.

3. School therapy sessions

Similarly, when the therapy sessions take place in the school, the parents' cooperation is required. Frequently parents are requested to help in preparing homework for sessions, which is usually taping recordings or videos of the child at home. Sometimes an impasse occurs at a transitional stage in the school-based therapy, and a family member is requested to come to one or more school sessions to facilitate speech in school. In such a case, the parent's help is required to plan and conduct the sessions with the therapist.

4. School-based talking-playing sessions

Whenever possible, whether or not treatment with a therapist is being implemented, it is recommended that parents go to the child's school or kindergarten between one and three times a week for short, enjoyable talking-playing sessions. These are informal sessions in which the parent plays and talks with her child in school or kindergarten. This can be done in the morning when the parent drops the child off at school before the school day begins, or at any other time that is convenient for parent and teacher. The parent considers where in the school the child will speak to her, which depends on the severity of the SM. Some children will speak with a parent or family member in a secluded corner of the class, while others need the security of a closed room in order to speak to the parent.

These sessions significantly boost the effectiveness of the therapy. For example, instead of the child speaking once a week in school during one hour in therapy with the therapist, he is now speaking up to four times a week in school—three times with a family member and once with the therapist. The therapist may guide the parent (after consultation with the teacher) regarding the location of the sessions and the possible inclusion of other children in the sessions.

Here is a concrete example to illustrate such a session: A mother (or father or sibling) might come twice a week to the child's kindergarten, sit in a secluded corner with the child, and play with Play-Doh for twenty minutes as other children come into the nursery. If the child speaks to his mother, he may continue doing so even after other children come within hearing range and eventually when they sit with him at the table. Another example could be of a child who will not speak to a parent in the regular classroom; he may have these sessions with his parent in a closed, private room in the school, perhaps inviting a friend with whom he talks outside school to join in. As he grows freer in his speech in these sessions with his parent and friend, additional friends may join in, and so his circle of peers with whom he speaks in school will be widened.

In order to maximize the effectiveness of these sessions, they should be planned with the therapist and the teacher so that they complement the concurrent stages of therapy and classroom functioning. They will be structured according to the same behavioral principles used in the therapist's interventions. Initially the child will speak to the parent in a private area, then the circle with whom he speaks will be gradually enlarged to include friends and/or staff, and finally his speech will be generalized to include additional settings in the school, such as public areas and the classroom. The aim is to enable him to speak to everyone in all settings. Parents who are implementing this program without a therapist's simultaneous intervention or guidance should read chapter 6, the Therapist's Manual in order to understand how to build a structured behavioral plan with small steps that shape and generalize the child's speech. This plan can then be implemented in the talking-playing sessions that the child has in school or nursery with the parent, and in effect the parent will be the operant therapist.

5. Inviting friends home, telephone calls, recordings

Inviting classmates home to play can considerably help your child to overcome SM. If he speaks to his friend at your home, then a big barrier will have been broken—the classmate will have heard his voice—and that will make it easier for him to speak freely in school. And if more friends come, and he speaks to them too, this will further advance his progress. Even if he fails to speak to his friends at home, but communicates nonverbally and enjoys their company, this will facilitate greater social competence in school.

Friends should be chosen who suit your child's personality and whom he likes. The teacher can advise you as to whom she considers to be compatible. When these play-dates take place, do all you can to ensure that they are enjoyable and go smoothly. A socially shy child may need some behind-the-scenes assistance. You could plan an enjoyable activity, a special or new game, an outing, or some attractive arts and crafts activity. You can also help ensure that the house is peaceful and that any antagonistic siblings (if an issue) are otherwise engaged. If your child has nurturing, fun siblings, it may be preferable for them to be present! Frequent, enjoyable play-dates truly facilitate beating SM. Telephone calls may be a first step in verbal communication with schoolmates and staff; encourage your child to speak on the phone to people with whom he already speaks freely face-to-face, and suggest calling staff or classmates with whom he has not yet spoken, if and when you feel your child is ready.

At the onset of therapy, it is worthwhile to purchase a taping device and play with it at home. In all likelihood it will prove productive. Recordings are a useful pre-direct speech step where a child's voice is present without him having to speak directly. Playing around with recording devices at home—iPads, MP3, office tapes, talking photo albums, taping on cell phones and cameras—often proves invaluable to therapy. Chapter 9 gives a brief list of apps that are very attractive to children and intrinsically record the child's voice during the game. Once your child enjoys playing with the recording device at home with family members, it can be incorporated into therapy. If he does not object, the tape could be played to friends when they come to play, or to the teacher in school in talking-playing sessions, perhaps making it easier for your child to speak directly once his friends have heard his voice.

Leaving WhatsApp messages is a step prior to a direct phone call, wherein the receiver of the message hears the child without the child being on the other end. However, the child knows that his voice and message have been heard by the teacher or friend. A series of steps based on WhatsApp messages could facilitate speech with a teacher: the first step could be sending the teacher daily WhatsApp messages that the child records at home—for example, what he ate for supper, what the weather is, and so on, and the teacher initially hears the messages not in the child's presence. After a few days, she hears the messages with the child, and then after a few more times, she hears the message and asks the child to repeat the last word of the message by whispering in her ear.

6. Desensitization outside school

The behavioral techniques used by the teacher, the parents and the therapist in school, may be required to help your child speak in settings or with people outside school. If your child does not manage to talk to friends at home, you may utilize a behavior shaping program that you can implement at home which will take your child from silence to speech in small structured steps. After the initial assessment of your child and in your intermittent meetings with the therapist and teacher, it will be apparent with whom the child has difficulty speaking. The therapist can help you plan the desensitization schedule for your child to begin speaking to such a person. This is a scale of steps to gradually approach speech; for example, first nonverbal communication, then playing a tape of the child speaking, followed by speaking on the phone, and finally using a "sliding in" technique (as described earlier).

To give a theoretical example: The first step at home may be inviting a friend with whom the child doesn't speak and playing a pre-recorded app of the child speaking with his family in the presence of the friend, followed by a game of catch played with the parent, child and his friend, requiring sound production, such as saying "shhhhh" or whistling each time you throw the ball. Once this is successfully played the small group may play Chinese whispers; initially the child whispers only to the family member, later also to the friend. Then a game of snap could be played in which when the child gets a card identical to that of another player, he says "snap". Some children will pass through all these stages in one play-date, others may require at least one session to master each task. When several sessions are required, the previously achieved games are played before attempting to master a new goal. The games should be played in a light and playful atmosphere, as this will help your child to keep his anxiety in check.

Many determined,dedicated parents have learned to implement these behavior shaping programs at home successfully; thus, they have a series of steps they can implement at home that enables their child to gradually speak to friends. Often the child understands that this series of games offers him a bridge that takes him from silence to speech, and he gladly embraces the procedure that offers him a way to speak to friends or relatives.

A further example of desensitization carried out by the parents outside school could be a child who doesn't speak to his grandparents and requires help in gradually speaking to them. A plan could be constructed in which the child first plays and shows his grandparents a talking album in which he has previously recorded himself describing the pictures in the album; followed by leaving WhatsApp messages on a cell phone; after which the child speaks directly on the cell phone; then he listens to WhatsApp messages together with his grandparents:and finally he speaks to them face to face.

Another example could be a desensitization schedule for a child who doesn't speak to waiters in a restaurant. The child could go with his parent once a week to a restaurant as a special treat; the first time, he points to "milkshake" on the menu to communicate his choice to the waiter;the next week he plays a prepared tape of himself saying "milkshake please"; and finally he says "milkshake." These are just examples, the structure and pace would be designed to fit the needs of each child, with a family member carrying out the desensitization procedure.

7. Lowering anxiety

An underlying premise of the treatment of SM is that the disorder is usually anxiety-based, so in order to free the child of SM, effort must be made in all settings to lower the child's anxiety levels.

At home,this translates into easing the pressure on the child to speak. Paradoxically, the more a child is coaxed to speak, the harder it may be for him to do so. This will express itself in how you speak to your child. Make clear to your child your manifest confidence that he will overcome SM. In all of the interventions described here, the lighter and more playful the tone, the more effective they will be in lowering the child's anxiety. As mentioned before, positive and negative pressure—both reprimanding a child and promising prizes for speech—may cause the child to be more self-conscious and anxious about his difficulty speaking.

8. Modeling

Parents must try to show their child that they are not overly anxious about the SM. It is natural that every parent of a child with SM is anxious about it, therefore parents may need to work on their own anxiety management, too. How parents cope with anxiety is a strong modeling example for their child.

Research has found that often (but not always) one of the parents of a child with SM has some anxiety issues herself. If you feel that you have anxiety that is affecting your parenting, this is an opportunity for you to discuss it with the therapist. You will not only improve your parenting skills, but also show your child how you are overcoming your fears, engendering a feeling of empowerment in the family. You might learn some cognitive-behavioral tips on how to work toward lowering your anxiety about SM. Two examples of cognitive-behavioral exercises are given in the worksheets at the end of this section.

Similarly, modeling social behavior can be very powerful. For example, if your family is fairly insular, and you work on opening your home to visitors, this may encourage your child to be more open to receiving his friends at home.

9. Increasing independence: enabling/protecting

When a parent sees his child feeling scared or anxious, it is his natural instinct to try and protect him from the perceived danger. And when there is an immediate extreme danger, it is indeed the parent's duty to protect his child, to pull him away from exposed electricity, for example.

However, with anxiety-provoking everyday situations in which the child needs to learn to function in order to lead a full and satisfying life, the parents' aim should be to enable him to acquire and practice coping skills. This involves conveying to the child your belief in his abilities and allowing him to be in situations that are challenging to a tolerable degree and will give him the experience needed to hone his skills. For example, when a shy child is asked a question by an acquaintance, it is tempting for the parent to answer for the child. But if the child, with some effort and a little discomfort, can answer, then the parent is depriving him of a valuable social skills building experience by answering in his place. There is a fine line between not asking a child to do something that raises his anxiety to an unbearable level, and encouraging him to express himself in tolerably anxiety-producing situations. If this is a relevant issue for you and your child, then it may be helpful to work with a therapist to consider how to discern and apply the fine line between enabling and protecting. Useful further reading is listed in the reference section.

Rescuing and the Five-Second Rule

We are so accustomed to immediate verbal responses within discourse that we may not wait for a child with SM to respond and may respond in her place. This is called "rescuing," and this is how it happens: an adult may ask a child which grade he is in, and the child hesitates to answer for all of three seconds—which seems to our ears to be an eternity. The parent wants to both ease the child's apparent discomfort and to conform to the rules of verbal discourse in which pregnant silences are awkward, and he answers instead of the child. This gives the child a message that the anxiety is too great for him to manage and that you do not expect him to be able to respond. The five-second rule helps parents give the child a chance to answer. If someone asks the child a question, the parent (or teacher) can count to five in his or her head, after which the adult can restate the question to the child, giving a couple of options for a verbal response that can't be answered by a nod of the head. For example, ask, "Are you in first grade or second grade?" Then wait a further five seconds. This procedure—which feels to the parents more like ten minutes then ten seconds—gives the child the message that his parent thinks that he is capable of answering and expects that one of these days, he might just do so. And actually, he might answer during the time that you give him to respond. But even if he does not, he will understand two things: his parent believes in him, and he was exposed to an uncomfortable situation for all of ten seconds and survived! This is one of the keys to treating anxiety disorders: habituation to the anxiety-provoking stimulus shows the child that he can accustom himself to the feared situation (adapted from Dr. Steven Kurtz).

In addition, at the age at which SM is most prevalent—around the beginning of elementary school—children are becoming more independent, functioning in large educational institutions, some traveling on school buses. Parents can assist their children by fostering **appropriate levels of independence** at home. This can include tasks such as tidying their room, bathing, homework, etc. Age-appropriate independent functioning gives a child a feeling of competence and control over his surroundings. This can help the child feel more able to function in school and have the confidence and courage to take steps toward speech. More about enabling in the section below.

10. Parenting a shy or socially anxious child

The dandelion child and the orchid child
A sensitive child has so many potentially propitious and invaluable attributes waiting to blossom in a nurturing environment. But what is a nurturing environment? How can parents help their shy child to bud and bloom?

A beautiful science-based metaphor and theory has taken root in recent years: the dandelion child and the orchid child (Ellis and Boyce 2005, Jay Belsky 2012). Many children are like dandelions; given a reasonable environment, they will grow and thrive. Others are like orchids; they are more delicate and need an environment tuned to their sensitivities. David Dobbs explains that "most of us have genes that make us as hardy as dandelions:able to take root and survive almost anywhere. A few of us, however, are more like the orchid: fragile and fickle, but capable of blooming spectacularly if given greenhouse care. Many introverted (and shy) children appear to have orchid genes; with the right environment and good parenting, they can grow up to be society's most creative, successful, and happy people."

This is encouraging and daunting at the same time—it means that your shy child, who may be struggling at the moment, has the potential to flourish and bloom as she develops. But is also means that she needs environments and parenting that cater to her sensibilities. We discussed in chapter 3 under "shyness" what strengths the shy child frequently has—including an increased sensitivity, which can foster greater empathy and awareness of others' needs, having stronger relationships (though perhaps with fewer people), being more original and less determined by others' tastes, and having heightened creativity, attention to detail, and thoroughness (Susan Cain 2013).

How can parents cater to the needs of the shy, spectacular, orchid child with his greenhouse requirements and vulnerability? Firstly be reassured that you don't have to be, and in fact can't be, perfect. Bruno Bettelheim speaks about "the good enough parent," and that is what you can aim for. But perhaps more thought and effort is required by the orchid child in order to meet his basic needs. Here follow a few general guidelines.

Understanding and sensitivity
The shy child's temperament must be considered before and during activities that for other children might be mundane, everyday occurrences. For the shy child, these may be daunting obstacles to be surmounted. Before any steps can be taken to assuage anxiety, the parent has to perceive that for this child, going to a birthday

party or a doctor or even an aunt's house could be cause for concern. Denying the child's anxiety may make him feel misunderstood and deficient. Take care not to label a child—for example, as shy or antisocial—because labels can insinuate boundaries of the child's potential and effect his belief in his ability to gain confidence and competence. Often when a child is labeled "a problem child," that becomes who he is in other people's eyes and sometimes even in his own. However, understanding when it is hard for the child and expressing your insight to him shows him that you see him and are there to help him overcome obstacles.

Guiding and helping her through adversity

An anxious child needs more help than others to navigate stormy (and calm) social seas. Once you are aware of an upcoming daunting event—say, an invitation to play at a new friend's home—you can try to help her in several ways. Firstly you can prepare her for the event: who will be there, games that will be played, and how long she'll be there, and you can discuss with her how to make it more manageable. In this way she knows what to expect, and she can accustom herself to the idea of the upcoming event. For example, you could suggest games she may enjoy playing with her friend. A second way to help could be during the feared event: you could stay there with her for a while or give her a cell phone to call you if she wants to return home. It is important not to discourage her from functioning in the most independent way she can manage comfortably; there is a fine line between overprotecting and assisting. The better you understand your child's fears, the more finely tuned your estimate of how much help she needs in any given situation will be.

Molding the environment to meet mild hothouse standards

You may need to modify certain aspects of your lifestyle to make your child's life less challenging. An anxious child may cope better when he knows in advance what to expect and has time to adjust and think of coping strategies. For example, it may be better for him to be forewarned when friends are coming round or if you are going out and a babysitter will be with him. He may need to get to know a babysitter in advance in order to avoid feeling uncomfortable when you are out. It is helpful for the child to know your schedule—if you will be home when he returns from school, who will do drop-off and pick-up, and so on. A critical decision that is often barely considered is the choice of kindergarten and school your orchid child will attend. Make sure that you consider options before deciding and look into available frameworks. This is discussed below in "Choosing Schools and Therapists." Where you live affects your child greatly—while he will not be the only factor in your choice of neighborhood, his needs should be considered. An area with sensitive schools, suitable friends, and an atmosphere of safety and security could be some of the considerations. Frequent geographical moves could be an added stressor requiring adaptation and flexibility.

Advocating for and being your child's case manager

A child with SM should be encouraged to express herself to others whenever she can, but there will be times when you will have to be her spokesperson. You may need to convey requests she wishes her friend's mother to know when she is on a playdate. In school she may be bullied and be suffering in silence, unable to reach out to the teachers. Banal details such as next to whom the child sits in school may be causing her distress and may be easily remedied by a word to the teacher. Try to investigate which teacher may be most suited to her, and do your best to have her placed in this teacher's class. Being your child's case manager when a therapist and a multilayered intervention are involved is no small task. Having your child's best interests in mind yet not pushing the frequency of

65

communication with the teacher beyond what is acceptable is walking a tightrope.

Stressing his strengths

When a child has difficulties, these challenges so often fill center stage, relegating his positive traits to the background. Communication between the child and his parents can become focused on what isn't there instead of all that is. A child with SM is always so much more than his difficulty speaking. Search out all those wonderful things about your child, and refer to them—you must be authentic and relate to real things you see in your child. Focusing on the positive often is an immediate lift-me-up for the relationship and your child's self-confidence. Apart from present strengths, such as intelligence, kindness, responsibility, and a sense of humor, look for and nurture abilities that he can be proud of and that can be a form of self-expression. Playing a musical instrument, singing, gymnastics, martial arts, or painting can do wonders for self-esteem and communication. Look for areas in which your child shows promise, and milk them to the maximum. This adjusts the relative focus on problems as contrasted with abilities.

Reframing her difficulties

When you are looking at your child through a rose-tinted lens, you can often see her difficulties in a positive light. For example, her sensitivity may make school and social relationships fraught, but they show that she relates to her feelings and often to others' feelings too. A child who doesn't want to talk because of pronunciation problems and the feeling that people will laugh at her has high levels of self-expectation and perfectionism—if well channeled, these can be positive traits indeed! My mother once reframed my tendency to cry too easily when relatives left by saying that it was because of my big heart. I remember the wave of relief that washed over me when I realized that I had a really good trait that sometimes (still) causes me embarrassment!

Belief in his ability to develop

Children perceive our expectations of them and often act accordingly. That explains some of the power of a positive relationship between parents and children—the parent projects his or her belief in the child, and that bolsters the child's belief in himself or herself. It helps to remember that we are always at a given point in a process, and in the case of most children with SM, with adequate help they will improve and overcome. Looking back retrospectively once a child has beaten his SM, many parents feel that if only they had known how things would turn out, and had they been able to fast-forward to a later time, they would have been far more optimistic. Try to be optimistic without seeing the future, because it may actually make the future brighter and make your child happier right now.

Independence/protection

We're back to the fine line between protecting and enabling. In our attempts to shield our child from anxiety, we may actually bolster her fear. If a child realizes to what lengths we go to ensure that she will survive a playdate, she may feel that a playdate is truly a dangerous endeavor. How can we know where to draw that line—to protect when needed, to enable whenever possible? Here again the answer lies in your understanding of what your child is capable of and being aware that your goal is to maximize independence and minimize protection, as long as it is within your child's comfort zone. Enabling may mean giving some behind-the-scenes or overt support, which helps your child to function, without blocking her engagement in a daunting task. What does this mean in practice? Think in each given situation, "Must I protect, or can I enable?" For example, if a child wants to come to play, and your child is reticent, perhaps you shouldn't tell the friend not to come; rather, you can help your child feel at ease and enjoy herself, perhaps by playing with them to begin with and then by supplying enjoyable activities for the children to play without you.

Anxious children may look for reassurance in the face of feared situations; yet giving too much support can give them the feeling that they are indeed facing danger. Whenever possible, encourage age-appropriate independence; for example, in dressing, eating, bathing, and other daily tasks. This gives the child a feeling of mastery over his world, which is necessary for self-confidence and is the best remedy for anxiety. Sometimes a parent will feel such compassion for her child who has suffered in kindergarten for several hours that she will try to compensate by coddling him in the afternoon at home. Be kind and loving, but don't compensate by waiving the child's independent functioning in the afternoons, which may strengthen his feelings of incompetence.

Enabling habituation to anxiety-provoking situations— fighting fear by facing fear

When a child fears a situation, and her parents prevent her from encountering it—say, going to a friend's birthday party—the child does not get the chance to experience the number-one eroding factor of anxiety: habituation. When exposed to a feared situation for long enough and in a bearable way (within or perhaps at the edge of her comfort zone),the physiological trappings of anxiety will fade, and the child will feel more at ease. Her conclusion will probably be that it was less fearsome then she expected, and perhaps she will be less reticent the next time she is invited. In contrast, if your child is scared, and you allow her to avoid the situation, the fear will remain or even become greater as you gave your unspoken confirmation that this is a situation to be avoided. When a child confronts her fears, a parent can give her positive reinforcement, like a smile or a hug or a small treat, saying, "That was impressive—you faced your fears!" It is so easy to fall into the snare of lavishing attention on scared or avoidant behavior; try to give your child plenty of attention for brave and independent behavior.

Boundaries and parental authority

Most parents will be touched and remorseful about their child's suffering in school and his inability to talk for hours at a time. When the child comes home and can finally give vent to his feelings and frustrations, parents may feel unwilling to impose rules and standards of behavior that they feel are appropriate. In this way parental authority and boundaries may erode, and the child may slip into immature or negative modes of behavior. This will only harm the child for several reasons. The child may develop behavior problems that could last long after the SM has been forgotten. These may include oppositional behavior when going to sleep or doing homework, lack of respect for parents, and shirking chores. It may delay the acquisition of independent, age-appropriate behavior. This may eventually spill over onto his school behavior and cause him additional difficulties there. I frequently meet children who have recently overcome SM for the duration of which they were allowed to abstain from all school-related work. It is then a challenge to close the academic gaps that have grown and to acquire acceptable modes of behavior. It sends the child a message that he needs these special allowances at home and school because he is in some way deficient. When parents have clear, appropriate, compassionate boundaries and rules at home, it actually gives the child a sense of protection—home is a haven in which Mom and Dad know best.

11. How to select a school

Part of parents' multifaceted and high-stakes job is finding a school and, if required, a therapist for their child. It is part of being the leader and visionary of your family. Your child will be spending many hours a day in school over the course of twelve years, and you want to ensure that you have looked for the most suitable framework for your child, both emotionally and academically. All too often these fateful decisions are barely considered. There may be a neighborhood kindergarten or a local school that are the default choices. Options may be limited if there are laws determining which school children in your area attend. Often there are more choices for kindergarten than for school. Look into whichever options you may have. Be sure to check not only the academic standards of the school but also class size, population, and how well it will cater to your child's emotional needs. Look at the sensitivity of the staff and its members' abilities to address special needs. Spend some time there;feel the atmosphere and the tone of the teachers. You want a friendly and warm staff that is able and motivated to intervene in order to help your child overcome SM. Do your homework, and speak to parents of children who attend the school to hear their impressions.

12. Choosing a therapist

While a therapist is not a product in your supermarket trolley, never lose sight of the fact that you are the consumer, and you must be discerning. The first stage is to research what is the treatment of choice for your child's difficulty. In the case of a child with SM and other anxiety disorders,current research points to cognitive behavioral therapy as usually being the most effective treatment. Then consider the proximity of therapists and what their areas of expertise are, and ensure that they have ample experience in treating SM. Ask friends and acquaintances for recommendations, and you can also join relevant chat groups to consider others' experiences with a therapist for SM.

Once you have set up an appointment with a therapist, make sure that initially you are interviewing her and not the converse. Evaluate what her outlook is and which methods she employs. Is contact with the school staff and parents an integral part of her treatment? You might check where she studied and trained. Find out how much experience she has and how successful her treatments were. You could find out what her estimation of the duration of the therapy will be. Ask her for references so that you could talk to parents whose children she has treated and consider their recommendations.

Consider her personality and way of interacting—does she exude warmth and care, is she intelligent and understanding, is she a good listener, and does she inspire your trust? So many parents have come to me having spent years and fortunes on assorted unsuccessful interventions. Your child's welfare is at stake, and you must be discerning. It makes all the difference to have a therapist in whom you feel you can put your trust so that you can embark on a joint expedition toward overcoming SM.

13. Selective mutism and older children

Much of this book is written with the younger child in mind, until around ten years old, some of which is applicable to older children and teenagers too. Chapter 8 is specifically about therapy with older children. How may you, as a parent, assist your adolescent who has SM?

A child who has had SM for many years may have suffered collateral damage along the way. The longer SM lasts, the more a entrenched it may become—this is how he sees himself in school, and perhaps other places too, over many years. As he grows up and his cognitive abilities develop, he will be painfully aware of the difference between him and his peers. He may feel deficient and incompetent in social encounters, and this may affect his self-image and self-esteem. Early intervention is always recommended so that the SM will impact the child as little as possible. Initially SM may present as a relatively confined disorder, affecting the child a few hours a day in kindergarten, but over the years, it may develop into a more generalized anxiety disorder or evolve into depressive symptoms. In other cases, teenagers may seem relatively unscathed, possess good social skills, and lead a relatively contented life other than the difficulties inherent in their SM.

Many older children respond excellently to therapy that involves home, school, and therapy, and many employ their burgeoning awareness to combat their SM. It is not unusual for older children to have their own—often hugely successful—ideas about how to combat their SM,such as moving to a new school, or inviting the whole class home.

For other teenagers, SM may be so entrenched that they need medication to assuage their anxiety and give them the courage to shake off old habits. A psychiatrist may prescribe anxiety-reducing medication; it is often very effective in conjunction with cognitive behavior therapy.

One of the difficulties for the parents of a teenager with SM is that along with the attempt to engage the young person in a course of treatment come all the challenges of adolescence. An adolescent is setting off on her path toward separation from her family—each in her own way—and often does it with a flourish that can include moodiness and oppositional behavior, experimenting with risky company or behavior, diminished communication, and withdrawal from family activities. All of these can further exacerbate the parent-child relationship, interfering with the parents' quest to help their child.

While this is not the place for a treatise on how to parent teenagers, here follow a few guidelines that may be helpful.

Maintain a channel of communication
This may be easier said than done. Try to be available and open to chat when your teenager wishes to share thoughts and experiences with you (this may be in the small hours of the night!) Try to listen, and hear what you child has to say—we are often so busy thinking of what good advice we have to give that we barely pay attention to what our teen is saying. Make sure that you hear and see him—the same mirroring process that is so important with infants is equally vital in adolescence.

Try to be loving, positive, and nonjudgmental
When engaging in conversation, show your love and positive regard,even when this does not appear to be reciprocal. Remember that you are the parent and that even when your child may be antagonistic, you can set the tone and take steps to help your child.

Keep some boundaries
Often, almost by definition, your teenager is trying to extricate himself from the shackles of parental restrictions. All that freedom is threatening, and despite what he may say, he needs some boundaries and parental presence to keep him safe and on course. Choose, perhaps together with him, what are the bared-down rules and constrictions, and try to stick to them. Don't be afraid to be present; your child still needs you. Stay interested in his life, friends, school, and hobbies.

Try to find a therapist with whom your teen communicates

It will be a weight off your shoulders and may greatly improve your relationship to work with a competent therapist with whom you may navigate the stormy seas of adolescence and SM.

Believe in your teenager!

We continue to develop throughout our lives as we contend with obstacles and gain understanding. Your teen may currently be battling her selective mutism, yet with treatment she is likely to improve. Teenagers often save their least palatable side for their parents; try to keep that in mind when talking to her. Your belief in her ability to confront and overcome her challenges affects her belief in herself—she sees much of herself through your eyes. That is parent-power and must be used wisely. Your belief in her is a strong therapeutic tool for change. You can try some guided imagery on yourself to fast-forward to a video in your mind of your child five years from now, see her chatting to friends, studying in university, or working in an office, traveling and leading a full life. Believe that she can change and grow, while at the same time taking every precaution to get her the best professional help available.

14. Language issues in bilingual families

If your family is bilingual and your child with SM does not speak the local language fluently, this is an issue that is usually most effectively worked on at home where the child is most relaxed. For a shy child who does not speak in school or kindergarten and is not proficient in the local language, breaking the speech barriers in school in his second, poorly mastered language may prove an insurmountable task. Parents are advised to find ways to encourage their child to speak the local language at home by employing a babysitter or a teenager to engage the child in conversation in the local language in low-pressure, playful activities at home.

Parents may need to consider their attitude toward the local language and attempt to incorporate it more in the home. Many bilingual children with SM express negative attitudes toward the local language, which is a further hurdle to jump over in order to speak freely at school. Here again, parents may decide to try to model more positive attitudes toward the language, perhaps by buying a newspaper or listening to TV channels or radio in the local language. Similarly, immigrant families who maintain a circle of friends who speak their language of origin may try to expand their social network to include those who speak the local language. Parents who are seen by their child to be speaking imperfect English to English-speaking friends in the home can be powerful models their children may be inspired to emulate.

15. Transitions

Starting a new kindergarten or entering first grade may be a stressful experience and, as such, may cause regression if it proves too anxiety provoking for your child. However, a new start can be a window of opportunity for growth. A new teacher with whom the child has not yet established his non-talking behavior can sometimes break the cycle when she implements a behavior shaping plan before the school year begins. If the new teacher is prepared to come to the child's home in the summer and carry out the home-based sessions described in the Therapist's Manual and then carry out a school-based session before classes begin, this may be sufficient to enable the child to speak to the teacher in school or kindergarten once the academic year begins. For a full explanation, read the description of these sessions in <u>chapter 6</u>, the Therapist's Manual.

During any transition from one class to another, the parents should try to ease the child's anxiety by enabling him to become familiar with the new place, teachers, and children before the move occurs. Staff must be made aware of the anxiety issues of the child so that they will attempt to be as sensitive as possible to his needs.

16. Keeping an open mind and a watchful eye

Parents are constants in the childhood and adolescence of their children and are in a position to follow up over time; they will witness pitfalls, transitions, and achievements. It is possible that after the SM has been overcome, your child will have residual anxiety issues that you may want to address. For example, if your child remains excessively shy, cognitive-behavioral techniques could help him gain confidence. Parents must keep an open mind and a watchful eye so that all is done to ensure that their child continues to grow in confidence and social skills over time.

CBT WORKSHEET 1

A basic premise of Cognitive-Behavioral Therapy Is that
Thoughts → Feelings → Behavior
Hera follows a (very simplified) example:

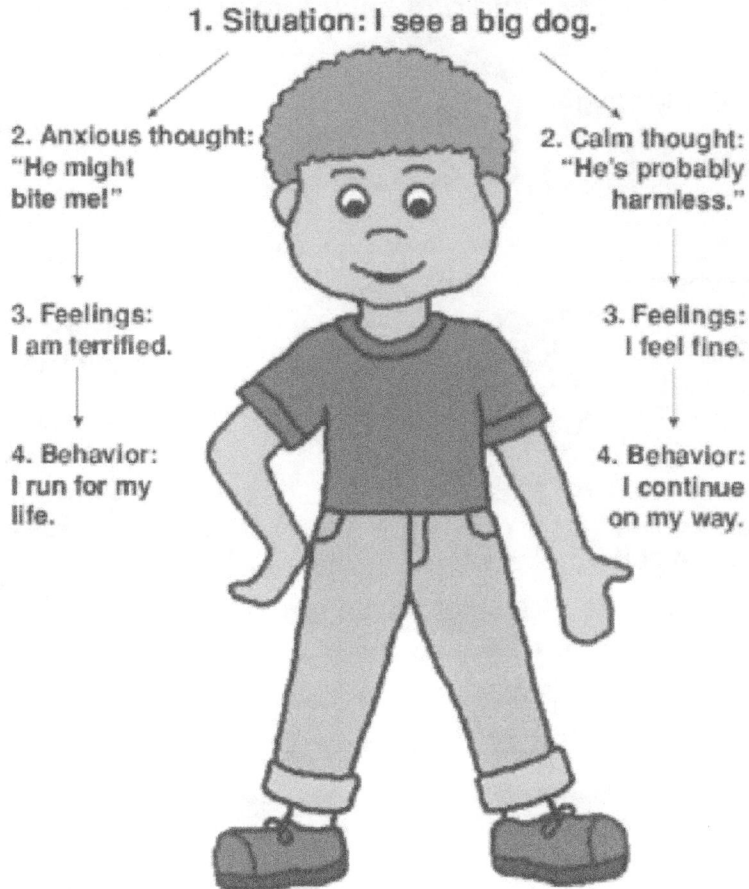

1. Situation: I see a big dog.

2. Anxious thought: "He might bite me!"

2. Calm thought: "He's probably harmless."

3. Feelings: I am terrified.

3. Feelings: I feel fine.

4. Behavior: I run for my life.

4. Behavior: I continue on my way.

Here we can see how our thoughts affect our feelings, which in turn affect our behavior. If we can learn to channel our thoughts in more productive ways, we can gradually learn to overcome our anxieties.

CXT WORKSHEET 2

Having a child with selective mulism can be anxiety provoking for parents, and if this parental worry is perceived by the child, it can, in turn, make the child with SM more anxious.

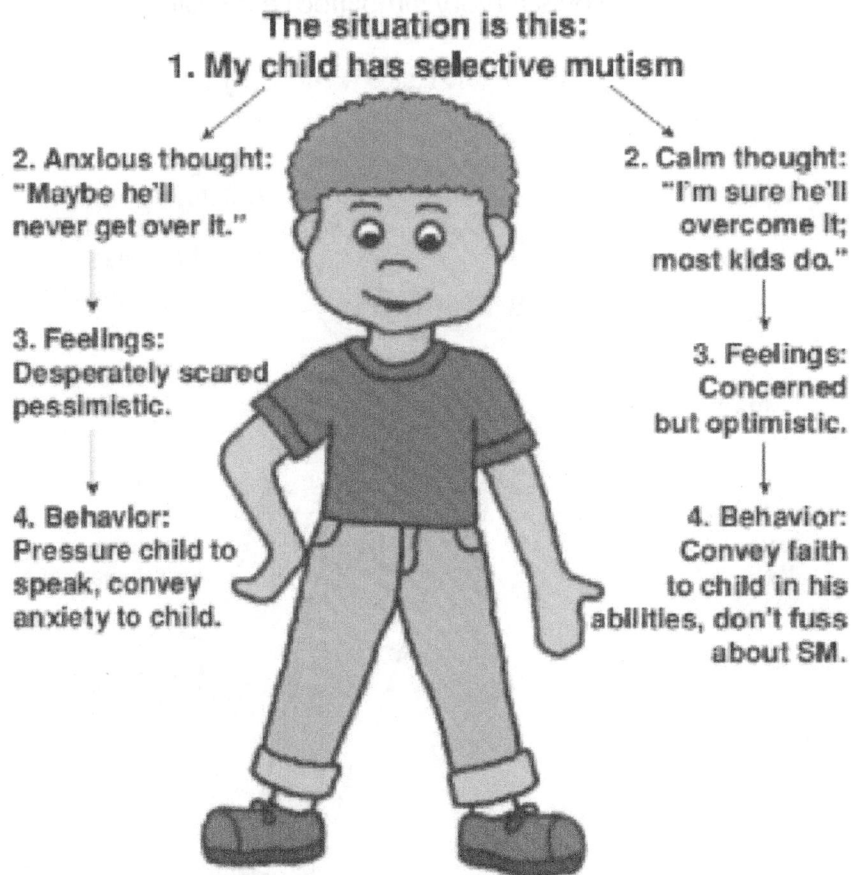

The situation is this:
1. My child has selective mutism

2. Anxious thought:
"Maybe he'll
never get over it."

3. Feelings:
Desperately scared
pessimistic.

4. Behavior:
Pressure child to
speak, convey
anxiety to child.

2. Calm thought:
"I'm sure he'll
overcome it;
most kids do."

3. Feelings:
Concerned
but optimistic.

4. Behavior:
Convey faith
to child in his
abilities, don't fuss
about SM.

Children know their parents so well! When we feel despair, our children absorb it and themselves feel more anxious. That is why when there are anxiety issues in the families of children with SM, and parents or siblings learn how to better control their anxiety, it has a ripple effect on the child too.

Teacher's Manual

still waters run deep

Contents of Teacher's Manual

4. Facilitating social interaction with other children
5. Building independence, assertiveness, and self-esteem in school
6. Blurring the distinction between home and school functioning
7. Transitions and home visits
8. Slotting in with the three-pronged intervention: therapist, parents, teacher facilitating progress on all three fronts

Introduction to Teacher's Manual

A challenge and a mystery confront a school or kindergarten teacher when a child fails to speak in her class. She may wonder: Can he speak, does he speak normally at home, why doesn't he speak, what is causing his silence, and is it something personal against me?

Then a host of further questions: How are his language skills, what are his cognitive abilities, how are his social skills, are there problems in his family, has some traumatic event caused his most unusual behavior?

And then still another bout of moot points: Should he be in my class, does he require special education; can I give him what he needs?

And finally, the most dramatic questions of all: Can he break free of his maladaptive silence, what is the treatment of choice, will he respond to the treatment?

Selective mutism often presents as a riddle. However, on further consideration, it is usually less mysterious than it seems. Much is now known about the causes and treatment of selective mutism, and on these pages answers will be given to all the questions posed above (and more...)

Firstly the answer to the last question: a resounding yes! Children with selective mutism usually respond well to the appropriate treatment and break free of their silent shackles in a relatively short-term intervention program. What's more, most of them function normally after they overcome selective mutism. They may remain shy and reticent but within regular parameters. In this manual, you will learn what SM is, how it can be treated, and how you as a teacher are in the eye of this storm, strategically placed exactly where the symptom is usually strongest—in school or kindergarten. In this treatment program, you may be a significant agent of change within a comprehensive program for the treatment of SM.

This chapter contains information specifically for you, the teacher, to enable you to help your student overcome SM. It is put succinctly, and includes a summary of sections of the other chapters for the very busy teacher with a bustling class to care for! If you have the time and inclination, reading the rest of this book will give you more depth and breadth about the causes and treatments of SM.

What is Selective Mutism?

Selective mutism (SM) is a childhood social communication disorder in which children consistently fail to speak in select situations despite the ability to understand and use language. Children with SM usually speak to family members at home, but do not speak at school. The speech patterns of each child with SM vary along a continuum of severity, from children who speak to everyone outside school and select peers in school, through children who fail to speak to everyone in school, including peers and staff. There is usually a striking contrast between the communicative child at home and the silent child in school. The vast majority of children with SM suffer from anxiety and many have some language difficulty. Most are shy and sensitive, and many are perfectionists and strong willed.

No link has been found between intelligence and SM, and no link has been found in the large research studies between traumatic events and SM. For a sensitive, anxious child, seemingly everyday events may be experienced as traumatic, such as being shouted at by a teacher, being embarrassed in front of a class, or being mocked by peers for a mispronunciation.

What Causes Selective Mutism?

Selective mutism is caused by the interaction between the nature of the child and external factors—nature and nurture. One can conceptualize this as various factors fitting into one of three groups: predisposing factors, triggers, and maintaining factors. (Adapted from Shipon-Blum 2007.)

Predisposing factors could include a child who is anxious, shy, hypersensitive or has a family history of shyness, anxiety, or selective mutism. This may include anxious parents and anxious behavior modeling by parents. Other predisposing factors could include speech impairments (usually expressive language), bilingualism, a negative self-image related to speech (e.g. not liking the sound of one's voice), and learning disabilities.

Triggers could include school or kindergarten admission, frequent geographical moves, the child's family belonging to a linguistic minority, or negative reactions to the child talking—bullying, shouting, mocking, etc.

Maintaining factors could include the following: the social isolation of families, misdiagnosis (that is, the child is wrongly diagnosed as having oppositional behavior, autism, retardation, etc.), or a lack of early and appropriate intervention. Other maintaining factors could be the lack of understanding by teachers, families, and psychologists; reinforcement of the mutism by increased attention or affection; heightened anxiety levels caused by pressure to speak; the ability to convey messages nonverbally; a lack of belief by significant adults in the child's ability to overcome the selective mutism.

When there is a combination of predisposing factors that heighten the child's vulnerability to SM, and triggers—events such as kindergarten admission or a geographical move—the scales could tip and bring about the onset of SM.

How Does Selective Mutism Present in School?

As explained above, each child with SM has his own configuration of where and with whom he doesn't speak. Some will not talk to anyone in school, while others will talk to staff and not to peers, and yet others will talk to friends and not to teachers. Many children with SM will whisper to one or two friends who become their spokespersons to the rest of the school. Some children will fully participate in all school activities except for those requiring speech, and some will participate in few activities. Some are very communicative using nonverbal gestures and facial expressions, while others may barely communicate nonverbally and may seem to be wearing a mask devoid of facial expression. Some children with SM may have a vibrant social life, while others may be socially isolated. At the end of the spectrum of severity of SM are children who appear frozen—they may not move unless guided by the teacher, nor eat, nor go to the bathroom. These children are often misdiagnosed as being autistic because that appears to be the case based on their behavior in school.

How does it affect the teacher?

A child with SM is often unobtrusive and undisruptive in the class. He will not be found to upturn tables or talk out of turn. This is why SM frequently remains undiagnosed and untreated—sometimes even unnoticed for many years. But for a teacher who strives to involve her students in class discussions and wishes to get to know the children and to further their academic and social development, a child with SM can be disconcerting. Furthermore, the implementation of what for many teachers is the intuitively obvious way to treat selective mutism—persuading the child to speak by using positive and negative methods (prizes or punishments)—can make things worse and rarely improves matters. It can be frustrating for teachers and it can feel personal, as if the teacher has done something wrong, when a child will not verbally respond to her. This is why it is usually necessary for a teacher to receive guidance on how to understand and help a child with SM.

Understanding the Child with Selective Mutism

While each child with SM has a unique configuration of functioning and emotions,certain reactions and feelings are common. One thing is almost always the case with a child who is not speaking in kindergarten or school:a child with SM suffers! He cannot be himself —the more spontaneous,communicative child he is in other contexts. He must expend effort to ensure that his radar informing him of who is in his proximity is always on, and control himself so that when his private space is encroached, or when he is in a setting in which he does not speak, he stays quiet. High and constant energy expenditure is required to maintain this awareness and control. This in itself is anxiety producing, however effortless the child with SM makes it appear.

The lack of verbal communication causes the child to miss out on social and learning experiences which would further his development. A child who cannot say what he wants will frequently be included in activities he wishes to avoid and conversely will be excluded from experiences he desperately wants to have. This is a recipe for frustration. This frustration is often taken out on his family when he returns home and can finally express himself. Sometimes the frustration expresses itself in school as the child makes his presence felt with his hands rather than his voice.

When a child with SM is unfortunate enough to be in a context in which he is misunderstood and considered to be unintelligent, unable to communicate, or oppositional, he may be inappropriately labeled and consequently placed in an unsuitable learning environment. This frequently exacerbates the child's difficulties. Parents confronted with a child who fails to speak in school frequently go through a period of heightened anxiety themselves. The parents' concern for their child and their grappling with schools and possible interventions as well as long-term projections and postulations regarding future implications for their beloved child can be overwhelming. To make matters worse, the parents' posturing to get appropriate intervention for their child can be misconstrued as over protectiveness and identified by the school as the cause, not the effect, of the child's SM.

For all these reasons (and many more), early intervention is vital. What's more, it usually works! Response to intervention using behavioral therapies for children with SM has been found to be highly effective. In addition, the following treatment plan is generally experienced by the child as an enjoyable, satisfying experience. Once children break the barriers and speak, they usually experience a surge of self- confidence.

How to Treat Selective Mutism

It is widely accepted today that behavioral methods with cognitive components are usually the most effective way to treat SM. It is also known that SM is usually anxiety-based, and that the family and school should be intimately involved in any course of treatment. In order for this to happen, it is vital to establish an open, communicative, and mutually respectful relationship between the teacher, the parents, and the therapist.

This treatment program aims to build bridges between the diverse settings in which the child lives, enabling him to move more confidently between the home and school. In other words, it aims to understand what allows him to speak at home and to try to incorporate those elements at school so that he will feel more comfortable there. At the same time, some factors at school may be conducive to assertiveness and independence, and the parents may wish to incorporate these factors at some level at home. This outlook is reflected in the locations of the therapy—at home and at school, as will be seen below.

This manual is presented as a part of a comprehensive treatment plan for therapist, parents, and teacher, each with their own tasks but working in conjunction with each other. This is in an ideal situation where there are the resources and the will to tackle SM from all three directions. However, if a full-scale intervention is not possible or it is thought that it is not called for, then this treatment plan offers a variety of ideas, interventions, and activities that can be implemented by the teacher, the parents, and the therapist alone without the full-scale program. In many cases, a partial implementation of the program by a teacher with the support of the parents can bring desirable results; often it is sufficient to help the child overcome selective mutism.

Overview of Therapy

The therapy plan before you employs behavioral methods and aims to **remove the symptom of failure to speak** in certain settings. I believe that, especially with young children, symptom removal is paramount because the symptom can affect the child's natural social, speech, and learning development as well as exerting a powerful influence on how the child feels about himself—his self-confidence, his social self-image, and his view of himself as "normal." In addition to this aim of facilitating speech,during the assessment stage other issues may have been found that can be addressed within this therapy, such as independence, assertiveness, and anxiety within the family. These may be incorporated as aims within the therapy, as part of the parents', teacher's, and therapist's interventions.

In some cases, children with SM have additional difficulties other than failure to speak. Some have speech impediments, and others may have additional anxiety issues that may require specific treatment beyond the scope of this plan. Once the non-speech is remedied, the child will be more able to participate in the requisite treatment for other difficulties should they exist.

When a child successfully overcomes SM, this in itself has a powerful self-affirming effect. The child learns that he has the courage to overcome difficulties, and this can have a ripple effect on further problems the child may have, especially anxiety-related issues.

Prior to the start of treatment, the therapist should interview the parents and the teacher in order to assess the child's speech patterns, his strengths and difficulties, and other factors relating to SM. After the assessment is completed, therapy sessions with the child may begin while guidance is given simultaneously to the teacher and the parents. The therapist will explain the therapy outline to the parents and will give ongoing updates regarding progress once therapy has started. Three-way meetings involving the therapist, school staff, and parents should be held at regular intervals.

Here follows a summary of the therapist's sessions with the child, then the parents' interventions will be outlined, and then I will focus on **what you as a teacher can do to help the child to overcome SM in school**.

The Stages of Therapy: Home-Based, School-Based

A primary aim of the therapy is to build on the child's optimum functioning, which is usually at the home, and to facilitate similar behavior in other surroundings. As such, the **therapy begins, whenever possible, at home**. The aim of these home sessions is to reach the stage wherein the child speaks directly and comfortably to the therapist.

In the initial sessions in the child's home, the therapist will engage in minimal small talk with the parent, trying to be unobtrusive to the child. The initial aim is that the child will talk in the presence of the therapist. Gradually over the course of the home sessions, the therapist will play with the child and other family members and will finally direct speech to the child and play alone with him. By the end of the home sessions' stage of the program, the child should be speaking directly with the therapist.

Once the child speaks to the therapist in the home, the **therapy is moved to the school. T**herapy will take place one to three times a week in a designated room in the school. Initially, the aim of the sessions will be for the child to speak to the therapist in the room in school. Activities may include games conducive to speech, listening to recordings of the child from home, and arts and crafts. The activities included in these sessions will be modified in accordance with the child's preferences.

Usually this transfer of location goes smoothly, and the child continues to speak to the therapist in the school-based therapy room. Sometimes the child is reticent to speak in the new school setting. If this is the case, the therapist will employ a variety of tools to facilitate speech. This could include recording the child at home and playing the tape in the sessions, including a sibling or inviting the parents to participate in the initial school sessions.

Once the child is speaking to the therapist in school, **the generalization stage** begins. Here the aim is **to broaden the child's speaking habits** to include as many people as possible, at first within the therapy room at school. The therapist invites classmates and staff to join in the sessions in small steps and employs behavioral techniques when necessary.

Once the child is speaking to several people in the therapy room, the next stage is to broaden the settings in which the child speaks. In order to achieve this, the sessions are moved either to an open space in the school, such as a hall or play area, or to a corner in the class itself. Here, using the same methods of playing, recording, and other activities used up to now, the child is enabled to speak in the classroom setting.

Parents' Interventions and Tasks

Here follows a summary of suggested parents' interventions to be carried out in conjunction with the therapist and teacher. For a fuller description of the parents' interventions, see chapter 4, the Parents' Manual.

Assessment: The parents' input is vital at the assessment stage, as they are often the only ones who are witness to their child's optimum speech functioning and have the sensitivity and intuition to consider and select realistic goals and time frames.

Home therapy sessions: The initial therapy sessions take place in the home and are planned and led by both the therapist and the parents.

School therapy sessions: Once the therapy sessions are moved to the school, the parents will help prepare the homework for the sessions, which is often recordings or films of the child, and they may be asked to attend certain school therapy sessions if the child's progress stalls at one of the transitional stages.

School-based talking-playing sessions: Whenever possible, it is recommended that parents go to the child's school or nursery between one and three times a week, for short talking-playing sessions. This will be described in more detail below, as it must be carried out in conjunction with the teacher and at her convenience.

Inviting friends home, telephone calls, recordings: Helping the child speak to peers at home will make it easier for him to begin to speak at school. Even if he fails to speak at home, inviting friends home will help develop his social skills. The teacher can advise parents as to whom she considers to be compatible for home play-dates. Telephone calls may be a first step in verbal communication with schoolmates and staff, and can be encouraged by parents. Recordings are a useful pre-direct speech step where a child's voice is present without him having to speak directly. Parents are recommended to accustom their child to play with voice recordings, which can be useful in school and therapy as described more fully below.

Desensitization outside school: The behavioral techniques that the therapist is using in school may be implemented at home, which will take the child from silence to speech in small structured steps. This could include helping the child to speak to friends or family members at home or helping him to speak in a restaurant or store. The therapist may guide the parents in the construction and application of a behavior modification program. Many parents have successfully implemented such programs independently, expanding their child's circle of friends and relatives with whom they speak.

Lowering anxiety: An underlying premise of the treatment of SM is that it is usually anxiety-based, and in order to free the child of SM, effort must be made in all settings to lower the child's anxiety levels. Parents learn to ease the pressure on their child to speak, minimizing or eradicating both positive and negative reinforcements, both of which may make the child more anxious about his SM.

Modeling: Research has found that often (but not always) one of the parents of a child with SM has some anxiety issues himself, and in these cases parents are encouraged to attempt to model overcoming their anxieties and broadening their social circles. When parents feel that this is relevant and desirable, they may receive guidance from the therapist on how to foster and model brave, outgoing behavior to their children.

Increasing independence: Parents are encouraged to consider how to increase their child's independence and feelings of competence at home, which will fortify their self-confidence and school functioning.

Bilingual children and immigrants: Bilingual children who are not confident in English should receive informal, playful language tutoring at home where they are more verbal and less anxious. For a timid child, overcoming selective mutism in a language in which he feels incompetent could be an insurmountable challenge.

Teachers' Interventions and Tasks

The teacher is a pivotal player in any attempt to ease the child's selective mutism because in almost all cases, the symptom—failure to speak—is at its strongest in her area of jurisdiction. It is also here in school that much of the fallout from the SM occurs. Apart from the constant self-control, frustration, and suffering that a child experiences having to maintain his silence day-in day-out for hours at a stretch, further negative side effects occur.

The child may perceive himself to be different and less competent than other children, having failed to master a basic communication tool in school. This may cause the child to develop a negative self-image, which may linger long after the SM is gone. It requires great sensitivity on the part of the teacher to convey to the child belief in his abilities and potential that goes so far beyond the narrow area of difficulty speaking in school.

The specific tasks that teachers can carry out in order to assist the child in his struggle to overcome SM fall into six general areas:

1. Developing a communicative relationship between the teacher and child

Often when confronted with a child with SM, the teacher feels that the basic key to communication is missing, so that a personal relationship between her and the child is not feasible. This attitude, while understandable, is not only misguided, it is damaging to the child. Usually a child with SM is very sensitive, and he cannot tell you or others with words the numerous things that may be upsetting him in the course of a school day. So for this child, even more than for others, a personal relationship with the teacher is vital in order to ease his troubled school experience. This same communication impediment can be improved by a personal relationship with the teacher, whereby he may gain the invaluable experience of a close relationship with an adult in school. This is a building block toward speech; as he becomes comfortable communicating nonverbally with the teacher and feels the positive effects on his school experience, his anxiety will decrease and he may feel braver in his attempts to talk.

But how can one build a communicative relationship with a child who doesn't talk? Indeed, it is not simple and calls for sensitivity, resourcefulness, creativity, persistence, and most of all, patience. The teacher must **set aside a five-minute slot every day** if possible, otherwise at least three times a week during which she will try to build a communicative, reciprocal relationship with the child. I know that this alone is a lot to ask of a teacher of a large bustling class. But usually this investment of the teacher's time generates ample dividends. The sessions should be pleasant, unpressured, and designed not to raise the anxiety level of the child. Initially, depending on the severity of the SM, the child may barely respond.

Take as a starting baseline whatever nonverbal communication the child is able to convey. This may be nodding, pointing, smiling, or eye contact. Build the initial sessions on questions that will not be alarming for the child but will show that you are interested in him and want to get to know him. For example, if a child nods and points, you could spread a picture of a variety of foods (or games, or places,or children in the class) and ask him to point to those he most likes. These reticent children may take a few seconds longer to respond than is common in most conversations. Be sure to wait those extra seconds and not to go on to the next question! Show him that you believe in his ability to communicate to you by giving him that extra time to respond. **Children usually perceive our belief in them, and this bolsters their belief in themselves**. Be sure not to expect or demand responses from the child that are beyond his current ability. For example, do not demand a verbal answer if the child is not able to talk in school, or pointing if the child barely nods his head.

When the child perceives your care and investment in him, he may feel more at ease and able to broaden his communications repertoire and you might discuss issues that could improve his school experience. For example, you could ascertain if he is happy sitting in his place in the class or being part of a certain reading group, or if he would like to participate in a certain project. In this way, he will deepen his connection to you and also see that he stands to gain from his communication in that it may solve some of his problems in school. This serves a double purpose. He is simultaneously experiencing a supportive, understanding, pleasant, communicative relationship with a teacher, and through it he is finding solutions to his difficulties. This will give him a taste of how much easier life will be once he can talk.

Finally, this personal relationship will be the sheltered cocoon in which the teacher may implement a behavior modification schedule enabling direct speech between the child and herself, as described below.

2. The teacher's behavior shaping plan

A behavioral treatment schedule, in many ways similar to that implemented by the therapist in her sessions, may be constructed for you to use in class. The aim would be to build on whatever communication the child is initially able to employ with you, and take small controlled steps toward speech. It may be helpful to start with a couple of home visits, perhaps the child will speak in your presence or to you at home. Even if he doesn't, it will show your interest in him, and slightly blur the boundaries between home and school. See point 6 below for more on home visits. The school sessions should be planned together with the therapist and parents.

It is important to **hold regular school-based sessions with the child, a few times a week**—a daunting task for a teacher of a large and lively class, but a key to steady progress.

The first step would be to build a reciprocal, communicative, pleasant relationship, as described in point 1 above. In the framework of this relationship, you could gradually work toward broader nonverbal communication, such as pointing, gestures for "like" and "dislike," and so on. Then you could try to utilize recordings. Using a small office tape recorder, you could ask a few easy questions, like what is your favorite color or how many siblings do you have, and then ask the child to record the answer at home and play it to you in your next session. Or it may be easier for the child to record a WhatsApp of himself reading at home and to send it to you every evening, which you will hear together the following day you in school. Once the child is playing recordings of himself reading to the teacher comfortably in school, the teacher may ask the child to read one of the sentences she has just heard on the tape. When listening at school to recordings made at home, it is vital that it takes place initially in a private room, so that the child will not be heard by all his classmates to begin with. If this is successfully carried out over a few sessions, the place at which the teacher hears the recordings could be changed to a more public area, perhaps a corridor, and eventually it could be next to the teacher's desk in the class. This should be done with great sensitivity, ensuring that each change is neither too early, nor too anxiety provoking for the child. The rule of slow but sure progress will allow each step to be within the child's bearable anxiety zone.

If no therapist is involved in the care of the child and available to guide you in the construction and application of a behavior shaping program, then it is advisable to read the Therapist's Manuals (chapters 6-8) thoroughly before implementing a treatment plan so that you will understand the basic premises that greatly facilitate progress, such as gradual progression and short, enjoyable sessions. The sessions can be adapted to be carried out by you or another staff member in school, and they are designed to guide the child gently from cooperation, to nonverbal communication, and ultimately to verbal communication using behavioral techniques.

Teacher-therapist mini-coaching conversations: I have found it most effective to coach teachers who are carrying out a behavior shaping program with a child, by building a structured intervention plan which is depicted in a chart, and having brief phone conversations with the teacher after each of her sessions. In these mini-coaching conversations we consider together the appropriateness of the goal set for the child in the recent session, the child's response, and plan together what to aim for in the upcoming teacher-child session. In a teacher's pressured and busy schedule, these 5 minute coaching/evaluating/planning phone calls with a therapist following each teacher-child session, keep up momentum, involvement and commitment. It encourages the teacher to be consistent in carrying out regular,scheduled,pre-planned sessions and keeps progress on track.

The following example of a stepladder of goals for a teacher's behavior shaping plan, is simplified and concise, and in all probability some of the stages would be repeated a number of times in order for achievements to be consolidated before moving on to the next goal. In addition, although it is omitted for the sake of readability and simplicity, in every session, **previously accomplished tasks are repeated before a new goal is attempted**. Obviously, this is just an example to give flesh to the idea of a teacher's behavior modification plan; for each child a tailor-made plan would have to be designed, based on his baseline of current communication in school, his strengths and difficulties. The program would have to be fine-tuned and altered depending on how the child responds to each attempted goal.

Example of a stepladder of goals for a teacher's behavior shaping schedule

Five minute sessions held by Ms. Clarke and Liz in kindergarten

Ladder of tasks Session #	Mini-coaching phone call with therapist after session	Result-Date
1. Ms. Clarke engages Liz in conversation in private room, Liz answers Ms. C.'s questions by nodding yes and no. Every night Liz sends Ms. C. a voice WhatsApp that they listen to together the following day in kindergarten.	10.12.2016	Liz nodded yes\no 10.12.2016
2. Ms. C. asks what Liz likes to eat, Liz points to pictures of food in a book in response.		
3. Liz plays a WhatsApp of her saying a phrase of a nursery rhyme, (looking at a storybook depicting the rhyme) to Ms. C.		
4. Liz plays a WhatsApp of her saying a phrase of a nursery rhyme to Ms. C. then says the same sentence to Ms. C. directly.		

5. Liz plays Chinese whispers with Ms. C. and Joan (Liz speaks to Joan outside school and whispers to her in school.)		
6. Liz plays a WhatsApp of her saying a phrase of a nursery rhyme. Liz plays hot/cold with Ms. C. and Joan, whispering hot/cold into a microphone.		
7. Liz, Joan, Ms. C. play "snap", Liz says "snap" when 2 cards are identical.		
8. Liz, Joan and Ms. C. play 20 questions, Liz answers yes and no to the questions.		
9. Liz, Joan and Ms. C. play " I went to the store and bought a….." each player adding an item in turn.		
10. Session 9 is repeated in a public space in the kindergarten when the other children are in the yard.		
11. Session 9 is repeated in the public area inside the kindergarten when other children are in the room.		

Using recordings or apps

Often, understandably, the teacher or kindergarten teacher doesn't have the time or mind space to embark on a full-scale behavior intervention schedule. However, I urge you, at the very least, to try a mini-intervention of listening to recordings of the child on a daily basis. When incorporated into a daily schedule, it need not take more than one minute of a teacher's time, and very often it precipitates a seismic shift in the child's functioning.

The idea is to hear the child's voice in school daily, with progressively longer recordings from week to week. A good way to start is for the child to send the teacher audio WhatsApp messages every day from the comfort of his home and under the guidance of his parents, perhaps in answer to an audio WhatsApp message sent by his teacher earlier on. For example, the teacher could send a voice WhatsApp question: "What is your favorite animal?" Then the child could answer, "A horse!" The teacher would then hear both recordings together with the child in a private place in the school. Once this has been repeated every day for a week, the bar could be raised, and the child could say a full sentence in response. For example, the teacher could ask, "Tell me the names of all the people in your family" or "What did you eat for supper?" or "What did you do over the weekend?" Then the teacher will hear the response that the child sent the following day in school in a private place. Once the child habituates to having his increasingly long recordings being heard by the teacher in a private space, the location in which the recordings are heard could be more public; for example, in the classroom during recess. Or perhaps it could remain in the private room, but the last word of the recording would be repeated by the child in a whisper to the teacher after they have heard it together. In this way, in a painless, brief daily intervention, the child's voice is heard in school. Keys to success here are constancy and frequency

—one minute a day sometimes yields dramatic leverage toward facilitating speech!

3. Lowering the child's anxiety level in school

As previously explained, SM is usually an anxiety-based condition. In the past, this sensitive child's response to an anxiety-provoking experience was to refrain from talking. This may have happened on the first day of a new kindergarten, or when shouted at, or when he felt insecure in his language or social skills, or when asked a question he felt uncomfortable answering. Since then the selective mutism has become ingrained in how he responds (or fails to do so) in some situations.

A sensitive child requires specialized hothouse conditions in order to blossom and thrive – see chapter 2 "Orchid and Dandelion Children." It is a challenge to provide this sheltered environment in school, yet this optimum setting enables the child to achieve his potential. In order to establish conditions conducive to starting to talk, steps should be taken to lower the child's anxiety in school. The **personal contact with the teacher** described above is a huge leap toward making the child more comfortable in school. Other steps can be considered within the framework of this teacher-child communicative relationship. Often children with SM find themselves sitting next to incompatible peers and have no way to express their distress. Try to find out **whom the child would be happiest sitting next to, as well as at which place in the class**—perhaps not right in the front where he is in the limelight and under the constant scrutiny of teachers. Similarly in kindergarten, at circle time, there may be children next to whom the child suffers, unnoticed.

A main way to lower the child's anxiety in school or kindergarten is to **refrain from putting pressure on the child to speak** when he is not ready to do so. Often in their enthusiasm to get the child talking, teachers feel intuitively that some coaxing in that direction would suffice to get him to speak. In fact, the opposite is nearly always the case. The less general pressure is put on the child to talk, the lower his anxiety levels will drop, and the more comfortable he will be. Once he feels at ease, he will be closer to being confident enough to speak.

Pressure to speak can take two forms: positive and negative. Neither is generally productive. Positive pressure can be the promise of a prize or a candy if a child says "good morning," and negative pressure could be not allowing a child to participate in an activity or receive a candy if he fails to answer a question. In many kindergartens, the teacher may ask the child to speak to her every morning for an entire year, is disappointed time and again, and the result is that every morning on entering the kindergarten the child is asked to do something that he is unable to do. That surely is an anxiety-provoking start (or middle, or end) to the child's day. Within the behavior-shaping program described here, small, structured, low-anxiety steps can be taken by the teacher to guide the child gently toward speech.

Schools and kindergartens abound with other potentially anxiety-provoking activities for a sensitive child in addition to speaking. Care should be taken to allow the child with SM to modify or circumvent these tasks. Here again, all rests on the personal relationship between the teacher and child, which enables the teacher to understand what exactly the child perceives as anxiety provoking.

This could include (and varies for each child) writing on the board, participating in plays and dances, leading the children out to recess, and giving out papers to the other children,to name just a few. Here there is a very fine line between respecting the child's nature by not asking him to do something that is too difficult for him, and **encouraging him to participate as fully as possible in kindergarten or school**. It requires great discernment on the part of the teacher to perceive where that line lies. While not wanting to cause the child anxiety, you want to involve him in school activities as much as he is able to do so within his comfort zone and work toward expanding his social and academic participation.

A final point under the category of lowering the child's anxiety is the **way in which you talk about the child's selective mutism**, both to the child himself, and to the other children in his class. The two keys are **normalization** and a **calm, optimistic** take on SM. When children ask, "Why doesn't Jenny speak?" your answer should be along the lines of "Jenny does speak perfectly at home, and I'm certain that she will speak here soon as well." In your words and tone you are showing the children that it is not so pathological—Jenny does speak at home—nor such cause for concern, as you have confidence in Jenny that she will overcome the SM. Once again, your belief in the child's ability to progress is a potent force for strengthening her self-confidence and belief in her ability to develop and overcome.

The same elements should shape the way you talk to the child about his selective mutism. This should seldom be discussed unless the subject is initiated by the child or it is decided otherwise in a broad therapy intervention plan. If your understanding of the child's SM is reiterated too often, this in itself can become a form of pressure. Your message should **be: "There are many children who find it difficult to talk in school who do manage to talk** after a while (normalization), we know how to help you overcome it soon (confidence and belief in the child's strengths)." In this way, the child learns that many other children also have SM, that it can be and usually is overcome, that you have confidence in his ability to speak normally, and that you can help him in his quest to speak.

4. Facilitating social interaction with other children

A child who does not speak in kindergarten or school will lose valuable communication and social skills experience. Depending on the form the SM takes, the child may be social and involved in reciprocal relationships with peers in ways other than speech, or he may be withdrawn and isolated. In all cases, the teacher's gentle intervention to enable maximum social interaction is recommended.

With a withdrawn child, the teacher should consider who may be compatible playmates and try to couple the child with SM together with those children. This could be in free play, in the seating place in the room, or in small groups. If you have developed a personal relationship with the child, you may be able to facilitate this social interaction by being a part of the small group initially until the child feels at ease without you by his side.

5. Building independence, assertiveness, and self-esteem in school

Selective mutism can infuse some children with a desperate sense of lack of control; they have lost the usual means children have of controlling their surroundings with their speech, such as requesting certain foods or social and academic activities, as well as voicing their unwillingness to be part of other goings-on with peers and in their studies. Again, the degree to which this sense of lack of control occurs varies from child to child, but it is intrinsic in the failure to speak of selective mutism. Teachers should attempt to return some control to the child by structuring the child's human and learning environment.

The first way this can be done is by **maximizing any communication abilities the child has;** if he can communicate by gestures, use these to the hilt. Involve him in choices; ask his opinion in a way he will be able to respond with the gestures in his repertoire. Construct further nonverbal gestures to enable him to convey to you common needs, such as going to the bathroom, feeling hungry, wishing to go to the yard, and so on. Use your creativity to find ways to give him a say in what he does. Encourage him to be assertive, both in the academic and the social choices he makes.

Consider what his strengths are and try to highlight these to fortify his self-esteem. Many children with SM develop alternative ways of reaching out to others, such as music and art. If this is the case with your student, give him a position in class that will make these abilities prominent and appreciated without intimidating the child by putting him in the limelight more than his comfort level allows. He may possess academic strengths; make sure other children are aware of his abilities and that he is made to feel really good about them. You could praise his work, frame and display it, read out his essays, or show his Lego construction, for example. In short, show him that you think him able and esteemed for who he is and what he does.

A powerful, insidious force at work in the relationship between the child and his teacher is her **belief (or lack of it) in the child**— his strengths, his personality and skills, and his ability to overcome his selective mutism. Teachers often feel hopeless, helpless, and desperate when considering the prospects of a child with SM. It may be hard to understand how a child who does not speak,contrary to all normal behavior and expectations and despite incessant cajoling and persuading, will be able to start speaking in school. Children perceive what you think and expect of them, and they may be convinced by a teacher's pessimism and feel hopeless themselves as a result. In stark contrast, a teacher's belief in a child's ability to overcome will be perceived by the child and strengthen his feelings of competence and his belief in himself.

A teacher's belief in a child is a powerful force indeed, with tangible, positive effects. But how can you conjure up this belief when it doesn't exist? Here the parents and therapist may come to your aid. From the parents you can hear about the child's ability to speak at home, to converse, argue, sing, and shout. Watch home movies of the child talking, and you will understand that this is who he is when freed from the shackles of his SM. From the therapist—and in my experience—you can learn that nearly all children with SM do overcome it in time, and with appropriate help this can be a fairly short process. You have no reason for pessimism, and good reason for optimism. If you let your newfound belief in the child shine through, you will buffer his self-belief and consequently help him to speak in school.

Sometimes it is tempting to "baby" a child with selective mutism. Because he does not speak, his teacher and friends respond for him. Often he would have given an answer through gestures, but those around him did not wait the couple of seconds more he required to give his response. **Return to him the responsibility to respond and make choices in any way he is able**, including gestures, such as nodding, pointing, and using previously decided upon signs.

Similarly, ensure that he is encouraged to be as independent as he can be. Lack of speech is generally no reason to exempt a child from hanging up his coat, unpacking his lunch box, or washing his hands. In extreme cases, selective mutism can present as a child who seems "frozen" and indeed needs help to take out his lunch box. But most children with SM are capable of some level of independent behavior if the staff controls the urge to coddle them. When a child sees himself engaging in independent functioning in school or kindergarten, this fosters within him a feeling of competence and self-esteem.

A word of caution about encouraging writing in place of speaking: It is tempting to use the written word once the child has mastered writing, as a way of communicating things beyond the scope of gestures. I am generally against using written communication for three reasons. It is far removed from verbal and body language, it is not a precursor to speech in the way that gestures are, and it can become entrenched as a good enough way of conveying thoughts and wishes, which may diminish the urgency of acquiring speech in school. However, every teacher must consider for herself the costs and benefits of encouraging written communication in the place of speech for each child.

6. Blurring the distinction between home and school functioning

For the child with selective mutism, school or kindergarten has usually been singled out as the place in which he does not talk, and home as the place in which he does. One of the aims of the intervention is to enable social communication and speech that is closer to the child's home functioning than his current behavior in school. This can be done in two main ways. Firstly, in your open,ongoing meetings and calls with the parents, try to learn what you can do to emulate certain aspects of the home environment in school. The **personal sessions with the child** described above are one way of building a caring, warm relationship in which you attempt to become closer to and more aware of the emotional needs of the child. This may resemble aspects of a close mother-child relationship as contrasted with a more distant teacher-child one. If a child uses email, you could supplement this contact by emailing and receiving emails from him when he is at home. Similarly, if he will speak on the phone, that could be a good way to start verbal contact when he is in the lower-anxiety surroundings of his home.

A second way, which is also a wonderful way to establish a trusting, personal relationship with the parents, is home visits. It shows the child how interested you are in getting to know him and takes you away from being associated exclusively with school. This may take the relationship to a further level of closeness. When visiting at his home, you should not demand any behavior the child has not shown at school—there should be no pressure to speak—but do show interest in his games and hobbies. He can show you his bedroom, yard, computer games he enjoys playing, and so on. You could also play with him a game of his choice. Do not insist on anything that the child shows resistance to doing. See if he is willing to show you a video of him talking without making any fuss on your part of the fact that he is talking. It could be a video of a vacation or some special family activity or birthday. In this way, in a light and pleasant atmosphere, you may hear his voice for the first time! If so, it will be most helpful to continue using the recordings in school, as is described in point 2 above. The visit must be planned together with his parents beforehand so that they will have a video of the child and a game to play at hand, and so that they will understand that no pressure will be placed (by you or them) on the child to speak. A general rule with children who are anxious is not to make too much of a fuss, not to put them in the limelight, not to express too much excitement about their achievements and attributes, as this hullabaloo could increase their feelings of anxiety. So when you do hear the child speak for the first time, be moderately pleased about it, as too much excitement may make him decide to stop talking!

7. Transitions and home visits

When a child moves from one educational setting to another—for example from one kindergarten to another, from kindergarten to school or from one grade to another—this may offer a window of opportunity for change and progress, or conversely it may be stressful and cause regression. Sometimes a fresh start with staff and children who do not have preconceived notions about whether the child speaks, enables him to begin to speak without causing a huge commotion of surprise and excitement among friends and teachers; commotion is usually anathema for an anxious or shy child. However, the opposite may be the case, as an unknown environment and the adjustment it entails may engender higher levels of anxiety and stress,causing the child to retreat further from social communication in school. Therefore,transitions must be approached with caution and sensitivity.

How then, to promote growth during transitions? **Home visits** by an as yet unfamiliar teacher may work wonders. The teacher should visit the home before the school year has begun; she has not yet been associated with school, and she is not yet necessarily included in the group of people with whom the child doesn't speak. The aim of the home visits initially is to hear the child's voice; then engage in some activity in which he speaks, though not directly to the teacher; and finally, engage in direct verbal communication with him. This may occur in one visit or it may (and usually does) take a few visits. The rule is to go slowly in order to enable the child to gradually feel comfortable enough to speak in the presence of a stranger. These home visits are similar to the initial home-based therapy sessions described in chapter 6, the Therapist's Manual, which you may want to read before embarking on this project.

Home visits must be planned carefully with the parents beforehand so that the teacher may slip into the home environment without fuss and without her focusing on the child in any way. The parents and teacher must plan to ensure that the child will be engaged in an enjoyable activity that requires speech and that takes place in the presence of the teacher.

During the initial home visit, the teacher should aim to be as unobtrusive as possible, a fly on the wall, enabling the child to speak in her presence. There should be no eye contact with the child, no initiation of any communication with the child;she should sit in an unobtrusive place and may engage in minimal small talk with the mother or father. In the Parents' Manual, parents are encouraged to record their child in a playful way for fun. They could play one of these recordings in the initial home visit as long as it is something that they have done before and won't be perceived by the child as something out of the ordinary. In this way, the child's voice would be present from the start. Once the child speaks in the teacher's presence, the next step would be to play a game with the child, teacher and a family member in which speech is required, but not direct speech between the child and the teacher. After this has been achieved, the teacher may try to have a direct conversation with the child, again, with sensitivity and gentleness. Finally, once the child is speaking to the teacher at home, one session between the teacher and the child should be held in the kindergarten or school, prior to the beginning of the school year, in which the child talks to the teacher while engaged in activities previously played in the home sessions.

This progression during the home visits from listening to recorded speech, to hearing the child speak, to direct speech with the teacher, usually takes a few sessions, and many teachers may not be available to invest so much time. In that case, one home visit will have to suffice. It should be noted, however, that when a teacher can take the time to go the child's home several times with a pre-planned strategy, it often circumvents months of working toward speech later on in school.

In addition to the teacher's home visits, the parents should be given a list of the children in the new class and encouraged to arrange play-dates so that the child knows some classmates on the first day of school.

Great sensitivity is required by the staff on the initial days of school or kindergarten so that all elements that may make the child less anxious and more confident will be in place. These include sitting him next to a friend and explaining to the other teachers the need to be gentle with him. Finally, if the child becomes acquainted with the physical school premises prior to the beginning of school, he will feel more confident navigating the logistics of getting to his room on the first day.

8. Slotting in with the three-pronged intervention: therapist, parents, teacher facilitating progress on all three fronts

As has been mentioned, fluid, open, and respectful contact between the school, the parents, and the therapist (in cases in which therapy is taking place) is most conducive to improvement. These three partners must share updates regularly so that the interventions of each side will complement progress on the other fronts. For example, if the parents report that the child is having successful play-dates with a certain classmate, it may be wise for the teacher to sit them together in class.

Once the therapy reaches the stage of school sessions, the therapist will have to coordinate with you in order to set a convenient time and place. At certain points in the school-based sessions, the therapist may wish to invite you to participate in order to generalize the child's speaking in school to include you. At a later stage, sessions will take place within the class, which must also be arranged with you.

Parental playing-talking sessions: It is recommended that parents come to school or kindergarten between one and three times a week for talking-playing sessions. These must be planned by the teacher and parent with the therapist's guidance to ensure that they will take place at a time and location that is convenient for the school. Playing-talking sessions are short, informal periods during which the parent plays and talks with the child in school or kindergarten. The parent considers where in the school her child will speak to her, which depends on the severity of the SM. Some children will speak with a parent or family member in a secluded corner of the class while others need the security of a closed room in order to speak.

These sessions significantly boost the effectiveness of the therapy. Instead of the child speaking once a week in school during one hour in therapy with the therapist, he is now speaking several times a week in school—for example, twice with a family member and once with the therapist. In order to maximize the effectiveness of these sessions, they should be planned with the therapist and the teacher so that they complement the concurrent stages of therapy and classroom functioning. They will be structured according to the same behavioral principles used in the therapist's interventions—initially the child will speak to the parent in a private area, then the circle with whom he speaks will be gradually enlarged to include friends and staff, and finally his speech will be generalized to include additional settings in the school, such as public areas and the classroom. The aim is to enable him to speak to everyone in all settings. You can read more about the playing-talking sessions in chapter 4, the Parents' Manual.

A warm, sensitive, and committed teacher can make the world of a difference to a child with SM. By implementing the interventions described here, either as part of a broader treatment plan together with a therapist and parents, or in conjunction with the parents alone, teachers can significantly help a child with SM break out of his silence and join the ranks of socially communicative, talking children in kindergarten and school.

Therapist's Manual 1

Behavioral Therapy for Young Children

still waters run deep

Contents of Therapist's Manual

Introduction to Therapist's Manual

Helping a child with selective mutism may seem to be a near impossible task for a therapist: How can you treat a child who does not speak, perhaps will not use body gestures, and may even appear "frozen" during sessions? And say you do manage to break the barriers during sessions in your clinic, and the child speaks and plays with you, are you really helping him, if in his everyday life his difficulty speaking continues unabated?

Selective mutism—the consistent failure to speak in certain settings or to specific people—necessitates a tailor-made treatment, which is usually based on **behavioral or cognitive-behavioral therapy.** The child with SM needs help in order to function normally in his home, school or kindergarten;in other words, a child suffering from SM needs **early intervention aimed at removing the symptom**—the lack of appropriate speech and communication. This symptom removal must take place in the child's natural environment, not in the sterile, disconnected setting of a therapist's office. This calls for some out-of-the-box thought and practice. The approach outlined in this manual is designed with this aim in mind—enabling the child to talk to everyone everywhere. It is largely behavioral treatment with sessions that take place initially at the child's home, and later on in his school.

It is widely agreed that the treatment of choice for SM is usually behavioral or cognitive-behavioral, with **pharmacological** treatment for anxiety supplementing therapy in stubborn or extreme cases. Yet so many children with SM undergo lengthy courses of play therapy, which often does little to assuage their selective mutism beyond the therapist's office. In practice, the whole range of psychological treatments is used for SM—family, speech, art, music and play therapy, to name a few.

While not denying the place of these and many other therapies,for young children the symptom of not speaking in school or kindergarten is often debilitating. Not speaking can become deeply entrenched and may cause or exacerbate numerous other problems, such as a negative self-image (feeling different and inadequate), social interaction difficulties caused by insufficient practice and exposure to social situations, delayed expressive language development, and a generalized anxiety disorder.

Therefore, therapy that is mainly behavioral with cognitive components (for older and more introspective children, more cognitive elements are included) is usually the preferred treatment. The aim of the therapy is to enable the child to function on a normative level: speak when speech is required, be able to answer adults and peers, and initiate speech with peers. Once this is achieved, there may be residual issues that require further treatment. These may be addressed more effectively once the child will be able to speak in therapy. The importance of early symptom removal is paramount, as it may limit malfunction in related areas (behavior, social skills, etc.) while the acquisition of normative speech will have an immensely powerful effect on the child and his environment, pulling him toward improved functioning in other areas.

This treatment plan is mostly behavioral, yet the process of therapy has numerous **dynamic characteristics** that must be implemented for treatment to succeed. The therapist must have those stalwarts of psychodynamic practitioners—empathy and listening skills—that enable her to build a warm and caring relationship with the child, the soil needed to nurture therapeutic improvement. Due to the sensitive, anxious nature of most children with SM,the therapist must be cautious not to overwhelm the child—to respect the child's shy nature and to communicate and express warmth and encouragement in a way that will not raise the child's anxiety levels.

It is vital to **include the child's parents and teachers in the treatment;** specific manuals are addressed to them. They should be involved in implementing change in the home and school or kindergarten. They should both be consulted for assessment and insight, and be intimately involved and guided by the therapist regarding ways in which they may facilitate progress. The initial therapy sessions take place in the home whenever possible, and fluid communication between the therapist, parents, and teacher is vital. The aim is to blur the borders between home, school, and outside the home. This approach builds on the child's strengths at home and enables him to generalize them to other contexts, making his experiences in diverse settings more consistent and productive.

Other treatment methods, in which the child is treated in a clinic away from the school, have the implicit problem of transferring any progress that has been made in the clinic so that the child implements that change in school. This rarely happens spontaneously as a result of therapy without employing agents for change within the school itself. Thus, when a child with SM undergoes seemingly successful therapy in a clinic, it may have little impact on the child's speech and social functioning in his life outside the clinic.

There is a perfect fit between the **educational or school psychologist, or the school guidance counselor**, and SM treatment in that the school psychologist is strategically based at the spot where the symptom is (usually) most pronounced. After several initial sessions at the home in which verbal communication develops between the therapist and the child, the psychologist can act as a bridge that allows the child to transport his functional speech from the home to the school, in controlled, structured, graduated steps. Having said this, this treatment program can be implemented by others, including speech therapists and teachers, as well as concerned,capable relatives and friends, who have the requisite understanding and characteristics and are available to hold sessions in the child's home and school.

Planning Therapy

Various points must be considered when planning treatment:

1. **The age of the child**. This manual is aimed primarily for the younger child; see chapter 8 for tools and the management of therapy with older children. Up to the age of about eight, therapy methods are primarily behavioral with some cognitive components. This means that goals and stages built by the therapist in the treatment strategy will be, on the whole, implicit, and not explicitly presented to the child. When working with an older child or teenager, the therapy is more transparent in its goals and methods. The therapist and young person work together to understand causes,emotions, and behaviors, building strategies and goals. Thus for the older child, the treatment is cognitive-behavioral, while for the younger child, emphasis is put on the behavioral axis. Another way of looking at this is that for the younger child, therapy mainly involves playing in a structured way that leads the child to improved communication, while for the older child it is mostly

about setting goals and finding ways to work toward those goals.

2. **Lowering anxiety**. Following on from the conceptualization of SM as anxiety-based, a twofold main aim of therapy will be to lower the child's experience of anxiety and to build up his emotional armor, strengthening his resistance to anxiety-provoking situations. Discussion of the cognitive understanding of emotions and behavior in SM with the child naturally causes an increase in anxiety—it is necessary and productive with older children, but with younger children is often not helpful and therefore can be largely avoided.

   This twofold aim of adjusting the environment in order to lower the child's anxiety levels therein and increasing the child's coping skills in anxiety provoking situations is a foundation of this therapy. Thus the teachers must consider ways to soften the threatening nature of school for the child with SM (see chapter 5, the Teacher's Manual.) These are often relatively simple changes to implement, such as explaining to all staff members that he should not be expected to speak and should be treated with sensitivity (not be shouted at), or ensuring that he sits next to a considerate child in the classroom or at circle time.

   Parents must consider ways in which they can diminish the pressure on the child to speak and strengthen both the child's belief in himself and his independent, competent functioning (see the Parents'

Manual). The message implicit (and when necessary explicit) of all those involved in the child's life should be: "We love and accept you exactly as you are; we know you can speak and believe that soon you will be able to speak everywhere." There should be minimal pressure to speak as this increases anxiety levels and, paradoxically, usually makes it harder for the child to start speaking.

Another important point to remember is that excessive praise or being placed in the limelight may be anxiety provoking for an anxious child. I have seen and heard of many instances in which a child speaks for the first time in school; the staff erupts with excitement and lavishes excessive praise on the child, at which point the child is deterred and stops speaking. A nonchalant, moderately pleased attitude should be adopted as the child takes steps towards speech.

Sometimes a child with SM fails to speak but does not seem socially anxious in other ways. The child may indeed not be socially anxious on the whole, yet he has maintained a maladaptive behavior that he originally took on in order to feel more socially comfortable. For example, a bilingual child who when entering kindergarten spoke English poorly, when assessed in first grade may speak perfectly and exhibit normal levels of social anxiety. Yet he cannot change his previously established silent social mores without intervention. Sometimes such children self-report after therapy that they had been waiting and hoping for a helping hand to pull them out of their self-dug hole.

In very stubborn or extreme cases, anxiety-lowering medication may be considered to supplement therapy. This is usually if the SM has become deeply entrenched and is not responding well to behavioral therapy, or if the child is suffering from generalized or other anxiety disorders as well as SM.

3. **Respecting the child's current comfort level**. Before commencing therapy, the child's baseline of speech and communication functioning, as well as the level of his anxiety in different settings, must be assessed. During therapy these must be constantly appraised so that the therapist can plan realistic goals based on furthering progress within the child's comfort zone.

4. **Small steps—great patience!** Therapy must proceed in small steps where the goals are moved gradually, enabling the child to proceed while keeping his anxiety level manageable. This often is perceived by the therapist and school staff as an unbearably slow pace, while in fact, it is the only way to proceed —in slow but sure steps. Not more than one variable should be changed from session to session, as explained below.

5. **Short, frequent sessions.** The sessions should take place at least once a week (twice or more is preferable) and should last between half an hour to an hour.

6. **Intensive interventions**. When it is possible to conduct an intensive intervention with sessions every

day for a number of weeks, the improvement is often striking and swift. Upping the notch to even more intense therapy usually brings about extraordinary results:the therapist spends a week with the child in his home and school during his waking hours and within that time can usually enable the child to talk, following the program described here. This is sometimes the method employed with children who live far from available assistance; the therapist flies over for a brief but usually spectacular intervention. Obviously, close cooperation with parents and school staff in planning and implementation is vital so that all agents of change are working simultaneously within this short period of time to help the child shed his selective mutism.

7. **Group Therapy**. The treatment method advocated here is eminently suited to group therapy when several children in the same school have SM. The therapy would begin for each of the children in his or her home with the therapist, and once each child individually speaks naturally to the therapist at home, therapy is relocated to a therapy room at school, initially alone with the therapist. Once each child speaks in the school therapy room with the therapist, a small group will be established with the other children with SM who have also previously spoken to the therapist in their homes. Children learn from seeing others overcome their fears and obstacles, and group camaraderie makes group therapy powerful and effective.

8. **Fun!** The sessions should be enjoyable for the child (and the therapist!) and should cater to the child's tastes and preferences. If he enjoys drawing, building, sports, etc. activities can be built around these preferences.

9. **Activities that lower anxiety levels while pursuing a goal**. When trying to attain a behavioral goal, physical activities or games can lower the intensity and pressure of mastering a new speech goal and therefore facilitate attaining that goal. For example, when the aim of the session is that the child speaks to a classmate for the first time, it is helpful to put it in the framework of a game, such as running games with a speech element, or throwing a ball and saying your name as you throw it. This will be elaborated on below.

10. **Addressing the triggers, predisposing factors, and maintaining factors**. In planning treatment, these factors must be borne in mind so that they can be included in goals to build long-term coping skills and social communication.

11. **Rewards**. In this program, rewards are conspicuously absent! The rewards intrinsic in improved social communication are such that any other prize pales in comparison, and is rendered redundant. Furthermore, the promise of a prize on the completion of a proposed goal can increase anxiety. Within the framework of a warm therapist-child relationship, praise and smiles are rewards indeed. The therapist can decide for herself whether to give

the child a candy or small gift to increase the pleasantness of the sessions. The way rewards can be effectively used with young children is when the rewards are not dependent on reaching a preset aim. Thus after sessions the therapist can give the child a small prize, which he can retroactively correlate to some progress made or some positive behavior in the session. The therapist can discern positive behavior, even when none is strikingly apparent, and reward this behavior. In this way, she will build in the child a feeling and expectation of success and progress.

With older children and teens, rewards can be incorporated and can indeed be motivating elements within a CBT treatment plan, as described in chapter 8.

12. **Bilingual children and immigrants**. Bilingual children who are not confident in English should receive informal, playful language tutoring at home where they are more verbal and less anxious. For a timid child, overcoming selective mutism in a language in which the child feels incompetent often proves to be an insurmountable challenge. Employing a capable, warm teenager to play with the child twice a week at home in English is one way of arranging informal, enjoyable language experience. This is discussed further in the Parents' Manual.

13. **Parent and staff involvement. This** has already been mentioned above, but due to the integral place it occupies in this therapy, it is repeated here: Parents and educational staff are guided to plan and

implement their own custom-built interventions which will be complementary to the therapist's treatment. Their principle aims are to decrease pressure on the child to speak in order to lower anxiety levels, and to take steps to foster social communication and ultimately speech. **It is vital that the therapist reads the manuals for parents and teachers** in order to be fully aware of the tasks they will carry out in the framework of the three-way therapeutic alliance. It is the therapist's job to oversee and coordinate the three parties to ensure that they work together and complement each other. Once a behavioral plan has been built to be implemented by the teacher or parent, the therapist must follow up to ensure that it is being carried out as planned and to assist in fine tuning it based on the child's reactions to it. Often the teacher's behavioral plan requires ongoing supervision to see that it is actually happening – a teacher of a bustling, large class is very likely to find it hard to be consistent in carrying out the intervention, and consistency is a vital ingredient of success in such endeavors. A chart in which the teacher may check each intervention, with a brief description of the child's response, to be emailed to the therapist once a week, may engender greater consistency. Thus the teacher's intervention may be a five minute conversation with the child each day, in which the child initially uses gestures, gradually progresses to taped messages, and eventually uses the spoken word. If the teacher jots down a progress record on completion of each five minute conversation, to be reviewed with the therapist once a week, it may cause these mini sessions to occur regularly. Often,more intensive coaching of the teacher, including a very brief report and evaluation with the therapist after each mini-session, is conducive to progress. See the chapter 5, the Teacher's Manual for a concrete example of a teacher's behavior shaping plan.

14. **Transitions**. While transitions can be stressful, they are also windows of opportunity for change. For example, when moving to a new school, home visits by a teacher before the academic year begins may enable the child to talk to his teacher at home. With careful planning, this may be carried over into the school through further school visits with the new teacher before the school year commences. Utilizing the transition and school vacation may well sidestep months of suffering and therapy by enabling the child to speak to his teacher before school begins. This is described more fully in the Teacher's Manual.

15. **Assessing and planning after each session**. In stark contrast to psychodynamic therapy, in structured behavioral therapy—where the aim is to work toward a goal in each session—assessment and planning after each and every session is vital. While part of the aim of therapy includes goals that may be hard to quantify, such as improved social communication and a sturdier self-image, the goals of progressive improvement leading to speech are assessable. In order to ensure that therapy is on course and progressing as surely as possible, it is indispensable to think and jot down after each session both how the session went and what the next

session's aim should be. It is all too easy to tread water and continue with the same level of functioning for several sessions—for example, if a child can speak comfortably with several friends in the therapy room at school, therapists may be tempted to repeat several sessions in a small group without advancing the child further to include additional friends or staff or moving the location of the sessions to a more public place. Meanwhile the child's life is on hold; much of his well-being is dependent on continued headway toward normal speech. When supervising therapists, I often give them the following table to be filled in following each session:

Assessing and Planning Each Session

Date of session	Goals and participants	Outcome (child's functioning)	Goals for next session	Activities for next session	Participants for next session
Wed 5.11	*Goals: For Don to speak to me in school therapy room Participants: me, Don*	*Spoke in a whisper in my ear, then in a loud whisper, played Chinese whispers and secret square*	*To speak one word in an audible voice*	*Chinese whispers, category game, maintaining large balloon in air, while saying aloud a word.*	*Don, me, (therapist)*
Mon 10.11	*Goals: For Don to speak to me in school therapy room in audible voice Participants: me, Don*	*Spoke in a whisper in my ear, and then in a loud whisper, played Chinese whispers and secret square, then played ball category game, the balloon game and said "boom" in a loud voice*	*To speak several words in an audible voice*	*Chinese whispers, ball category game, maintaining large balloon in air, while saying aloud a given word, then same game but say two words and then three words while maintaining the balloon*	*Don, me, (therapist)*
Wed 12.11					

Obviously the therapist cannot stick blindly to the planned aims and activities but must use her understanding and empathy to modify steps on the spot, according to how the child responds and whether the planned activities are more or less daunting for him than you anticipated. A therapist will often take a step back if the planned task proves too anxiety provoking for the child, or go further than planned if it seems that the child is able to do so.

Three Main Tools of Behavioral Therapy

In addition to the dynamic tools of empathy, listening, building rapport, and a warm, supportive relationship, three main behavioral tools are employed at different stages of the therapy.

1. **Desensitization**. A hierarchy, or stepladder, of imagined and real nonverbal and verbal communication is constructed. The child gradually passes through the steps, feeling less anxious and more relaxed, until he reaches face-to-face verbal communication. For example, he may first speak on the phone, then in a voice recording device, then in a talking picture frame or album (a photo album in which alongside each photograph a short message can be recorded), then whisper to the teacher, and finally talk directly to the teacher.

2. **Stimulus Fading**. The child's speech is constant, but the setting or the people present to hear his speech change. The child initially talks to the therapist at home, then in a room in school into which children and adults are gradually

introduced. Then the setting may be broadened to facilitate generalization. Thus after the child speaks to the therapist and some friends in the closed therapy room, the little group is removed to the kindergarten shared space or classroom, and the child hopefully continues to speak within the open space. It is vital never to change more than one variable at a time, to ensure that the child is comfortable with the current setting and people before changing, and to make the steps as small as possible to ensure that the child's anxiety levels remain bearable.

3. **Shaping**. Here the child's speech patterns are developed, and are rewarded at each step —either by the praise and positive regard of adults, or with small prizes. The child may begin without social communication, then gradually build a relationship with the therapist in which he feels sufficiently at ease to communicate nonverbally, after which he works toward eliciting sounds, consonants, words, sentences and ultimately spontaneous speech.

Stages of Therapy

Below are the four main stages of therapy: home sessions, school-based with the therapist, school-based with the therapist and peers and/or staff, and out of the school therapy room and into the classroom. These four main stages will be followed by the smaller steps of the sub-stages, with suggested activities within each stage. These stages are made up of steps on a desensitization ladder of goals. As the child completes the goals and ascends the stepladder, he moves incrementally toward speech and improved social interaction.

Progression from one stage to the next depends on the pace at which the child has attained previous goals and an estimation of the boundaries of the child's comfort levels. When the therapist is unable to carry out sessions in the home and school, this therapy can be adapted for implementation in the clinic, which is described in chapter 7.

The sessions outlined below are just examples of how therapy could proceed. **They should be modified according to the child's level and type of SM, his progress, and the therapist's intuition**. They may proceed faster with several sessions rolled into one,or may require smaller steps and more sessions. Remember to **always begin sessions with activities that the child has successfully accomplished previously** before attempting a new goal. There is huge room for the **therapist's creativity** in finding activities that appeal to the child, lower his anxiety, and are conducive to a warm therapist-child relationship. For a list of games and activities that are conducive to speech and social interaction, and may be used in the therapy sessions, see Appendix 2.

Prior to beginning therapy, the child should be assessed, his speech patterns and baseline estimated, and parent and teacher interviews conducted, along with consideration of the predisposing and maintaining factors outlined above.

As well as facilitating a verbal, communicative relationship between the therapist and child, home sessions offer an opportunity to develop a supportive, productive relationship with the parents. At this time, initial guidance sessions may be held with the parents, helping them to nurture independence and social confidence in their children.

At the beginning of the therapy, <u>several tasks should be given to the parents</u> that will be helpful later on. In order to maximize the effectiveness of therapy, parents should be active partners with their own tasks to fulfill, as is described in full in the Parents' Manual.

Firstly, **parents should take it upon themselves to invite the child's classmates to their home as frequently as possible**. They are responsible for ensuring that a good time will be had by all and for preparing enjoyable activities or games for these play-dates. If the child speaks to the friend in these visits, the course of therapy will be greatly eased.

Secondly, the therapist, parents and teachers should, when possible, plan **parent visits to the school at least once a week for talking-playing sessions**, during which they work according to a desensitization ladder of goals in which the child will speak to his parent/family member. For example, on the parent's first visit to the school, she may sit with her child in a secluded area of the yard and elicit speech from him. The following week she may sit in a less secluded part of the yard and the next week in a room within the school building. Similarly, the parent may initially sit with the child alone, and then gradually invite friends to join in the sessions. In this way, there is a parallel, parent-induced process of desensitization occurring together with the therapist's intervention. This is more fully described in <u>chapter 4</u>, the Parents' Manual.

Thirdly, **even before therapy begins, it is advisable for the family of the child to play with taping or filming devices** in which the child and other family members record themselves for fun so that the child grows accustomed to being taped or filmed; this will be used later to facilitate therapy.

Stage 1: Home Sessions

Whenever possible, first sessions are conducted in the child's home or wherever the child speaks most comfortably. These must be planned in advance with the parent or sibling who will be present at the initial sessions. The idea is that the therapist will slip inconspicuously into the home setting, enabling the child to continue talking in her presence. Once the child speaks openly with the therapist at home, the sessions can be moved to the school or kindergarten.

As mentioned before, it is important that the child is reasonably comfortable with the aim of each therapy session, and whenever possible, the sessions should be fun. This serves two purposes: When a child enjoys an activity, it distracts him from the intensity and stress of his endeavor to attain speech goals, and paradoxically makes them easier to attain. It also does wonders for motivation, engaging the child in the process of conquering selective mutism.

Here follow **concrete examples of how the stages may look**, following the principles outlined above. These descriptions are provided in order to give the therapist a picture of how to proceed with therapy. Clearly, **each child has his own baseline of speech in diverse settings, and will react in his unique way and pace to therapy; the stages and activities will have to be amended accordingly**. The therapist must use his understanding, judgment, and intuition to modify the sessions to fit the child.

Session 1-i
Location: Home

Aim: The child should speak naturally in the presence of the therapist. In the initial session in the child's home, the therapist directs small talk to the parent or sibling, does not address the child directly, avoids eye contact with the child, and makes herself so unobtrusive as to almost blend in with the furniture! In planning the meeting, the parent and the therapist must think of a way to ensure that the child is in the room with the therapist and the parent. This can be done by planning an activity that will be enjoyable and will keep the child in the room, yet won't be bombastic or something that the child has never done before—which could raise the child's suspicions and anxiety that something is aplot!

Activities: The parents should decide on activities according to the child's preferences—they should be enjoyable and engaging, and may include baking cookies, card games, board games, building activities, arts and crafts, etc. A family member leads the activity; the therapist is a fly-on-the-wall. (For a fuller list of possible activities see Appendix 2: Games and activities.)

Session   1-ii
Location: Home
Aim: The child should play a game with family member(s) and therapist without the therapist directing speech to the child.
The parent plays a game or involves the child in an activity, and initially the therapist observes. Once it is clear that the child is speaking comfortably in the therapist's presence,the therapist joins in the game, but does not direct speech to the child.

Activities: May include board games, memory games, lotto, puzzles, construction games, arts and crafts, sports, cooking, etc.

Session 1-iii

Location: Home
Aim: The child will play a game with family member(s) and therapist, including direct speech between therapist and child. The child will be taped or filmed for fun by a parent during the session and will play the tape back to family members.
Initially a game is played with family members and the therapist without direct speech between the child and the therapist; once it is ascertained that the child speaks freely during this game, the therapist and family members play a game that includes direct speech between therapist and child.

Activities: As in session 1-ii.

Session 1-iv
Location: Home
Aim: The child will play a game just with the therapist, including direct speech between therapist and child. The child will be taped or filmed for fun during the session and will play the tape back to family members.
The therapist and child play games with direct speech between them. The child is taped by the family and plays back the tape to the family members in the presence of the therapist.

Activities: In the final home-based session, it is useful to play games or engage in activities that can be repeated during the following school-based session, such as board games, cards, and arts and crafts. The game hot/cold can be played—it is a good way to start the following school-based sessions and should be introduced at the home. The child hides a candy, and the therapist searches for it as the child says hot or cold depending on the proximity of the therapist to the treat. Then roles are reversed.

If, by the end of this session, the therapist and parents feel that the child is at ease talking and playing with the therapist, then the following sessions can take place at school. Sometimes, further home sessions are required before the child reaches a satisfactory level of comfort to enable changing locations.

Finalizing the home-based sessions

At the end of the home-based therapy sessions, the therapist should explain to the child that from now on the sessions will take place in school. The therapist should explain this in a light, natural way by saying that she works in the child's school, takes out children for enjoyable activities, and will take him out for sessions in school from now on, sometimes alone and sometimes with friends. She should explain that usually children really enjoy the sessions, as they involve games, arts and crafts, etc.

There may be cases in which it is not possible to carry out home sessions. For example, parents may be resistant or there may be children who do not speak at home. In these cases, therapy begins in the school or clinic and starts from the point of non-speech with the therapist. This is discussed in chapter 7.

Whenever possible, it is highly preferable to hold initial home-based sessions before tackling the selective mutism in school; it shortens the length of therapy, involves parents and families in treatment, and enables the therapist to understand the child's optimum functioning.

Stage 2: School-Based with Therapist

The transition of therapy from home to school is delicate and requires sensitivity and understanding on the part of the therapist so that it may be carried out while maintaining the level of speech that had been reached between the therapist and child during the home sessions. When speech that has been elicited at home with the therapist can be successfully transferred to the school, it greatly speeds up the process of establishing normal speech at school. Remember that **the sessions outlined below give a general idea of how therapy might proceed; in reality they will need to be tailored to the needs and pace of each and every child**.

Before moving the therapy to the school setting, the therapist must update the teacher regarding progress and arrange with her a suitable time and place for therapy to continue. The therapist should have a private room in the school that will be available for the therapy sessions and should be stocked with the required materials —arts and crafts supplies, games, and recording equipment. The teacher should be advised on how to explain the sessions to the rest of the class. Normalization is the guiding principle. Therapy should not put the child with SM in the limelight in the eyes of his peers. A sample explanation by the teacher could be the following: "Sara sometimes takes children to her room for various activities. She will be taking Johnny for the next few weeks."

The start of school-based therapy sessions is a time to consider what the teacher can do to hasten the child's improvement. Simultaneous with the parents' and therapist's interventions, there should be **a parallel and interconnected teacher's intervention**. The teacher should consider four main goals: establishing a communicative relationship with the child, helping the child to take gradual, controlled steps toward speech, lowering the child's anxiety, and building his self-confidence in school. This is fully described in the Teacher's Manual. The therapist should read the Teacher's Manual and sit with the teacher to consider how to implement the described interventions.

For example, the parents could tape the child every day at home, following which the teacher could listen to the recording together with the child every morning in school, at a fixed time in a private setting. In this way, the teacher will be hearing indirect speech from the child every day, and the barrier keeping the teacher from hearing his voice will come crashing down!

Session 2-i
Location: School therapy room
Aim: The child should speak with the therapist in a therapy room within the school. Please note that this is described here as one session, but may require several in order for the child to interact and speak freely with the therapist in school.

The therapist takes the child to the therapy room inside the school. Whenever possible, she should have a tape of the child speaking at home that was recorded by the parents during the previous home-based sessions. WhatsApp voice messages sent to the therapist serve this purpose well. This recording can be played as soon as the child comes into the room and initiates the session by breaking one barrier—his voice is present in school, on the tape or phone.

Games can be played which require minimal or rote speech. A good way to proceed is to play hot/cold—which has previously been played at home—in which the child must say "hot" or "cold," guiding the therapist towards a hidden treat, and may simultaneously bang a tambourine louder or softer.

Other examples of games requiring a defined amount of speech are happy families or throwing a ball to one another saying your name (or other category such as clothes, foods, colors, etc.) each time you throw it. If the child speaks to the therapist, further games previously enjoyed at home can be played. If the child fails to talk, games should be played that require nonverbal communication and noise production, including playing musical instruments and banging.

A note about whispering:

Sometimes when a child with SM begins to speak in school, he whispers. The therapist should consider how to help the child achieve audible speech, as whispering can itself become an entrenched and nonfunctional way of communicating. The therapist should work toward raising the volume of the child's speech using behavioral shaping methods. The parents can be helpful here again. For example, if the child is talking to the therapist in school in a whisper, a parent may be invited to join in a session at the school with the therapist and child. The **parent-child session** would take place in the school therapy room, initially without the therapist. The parent begins the session playing with the child games that require speech, such as hot/cold, blind man's buff, card games, recording activities, and ball games that require speech (for example, each time a ball is thrown the thrower has to say the name of the person to whom he is throwing it). The parent does not accept whispering, and once the child is speaking at a normal volume, the therapist comes into the room but does not join in the game. Gradually, the therapist approaches the child and his parent and eventually joins in the game. This may occur in one session, or may require several parent-child-therapist school-based sessions.

Sometimes the child stalls at the whispering stage, and activities in which the **child's whisper is amplified** may be needed. This could include games in which the child speaks into a microphone or makes the volume display on a tape recorder show increased volume. Use of a Madonna microphone which the child wears is often fun for the child and allows him to be mobile during games. For example, the child may already be whispering answers and plays hangman with the therapist, during which he whispers each letter he guesses into a microphone so that it can be heard out loud. Similarly, this could take place within a game of twenty questions or I spy with the child answering into a microphone. Again, this could occur in one session, or it may take several sessions of structured steps. If this does not spontaneously engender speech, a graduated series of steps can be planned in which the child speaks into a microphone when the therapist is outside the room, then he speaks into a microphone when the therapist is inside the room looking away from him, and finally she looks at the child when he talks. Then the volume is lowered on the amplifier so that the child must speak louder to be heard, and finally the volume is switched off, leaving the child speaking aloud without amplification.

If the child succeeds in talking to the therapist in the initial sessions, then the therapist can jump to session 2-vii, below. If the child does not speak to the therapist in the initial school-based sessions, continue with sessions 2-ii to 2-vi below.

Sometimes the child fails to speak to the therapist in these first sessions, in which case a structured behavior shaping program can be utilized with the help of the parents. An example of this is outlined below in sessions 2-ii to 2-vi. It should be adapted to the needs and pace of each individual child.

Session 2-ii
Location: School therapy room

143

Aim: The child should speak to a parent/family member in the presence of the therapist in school.

The therapist arranges for a parent or family member with whom the child speaks to meet the child in the therapy room. The parent and child remain alone in the room for half an hour after which the therapist enters. During the time in which the parent and child are alone, they should engage in activities described above—playing a recording of the child, then playing hot/cold, board games, or arts and crafts that the child likes and that require at least some speech. When the therapist enters, she remains in the room but does not comment or participate in the activities; she may be engaged in looking through her papers or any other quiet activity that enables her to be in the room, and to hear the child without focusing on him. This may occur in one session or may take several sessions.

Session 2-iii
Location: School therapy room
Aim: The child should speak to a parent/family member and the therapist in school.

The family member comes again to the school therapy room, engages the child in activities requiring speech, and after a few minutes, the therapist enters the room. If the child seems ready, the therapist joins in the activities and speaks to the child. If the child speaks directly with the therapist, continue with session 2-vi. If the child is reticent to speak to the therapist, further sessions are required. If after further sessions it seems that a more structured approach is required, stimulus fading can be tried as described below.

Session 2-iv
Location: School therapy room
Aim: The child should speak to a parent/family member and the therapist in school using stimulus fading

("sliding in").

This is a version of stimulus fading developed by Johnson and Wintgens (2001). Here the parent engages her child in an activity in which rote speech is required, and the therapist gradually comes within hearing distance and eventually joins in so that the child speaks to her. For example, the parent and child could throw a ball to each other, and each time they throw it they have to say a number in turn. They begin the game alone in the room. After a while, the door is opened and the therapist, who is sitting outside the room, hears the child's voice. After this, the therapist enters the room and sits with her back to the child. Finally, the therapist will sit facing the child and will then join in the game. This may be done in one session or may need to be broken down into several sessions. The sliding in procedure should be explained to the child before carrying it out, in a way in which the child will feel the least anxiety possible. The therapist may include a small treat in the center of the circle of people engaged in "sliding in", and the child could receive a candy after each round of the game. The remainder of the time in each session once the sliding in is finished, if the child is not ready for further verbal communication, can be taken up with games played by the therapist, parent, and child that require nonverbal communication, listening to tapes of the child previously recorded at home, and playing games that generate noise, such as musical instruments.

Session 2-v
Location: School therapy room
Aim: The child should speak to a parent/family member and the therapist in school.

Once "sliding in" is successfully carried out, the parent should continue to come to sessions until the child is speaking comfortably to the therapist; activities should be undertaken that employ rote language and gradually more spontaneous language can be

145

encouraged. This may occur in one session or may require several meetings. The therapist and parent must use their understanding and intuition to decide at which point the parent need not come to sessions.

Activities: May include hot/cold, ball games, card games such as happy families, commercial and board games (such as Bingo, Lotto, Guess Who, Submarines, Taboo), arts and crafts, etc.

Session 2-vi
Location: School therapy room
Aim: The child should speak to the therapist in school without the family member.

Once the child feels comfortable speaking to the therapist in school in the presence of the family member, sessions should continue without the family member present. The therapist should play games and engage in activities that the child has enjoyed in previous sessions to give a feeling of continuity. The sessions can be structured so that they start with games employing one-word answers, gradually progressing to activities that require more language and, eventually, spontaneous speech. Ample use should be made of playing prerecorded songs, stories, or speech of the child.

Activities: Could include hot/cold, Chinese whispers, word guessing games such as I spy, twenty questions and hangman, card games such as happy families, board games such as Guess Who and Secret Square, activities employing a combination of physical activity and speech such as ball games and blind man's buff, arts and crafts, etc.

A simple activity that encourages young children to speak utilizes a small notebook and stickers. Each page in the notebook is divided into a number of squares, and the therapist displays on the table before her an array of tempting stickers, such as animals, flowers, cars, and so on. The child must request the sticker she would like; for example, the child must say, "Please, can I have the red flower or big elephant or yellow smiley?" after which she gets that sticker and adheres it onto one of the squares on her paper. Once all the squares on one page have stickers, she gets a small candy or prize. This is a combination of behavior shaping together with the distraction and attraction offered by colorful or sparkling stickers.

Session 2-vii
Location: School therapy room
Aim: Consolidation of the child's speech with the therapist in school without the family member.

In the previous session the child managed to talk to the therapist in the school therapy room without the parent/family member present. This can be consolidated before peers are included in the sessions. The therapist must use her intuition to decide how many such sessions are required. In these meetings, the therapist follows the format of previous sessions, partaking in activities that require the child to speak and varying these activities to include games that the child did not play previously with his parents. Once the child is comfortable speaking to the therapist, he is ready to progress to Stage 3.

Activities: Could include hot/cold, Chinese whispers, iPad apps requiring voice production as described in chapter 9, ball games, guessing games such as I spy, twenty questions and hangman, word games like child and therapist making up a story taking turns adding one word at a time, and "I went to the store and bought..." with therapist and child adding bought items in turn and recalling previously mentioned items, card games such as happy families, board games such as Bingo, Lotto, Submarines, Guess Who and Taboo, arts and crafts, etc.

Stage 3: School-Based with Therapist and Friends/Teachers

Once the child is comfortable speaking to the therapist alone in the therapy room in school or kindergarten, the next variable to change is the people present in the room, usually starting by including peers in the sessions. At the beginning of therapy, the parents were encouraged to invite the child's friends to their home and to ensure that pleasant activities took place during these play-dates. Now with input from the teacher, the parents, and the child, the therapist determines who are the child's best friends and with which friends he speaks at home and at school. If he speaks with certain classmates at home or in school, these should be the first ones to join in the therapy sessions. Permission must be requested from the parents of the children to be added to the sessions, as well as from the teacher.

A similar process occurs in this stage to that outlined in Stages 1 and 2. The therapist invites children to join the sessions, changing one variable at a time so that the games are similar, but an extra person is added. Once the child speaks with the therapist and one child, another child is added. To illustrate this process, here follow postulated Stage 3 sessions.

Session 3-i
Location: School therapy room
Aim: Child should speak to therapist and classmate in therapy room.

A classmate is invited to join in the session. It is preferable that this is a child with whom the child speaks at home and whose company the child enjoys. The plan in this session is to go from taped speech, to whispered speech, to rote speech, to spontaneous speech. Here again, the child may pass through all these stages in one session, or several sessions may be required.

Activities: It is advisable that the session begins with playing a video, WhatsApp voice message or iPad game featuring the voice of the child that has been used in previous sessions. In this way, his voice will immediately be present in the room. The next activity could be Chinese whispers, where the child with SM is always the middle child so that he only has to whisper and not say the word out loud. The next activity could be a game employing sounds or rote speech out loud,such as throwing a ball and saying your name as you throw it. The following activity could be playing happy families where a certain card must be asked for.

Some children will not progress through more than one of these stages in the first session, and others will go through to spontaneous speech with the classmate in one session. If the child stalls at one of these activities, it is a sign that he may require a few sessions to get through all the stages. In this case, the pace must be slowed so that the child may have one session in which a tape of his voice is heard and simultaneously engage in games in which nonverbal communication is called for. In the following session the tape could be heard again, and Chinese whispers would be played. In this way, in each session a small new step is introduced.

If a child fails to progress through a given stage as expected, the therapist must return to the previous stage and reincorporate whichever elements she thinks would stimulate progress. For example, if a child fails to talk with a friend, one of several courses of action could be required: It could be that he needs more sessions to consolidate his speech with the therapist; perhaps a parent should come in for one or two sessions with the child and his friend; maybe what is needed is that the therapist should conduct a couple of home-based sessions with the child with SM together with his friend, after which she would meet with the child and his friend in the school therapy room.

Session 3-ii
Location: School therapy room
Aim: Consolidation of child speaking to therapist and classmate in school therapy room.
The child plays games requiring speech with his classmate and the therapist, starting, as always, with games successfully played in the previous sessions and adding further activities and games. Thus his speech in this setting will be consolidated.

Activities: Could include hot/cold, Chinese whispers, voice recordings, iPad apps such as "Puppetpals" and "Doodlecast Junior", throwing a ball and saying a name or object within a category, happy families, lotto, Guess Who and Taboo, taping the children and playing it back to them, puppet shows, charades, word games, I spy, twenty questions, hangman, arts and crafts etc.

Session 3-iii
Location: School therapy room
Aim: Child should speak to the therapist and two classmates in school therapy room.
Here an additional classmate joins the session. This should preferably be a classmate liked by the child and one with whom he has spoken outside school. The process is parallel to that in session 3-i, beginning with taped speech from previous sessions or from home, followed by games requiring individual words or rote speech,

and then activities requiring more spontaneous speech. As above, the child may progress through all these stages in one session, or it may take several sessions.

Activities: As above in 3-i and 3-ii, and in <u>Appendix 2</u>.

Session 3-iv
Location: School therapy room
Aim: Consolidation of child speaking to therapist and two classmates in school therapy room.
The child should play games requiring speech with his classmates and the therapist, starting, as always, with games successfully played in the previous session, and adding further activities and games.

Activities: Could include apps and voice recordings, hot/cold, Chinese whispers, ball games, word-guessing games such as twenty questions, hangman and I spy; word games such as the children and therapist making up a story taking turns adding one word at a time, and "I went to the store and bought..." with therapist and children adding bought items in turn and recalling previously mentioned items; card games such as happy families and Story Cards; Bingo, Lotto, Submarines, Guess Who, Taboo, blind man's buff, arts and crafts, etc.

Session 3-v
Location: School therapy room
Aim: The child should speak in the school therapy room with three classmates or a varied configuration of classmates.
The idea for the remainder of the sessions in this stage is to either add further children or to vary the configuration of children in the sessions, so that each session includes one or more children with

whom the child with SM has spoken and a new classmate with whom the child has not yet spoken in school. The activities are similar to those in the other Stage 3 sessions, and the rules are the same: to change one variable at a time, and if the child stalls, either to go back to the last stage in which he successfully achieved the goal and consolidate it before going further, or to make the steps taken toward new goals smaller and more gradual.

One method to increase generalization in order to include peers and even staff in one fell swoop is to **prepare a puppet show or a play with a group of children** in the therapy room and then to **film it and play it to other children and/or staff**. Alternatively, one could invite a group of children and teachers to come into the therapy room and see the performance once it has been prepared. This depends on the child's response to the idea of performing; sometimes in the guise of a character in a play or puppet show, speech is possible in front of people with whom the child has not previously spoken. A cardinal rule here is to be open with the child when suggesting the show and not to go forward if it seems to be too anxiety provoking.

It is possible at this stage to **invite staff with whom the child does not speak into the therapy room**, much as has been done with classmates. This is done by inviting a teacher either by herself, or together with a couple of children with whom the child already speaks in the therapy room and playing tapes and games in a way similar to how classmates were included in session 3-i. Often the teacher can be included in the last few minutes of a session with peers, in which a recording of one of the games is played to her and then an activity on the current rung of an exposure ladder of speech with the teacher – perhaps Chinese whispers or the ball category game. Here the therapist must judge which will be the child's path of least resistance, either generalizing the child's speech by taking the group outside the therapy room or including adults within the therapy room. The choice should be made according to what the therapist feels will cause the child less anxiety, and her estimation of what is likely to be more natural and effective.

Once the child speaks comfortably in the school therapy room with the therapist and several children and/or teachers it is time to generalize the speech to the wider context of the school beyond the four walls of the therapy room.

Stage 4: Taking the Therapy out of the Therapy Room and into the Classroom

Now that the child speaks freely in the therapy room, the aim is to enable him to speak in the larger school environment. The same behavioral techniques previously employed in stages 1 to 3 are used here. At this stage, the sessions initially take place in a public space in the school such as a corridor or yard and ultimately are held in the classroom. It is frequently the case that as there is improvement in the therapy room, parallel processes will occur in other contexts, and the child will begin to speak in the classroom or yard. Usually, however, some structured help is required to shape speech so that it fully generalizes to the classroom.

Session 4-i
Location: School—public space (corridor, hallway, yard, etc.)
Aim: The child should speak in a school common space with the therapist, or with the therapist plus one classmate.

As in all the above steps, one variable is changed at a time, in this case the setting. The therapist will have to judge whether it will be easier for the child to speak in this new setting with her alone, or with the therapist plus one peer with whom he has spoken in previous sessions in the therapy room.

The context should be a public space in the school that is sheltered —not too much through traffic—where the little group can sit at a table and play games. The activities should be those successfully performed in the previous stages, again ordered according to verbal output, from recorded speech, to one word or rote responses through to spontaneous speech.

For the sake of clarity, this is presented as one session, but in reality, it may take several sessions for the child to reach spontaneous speech in this public setting.

Sometimes it is easier for the child to begin in an outdoor setting such as the schoolyard, and once the child is comfortable speaking outdoors, the little group may be moved to an indoor common space.

Activities: Could include playing with iPad apps such as "Talking Tom" "Story Wheel" and "Sparklefish", listening to previously recorded WhatsApps, hot/cold, Chinese whispers, guessing games such as I spy, twenty questions, and hangman, word games with physical activity like throwing a ball and saying a name within a category, recording one another and listening to the recordings, playing with mobile phones (for example members of the group phoning one another from varying distances and locations within the school), Go Fish, board games such as Taboo, Guess Who and Lotto, arts and crafts etc.

Session 4-ii
Location: School—public space (corridor, hallway, yard, etc.)
Aim:The child should speak in the school common space with the therapist and several classmates.
Once the child speaks in the common space with the therapist and one child, several children can be added, starting with those with whom the child has previously spoken. The same caution should be taken to ensure that there is a gradual increase in the speech requirements of the activities employed, moving from low speech output to spontaneous speech.

Activities are as above in 4-i.

Session 4-iii
Location: School—classroom (in a relatively sheltered corner of the room)
Aim: The child should speak in the classroom with the therapist.
The therapist and child sit in a corner of the classroom; the child should have his back to the rest of the class. The activities again should be those previously enjoyed, and requiring gradually increasing amounts of speech output—beginning with a game that requires little speech, such as happy families or arts and crafts, and moving on to games which may require more speech or, alternatively, gradually incorporating conversations between the therapist and child.

Frequently the child will speak quietly or in a whisper, and it may take a few sessions to shape his speech so that it is audible to other people present in the classroom. It may be preferable to hold the first kindergarten or classroom session during recess when the classroom is empty, followed by sessions during periods where the rest of the children are in the room.

Activities: May include Chinese whispers, guessing games such as I spy, hangman and twenty questions, word games including child and therapist making up a story taking turns adding one word at a time, "I went to the store and bought..." with therapist and child adding bought items in turn and recalling previously mentioned items, card games such as happy families, commercial and board games such as Bingo, Lotto, Submarines, Guess Who and Taboo, games requiring physical activity together with speech such as ball games played while sitting down opposite one another, arts and crafts etc.

Session 4-iv
Location: School—classroom (in a relatively sheltered corner of the room)
Aim: The child should speak in the classroom with the therapist and a classmate.
This is as above in session 4-iii but includes a classmate with whom the child has spoken in previous sessions in the activities. If it is felt that consolidation is required, several such sessions can be held, including more children, and varying the children participating in the sessions.

Activities: As in session 4-i, appendix 2 and chapter 9

Session 4-v
Location: School—classroom (in a relatively sheltered corner of the room)
Aim: The child should speak in the classroom with the therapist and the classmate.

This is as above in session 4-iii, but now the child faces the classroom from the corner where previously he had his back to the other children.

Activities: As in session 4-i, Appendix 2 and chapter 9

Session 4-vi
Location: School—classroom (in a relatively sheltered corner of the room)
Aim: The child should speak in the classroom with the therapist, classmate and teacher.

Here the teacher is included in the little group in the classroom corner. As before, small steps are taken within this stage. First the teacher is passive but close to the group as they are playing a game in which rote speech is required. Next she joins in the game without speaking directly to the child, and finally she engages in direct speech with the child. Again, this may occur in one session or in several. If the child finds it hard to speak to the teacher or in her presence, it may help to listen with her to recordings or apps, or to prepare and perform a puppet show or play for the class, as described in session 3-v above.

Activities: As above in session 4-i, Appendix 2 and chapter 9

Session 4-vii
Location: School—classroom, at the child's desk
Aim: The child should speak in the classroom at his desk with the therapist.

Here the aim is to generalize the child's speech further so that he speaks sitting at his place in class,or at a group table in kindergarten. The therapist sits with the child at his desk during a regular lesson and elicits speech from him in a gentle and nonthreatening way. It is important not to be satisfied with a whisper, but to elicit audible speech.

Activities: The child participates in whatever the class is doing.

Session 4-viii
Location: School—classroom, at the child's desk
Aim: The child should speak in the classroom at his desk with the teacher, while the therapist is by his side.
The therapist sits next to the child at his desk during a regular lesson and the therapist elicits speech from him. Then the teacher asks him an easy question close up, which the child answers. If the child seems ready, the teacher can then ask a question (which is easy, requires a one-word answer, and whose answer is certainly known by the child) in front of the rest of the class.

Activities: Whatever the class is doing.

Session 4-ix
Location: School—classroom, at the child's desk
Aim: The child should speak in the classroom at his desk with the teacher when the therapist is not by his side.
The therapist sits next to the child at his desk during a regular lesson and the therapist elicits speech from him. Then the teacher asks him an easy question close up which the child answers. After this, the therapist moves away from the child, and the teacher asks him another easy question from close up. Finally the therapist goes out of the room, but remains by the door, visible from within the class, and the teacher again approaches the child and asks him a question requiring a verbal response.

Activities: Whatever the class is doing.

Further sessions consolidating the child's speech in the classroom or kindergarten will most likely be required, enabling the child to continue speaking without the presence of the therapist.

At this point it is hoped that the child is responding verbally to questions from his teacher and interacting verbally with his peers. It is possible that pockets of selective mutism remain within the school —perhaps difficulty talking to other staff members, older children, etc. Similar methods can be employed to tackle these last bastions of non-speech, and **it is important not to end therapy prematurely**. When it is not viable to continue therapy, and the child now speaks with his teacher, it is often possible to guide the teacher so that she can ensure that the speech generalizes further until the child can respond verbally to any person who addresses him in private. Similarly, there may be some situations outside the school in which the child still fails to speak, such as to certain family members, in stores, etc. Here the parent may be guided as to how to further develop the child's speech and social communication. This is described more fully in the Parents' Manual.

It is clear that for some shy children, many social tasks may remain daunting, such as speaking in front of a class, going to friends' homes for the first time, and so on. In much the same way as described above, stepwise behavioral interventions can be useful and may be implemented by the teacher, parents, or therapist. For example, if a child finds it hard to speak in front of the class, he may be encouraged to speak about something he knows well in front of a small group and be praised for so doing. Similarly, a child for whom going to a friend's house for the first time may be daunting might be helped by a gradual program implemented by his parents. For example, first the friend comes to his house, then he goes to the friend's house with his parent. After that, the parent accompanies him but stays for a brief time, and finally the child stays alone at the friend's house. Small but sure steps that allow gradual exposure are best.

Once the therapist terminates therapy, a case manager in the school should be appointed—this could be the teacher, assistant, or school psychologist—who will consider the child's ongoing functioning in school and implement interventions when needed. The school case manager may have to ensure that new staff members are aware of the child's sensitivity, or consider in advance possible pitfalls intrinsic to transitions, so that steps can be taken to safeguard continued improvement in the child's social communication skills.

Sometimes, once normative speech is acquired, other difficulties become apparent that require treatment. These could include speech impediments requiring speech therapy, shyness in social situations causing discomfort or other emotional issues that call for continued therapy. Now that the child speaks, these issues can be addressed and hopefully eased, with the now verbal child participating in the required treatment.

Usually the acquisition of normative speech exerts a powerful effect over related areas in the child's psychological makeup and social development; he is now able to benefit from the wealth of social situations open to him where previously he was withdrawn. He may now see himself as a normal child who speaks when spoken to and who does not have to exert constant control not to talk. His anxiety level drops, and his self-confidence soars.

Here follows an illustration of the treatment methods described in this chapter with five-year-old Rona. All names are changed, and I have included some composite characteristics to blur the identities of the children and their families. All the descriptions are true to actual therapeutic interventions. In this first case study I will describe the sessions in detail, the two that follow later in the book will be more general portrayals of how therapy proceeded.

Therapy with a Five-Year-Old Girl in Kindergarten
--*-* Rona *-*-*-*

"She was a girl suffering, silently crying out for help."

Background
Five-year-old Rona was a china-doll-pretty redhead. She looked fragile, and her behavior the first day I saw her, on a fresh winter morning, exuded vulnerability. She stood stationary and silent in the midst of a swirl of activity and noise in her bustling, effervescent preschool class. Every child (and there were many) seemed to be talking or laughing or shouting or complaining, and most were in motion. Rona was still.

In the meeting with her parents and teachers, the following picture emerged: Rona was the second child in a family of five children. Her family moved to England from Argentina shortly before she was born; Spanish was the language spoken at home, although the siblings sometimes conversed in English. Her parents were educated and devoted to their children; the family environment was rich with books, toys, arts and crafts, not to mention love and caring, with a good sprinkling of healthy limits and rules. Both parents appeared reserved, somewhat shy, and most concerned about Rona's selective mutism.

Rona had never spoken in kindergarten. She had been in a private small playgroup until this year and had been fairly relaxed, participating in most activities, although she had never spoken to children or staff. But on entering this kindergarten with forty children, two bubbly, larger-than-life teachers, and all the consequent commotion, she shut down and froze. She spoke to no one and participated in nothing. She would remain wherever she was, until her teacher led her by the hand to a seat or to the yard. Her facial expression was frozen too; she made no gestures except the most faintly perceptible shake or nod of her head meaning yes or no. She never laughed or smiled, and she didn't cry or sob with any sound; sometimes you could see tears running down her silent, expressionless face.

At home, the picture couldn't have been more different. Rona was full of life and movement and song and, most of all, incessant chatter—as if the long, silent mornings in kindergarten were offset by the constant flow of words and activity at home. She would play with her siblings, fight with them, demand her mother's attention, put on a play or a puppet show, organize a board game, and ride her bike—except when strangers came to visit; then she was restrained and shy and spoke in a whisper, if at all.

The kindergarten staff was skeptical that change was possible in a regular kindergarten and felt that a special-education class was indispensable; Rona's parents and I begged to differ. The teachers were willing to allow therapy to take place in a storage room attached to the kindergarten but could not commit to being active partners in the process.

Rona: Therapy

Home-Based Sessions
Session 1: At home. *Prior to the first session, I met with Rona's parents and explained to them the expected course of therapy, beginning with home sessions.* **My aim in the upcoming initial**

session was to merge into the background, hopefully enabling Rona to be her usual rambunctious self in my presence. Her mother was to be responsible for ensuring that enjoyable activities would take place and that there would be chatting or banter while playing. Before each ensuing home session, I would plan with the parents what would happen based on Rona's response to the previous session. This joint planning is indispensable in home sessions, because it is the parents who engage the child in play as she habituates to the therapist's presence.

I knocked on the door and sat down in the kitchen, which was open plan and adjacent to the large living room area in which Rona and her sisters were painting. I sat with my back to the children and sipped a coffee with Rona's mother, Miri, while chatting quietly and laconically with her. I did not greet the children, nor look in their direction, and I appeared to have no interest in them.

*The living room was cluttered with toys, and the dining table was covered with a nylon protective sheet, barely visible under paints, brushes, papers, glitter, scissors, and glue. As I entered the house and sat with Miri, the girls continued painting, but initially a hush fell over them so that they barely spoke to one another, and when they did so, it was in a whisper. After a few minutes, during which I was clearly neither interesting nor interested, the volume rose, and the chatter was restored. Rona was dominant, instructing her siblings about color and technique, laughing, joking, and chiding. She was also demanding, and soon I was deserted by Miri, who moved over to the budding artists, and the volume and laughter rose higher still. I resisted the temptation to become more visible and turn around or to draw near to the table. I stayed quiet and noninvasive in my kitchen seat with my back to the girls. By the time I rose to leave, no hush ensued, the chatter continued, and I said good-bye to Miri alone. **My*** *first goal had been achieved—Rona spoke absolutely freely in my presence.*

Session 2: At home. *My aim for the second home session was for **Rona to speak freely in my presence**, this time I would be less of a wallflower, and **my presence would be more prominent**, although I would not look at her or speak directly to her. As in every session, before progressing to the new goal, I repeated the previously achieved goal first: I entered the home, sat down in the kitchen, and chatted quietly with Miri. Rona was again engaged in artwork at the living room table, and this time there was no pause in the chatting as I entered, but the instructions, requests, complaints, and laughter continued unimpeded by my presence. Rona had habituated to me being there! After about fifteen minutes, I moved from my place in the kitchen and sat closer to Rona on the living room sofa. Rona had her back to me but was aware of my proximity, turning around and observing me every now and then. After a few seconds of hesitation, she asked her sister to pass her the glitter glue, and the clamor resumed. A few minutes later, she tired of the gluing, so Miri sat with the girls and played go fish with a funny card set of families of caricatured fish. The game was noisy and funny and reached near-altercations at times. What it was not was quiet! The second session's aim was successfully achieved!*

Session 3: At home. My aim this session was to join Rona and her family playing a game requiring speech. A possible further aim was for Rona to speak to me within the context of this game. *I entered the family home and sat in the living room, as the children were playing a rowdy game of go fish. After two rounds of the game, I approached and sat at the table. The noise level remained constant, which encouraged me to take it one step further. After another round (in which Rona won, employing questionable means), I asked Miri if I could play too, and joined Miri, Rona, and* *her two sisters. To begin with, Rona didn't ask me for a card when it was her turn, but after a few turns, she looked down and asked me, "Do you have a green card?" Victory! Fortunately I had not only one but three green cards, and there were smiles all round. In the following rounds of go fish, Rona did not hesitate to ask me for a card—albeit in a quiet voice. Mission accomplished for this session —direct speech with me.*

__Session 4: At home__. Last session, Rona jumped two rungs up the ladder in that she spoke directly to me within the game go fish; __my aim this session was direct speech with me not within the context of a game__. As always, the session began with a task that Rona had already mastered: we played go fish with two siblings, and without pause, Rona mercilessly asked me for cards. After a couple of games, we moved on to "I spy," in which Rona had to ask me or answer me in order to guess which item had been chosen. Then I took out a few tiny, colorful chocolate candies and asked the children to tell me which color candies they would like. Rona gleefully complied. Finally I asked her if she would like the same chocolate the next time I came. She embarked on a speech describing her favorite candies, ending with a list of acceptable candies that I could bring to the following session.

__Session 5: At home. My aim was to consolidate the spontaneous speech with Rona and to play a game with just the two of us__. On entering Rona's house, I was greeted with yelps of joy from all three sisters and invitations to see the paper chains that the children were making. The banter was constant, and there was no need for me to facilitate speech by playing a structured game, but I nevertheless implemented a series of activities that I planned to include in my first kindergarten session with Rona the following week. It began with Chinese whispers, then throwing a ball between the children, each one saying a girl's name as they threw it.

This was followed by two games on the iPad; first, Talking Angela, in which you say something to a cat, who repeats it in a high voice. All the children loved to say funny and slightly risqué words to the cat, who repeated them unabashedly! The second game was "Puppet Pals," in which the children photographed themselves and then made up and recorded a puppet show on the iPad, in which their faces were superimposed on puppets, and as each child spoke, the puppet mouthed her narration accordingly. The children adored this game, and several two-minute long silly and sillier puppet shows were saved on my iPad.

A huge therapeutic accomplishment had been achieved—Rona was speaking freely and joyfully to a new person in her home, who was not one of the select few close family members with whom she had communicated previously. At the close of this session, I felt the time was ripe to make the move to Rona's kindergarten. I made the explanation I gave to Rona about this change of location as unthreatening and playful as possible. I told Rona that I sometimes visit various kindergartens to play with children, and that during the following week, I would be coming to hers and would take her into a small room to play some of the games we had enjoyed in her home. She was pensive, digesting the turn of events, but after a few seconds, returned to her squealing, happy self.

Kindergarten-Based Sessions with Therapist
Session 6: In kindergarten. *The night before our first kindergarten session, Miri told Rona that I would be coming the next day. Her response was, "I want her to come home, not to kindergarten." Prior to the first kindergarten session, I had a meeting with the entire staff and Rona's parents in which I outlined the expected course of therapy, and we shared our perceptions and understanding of Rona's current functioning and emotional state. I made sure that I would have a room and that Rona would be available when I came.*

At this meeting we also discussed what the teachers and the parents could do to complement therapy—the suggestions are included in interventions described in the Teacher's and Parents' Manuals. Rona's parents were unable to come in for talking-playing sessions, but they were working full steam ahead on playdates with friends from the kindergarten, during which Rona was full of the joys of life and speaking freely. They were also recording her frequently at home on a small office tape recorder, and she enjoyed both recording and hearing her voice played back.

The teaching staff vacillated between despair and distance—they thought that the SM was maintained by Rona's manipulative behavior, and they felt despondent at their inability to help her. I gave them some theoretical background about SM and explained that it was out of Rona's control and was not a personal slight against them. The teaching staff was advised to refrain from pressurizing her into talking—which was happening constantly, making Rona feel like an abject failure several times every day. On the other hand, they were encouraged to include her as fully as possible in the day's activities, employing whatever communication Rona was capable of. I usually encourage the teacher to try to build a communicative relationship with the child with SM using gestures, but this teacher was so boisterous and overpowering that I thought it might be overwhelming for Rona. Instead I suggested that a sweet, young, shy teacher's aide might try to build a nonverbal communicative relationship with Rona, talking to her and eliciting Rona's response of nodding and pointing. I also gave the aide the job of ensuring that at no time would Rona stand frozen like a statue in the kindergarten; she would be brought to a table, given some activity to do, and be involved as much as possible in whatever was going on in the kindergarten.

*I installed myself in the small storage room that was to be my therapy room and called Rona to join me. This was a very different Rona to the bubbly girl I had met at home: no facial expression; stiff, hesitant movements; and eyes focused firmly on the ground. She was truly a shadow of herself, emanating a wish to withdraw from the world and into herself. She was a girl suffering, silently crying out for help. She showed the slightest glint of recognition in her eyes as she accompanied me to the therapy room, a tiny cubbyhole of a room adjacent to the kindergarten main space. The door was firmly closed, and it was just me and her alone. **The aim of this session was for Rona to speak freely to me in the kindergarten therapy room**.*

I took out my iPad and told her I was going to play some of the puppet shows we had recorded at home in the previous session. She displayed no reaction. I played her the first puppet show; there was a twinkle in her eyes. Then the second puppet show; there was a half-smile on her lips. It was a huge achievement: for the first time ever, Rona's (recorded) voice had been heard loud and clear in kindergarten. Then we played Chinese whispers—slightly stilted to play it with two people, but it served my purpose. She whispered in my ear when it was her turn and said in a louder whisper the word I had whispered in her ear. Next huge achievement: whispering to someone in kindergarten. We played a last game—throwing a ball to one another, with the thrower saying one item within a chosen category. We started off with colors. She knew many, and we kept going for a while. Then we moved on to girls' names, then boys' names, then words that remind one of vacations, then items found in the home, and so on.

This was excellent progress all in one session, and I decided to spend the last twenty minutes doing some arts and crafts. We decorated a tiny photo frame with colors and stickers. This allowed

Rona both to engage in spontaneous speech and to finish this most sensitive session with a less-demanding activity.

And she did talk to me—quietly, but not in a whisper; I asked her about her friends and the teacher, and we joked and chatted. Over the course of one hour, her entire demeanor had metamorphosed from an anxiety-frozen, totally withdrawn, non-expressive girl to a relaxed, engaged, playful, talkative child! How did this happen? I literally brought a piece of her home to the kindergarten. I had established my relationship with her at home, where she was most relaxed, and then enabled her to generalize that connection to me so that gradually over the course of an hour, she could talk and interact with me in the room. No pain, no convincing, no power struggles, no soul searching—just playing in a structured, gradual, planned fashion.

Sessions 7 and 8: In kindergarten. The following two sessions were spent consolidating our warm, chatty relationship by playing the games we had played in the previous session, as well as others. I started both sessions playing something prerecorded on the iPad and then with a series of games that progressed gradually from minimal speech through to a few words and finally up to spontaneous speech. The sessions were fun and relaxed, and we both looked forward to them.

The time had come to include her peers in our sessions. Rona's mother had been dutifully inviting friends regularly to her house, and by this time, Rona was speaking to a number of them at home. Rona chose Naomi, with whom she was relaxed and chatty at home, to join in the next kindergarten session.

Kindergarten-Based Sessions with Therapist and Children

Sessions 9 and 10: In kindergarten with Rona and a friend. *Rona and Naomi were the participants of the ninth session. She had spoken to Naomi at home but not a word or even any nonverbal communication in kindergarten. Both were excited about coming, although with Naomi in the room, Rona initially reverted back to her expressionless, near-frozen posture.* **The aim of these sessions was to enable Rona to speak and play freely with Naomi in the kindergarten therapy room***. As soon as we had seated ourselves on the green kiddie stools, I whipped out my iPad and played a couple of prerecorded puppet shows. Naomi was hearing Rona speak in kindergarten. Then I played a video Rona's mother had sent me of Rona and Naomi playing noisily at home, replete with laughter and joyful screeching. I noted with relief something that I commonly see when a child with SM hears a prerecorded movie or audio recording of herself before others in the school setting for the first time: a visible change in body language, a physical relaxing of her shoulders and facial muscles, and a sigh of relief. Her voice had been heard by Naomi; a big hurdle had been surmounted. The next activity was Chinese whispers, where I whispered something to Rona, and she whispered it to Naomi. Success! After a few rounds, we moved on to Talking Angela, where each person had to say her name to the cat app, who repeated it in a distorted voice. Rona was quiet, whispering at first, but Angela does not respond if the voice is too quiet, so the second time around, she said her name in a barely audible voice. Then we moved on to saying any name to Talking Angela, and as the rounds progressed, so did the volume of Rona's voice and the squeals of laughter at the sound of the distorted voice. The final game was throwing a ball to one another, with the thrower saying types of food. By this time, Rona was full of the joys of life, throwing with gusto and saying the food names in a clear voice. Her eyes were firmly on the door much of the time, ensuring that no one but the three of us was privy to her speech and spontaneity. When the session ended, Rona and Naomi returned to the kindergarten,* *and the expressionless mask settled on Rona's face once again. But the two girls went to their places holding hands, and Rona had more of a bounce to her step than she had had one hour earlier.*

The aim of the following session was to consolidate the verbal communication with Naomi and to loosen up Rona's movement and self-expression. We played the aforementioned games, as well as additional games that involved speech together with a motor component, including duck, duck, goose—participants sit in a circle, as one person runs around the others, taps them on the head and says "duck" as she passes. When she eventually says "goose," the person who she taps must catch her before she returns to and sits down in her place; otherwise, she becomes "it." We also played blind man's bluff—a player is blindfolded and must catch another player and then guess who has been caught based on her voice. Rona gradually offered speech that was not an integral part of the game; she told us that she had been to a wedding the previous night, along with other personal tidbits and requests. The session was great fun, and as long as the door was shut tight, Rona was free with her speech and movement.

Simultaneously, I was guiding the kindergarten aide, Sari, to develop a nonverbal relationship with Rona and ensuring that at no point was she standing alone frozen in the kindergarten but rather led to a seat and encouraged to participate. Rona's mother reported that Rona was more comfortable in kindergarten now that she had an adult ally in the form of the aide. Sari was astounded to discover that it was possible to develop a communicative relationship with such an inhibited child: Rona utilized minimal tools of communication with Sari, including barely perceptible nods and shakes of her head and the smallest upturn of her lips—the hint of a smile. Yet Sari was building an understanding, warm relationship with Rona. For Rona this was the difference between being totally isolated and unable to communicate her needs during the entire school day, and being able to express herself and consequently yield some control over her kindergarten experience.

Sessions 11, 12, and 13: In kindergarten with Rona and several friends. *The same approach was implemented with an increasing number of peers. Each session, an additional child was included in the little group, and a similar progression of games was employed: from recorded speech, to whispered speech, to minimal speech within a game, to speech within a game employing motor activity in order to lower the level of anxiety, to the miraculous emergence of spontaneous speech. Rona understood that she could talk to any friend in this way, and she left each session beaming with satisfaction. What an empowering feeling to be able to talk to people in kindergarten within the space of an hour. At home her mother reported that she was happier, calmer, and more self-confident then she had ever been.*

Sessions 14 and 15: In the kindergarten therapy room with Rona and several friends, preparing a puppet show. *The time had come to accelerate the progress, and I decided to prepare a puppet show in the therapy room with a group of five children, which we could then show to the class, either live (I reckoned that to be unlikely) or filmed. Either way, the whole class and staff would hear Rona loud and clear, and this would set a new reality. I brought in a book about animals looking for their mothers and lots of hand puppets, and we delegated roles. I was the narrator, and each child spoke her part as dictated by the story. The children were bubbling with enthusiasm, and the puppet show was rehearsed and deemed ready to film. Much fun was had by all, and our group sat down to discuss how to show it to the kindergarten. Rona was distressed when I suggested showing it to the whole kindergarten, whether it be live or filmed. Finally, she agreed to show it live to groups of five* children at a time, who would be invited to the therapy room to see the show.

For the following session, we prepared popcorn in plastic cups and one row of five chairs, ready for the audience. Rona seemed jumpy and unsure of herself. We practiced the puppet show once more and invited the first group of five children to come and watch the show. It went as planned, and Rona said her part, in a quiet yet distinctly audible voice. As they took their bows, Rona looked thrilled and incredulous that she had spoken in front of five of her peers! Just like that! The next group of five children took their places and saw the show, followed by successive groups, until all thirty-seven children in the kindergarten had heard Rona speak! The final group came with a value-added supplement—the teacher and the aide, Sari. By now Rona was an old hand at performing in front of people with whom she had never previously spoken, and she didn't miss a beat, speaking loudly and clearly. The teachers were stunned. **The aim of these sessions had been accomplished: to speak in a live puppet show before all the children and staff of the kindergarten!**

Session 16: In the kindergarten common space with Rona and Naomi. The aim of this session was **for Rona to generalize her speech so that she spoke not only in the therapy room but also in the kindergarten common play room. Talking tasks would be introduced—the children would speak to each other during the week at specified times, not confined to within the sessions.** Here the variable to be changed was the location of the therapy: we were going to leave the secluded, safe space of the therapy room (a glorified storage room!) and venture forth into the common space where all the children played. I sat with Rona and Naomi in a quiet corner of the kindergarten and took out my iPad with a video of the puppet show we had performed the previous week. Rona was wary and did not want other children to approach, so we kept the rest of the class at arm's length. After seeing and hearing the video, I played Chinese whispers with the girls, and Rona spoke in a whisper even when it was her turn to say the word at the end. We then played go fish, and she spoke in an audible whisper. She seemed uncomfortable and wary. I then played my trump card: I took out a packet of small, colorful candies from my bag, and I covered my eyes with a scarf. In turn, each of the girls could take a candy if they told me which color they wanted. Rona had to speak loudly enough for me to hear in order to get a candy. To begin with, I could barely hear her whispering, and told her that I couldn't hear. So she said in a quiet voice, "Purple," and took the candy. We continued to play until each girl had a little mound of candies in her hand and a large grin on her face!

Talking tasks were introduced: I drew a chart with each of the five school days between this meeting and the next, and once a day in kindergarten, the two girls had to say to one another what they had eaten for breakfast and then put a sticker on the corresponding square to show that they had accomplished their talking task for the day. When I next came, I would review the chart, and if they had completed the task every day, they would get a small prize. This would mean that Rona would (hopefully) speak to her friend once a day in kindergarten, for the first time ever, not in my presence!

Sessions 17 and 18: In the kindergarten common space with Rona and several friends. The games that we played in the previous two sessions were repeated in these sessions, as Rona gradually spoke in a more consistently audible voice. All the children and staff had heard her in the puppet show we had performed a few sessions back, and this enabled her to talk now in a secluded corner of the kindergarten. But it was not easy for Rona, and she needed these sessions to enable her to speak more confidently and audibly.

I started the sessions with the candy game, in which she had to speak audibly to get a candy, so that each session began with Rona speaking in a quiet but distinctly audible voice. At the end of each session, I reviewed the talking-task chart for the past week, and the girls chose a small prize. Then I gave them a talking-task chart to be completed during the forthcoming week. This involved playing one of the games we had just played on a daily basis and putting a sticker on the chart for each respective day. As Rona worked through her daily talking tasks, a small miracle called "parallel progress" emerged: Rona spoke to Naomi not only within the confines of the talking tasks but was observed whispering to her in free play and speaking quietly to her during arts and crafts.

Sessions 19 and 20: In the kindergarten common space with Rona, several friends, and the teacher's aide, Sari. As the sessions proceeded, Rona spoke in a consistently audible voice, and I felt it was time to try to include the teacher's aide, Sari, in the sessions. We began session 19 with Rona, Naomi, and Rachel, first recording a Puppet Pals show together, then playing go fish and Twister, in which Rona spun a dial and announced to all of us where we had to put our feet and hands, until we all got into an impossible tangle. Next we played Secret Square, in which one player puts a counter under one of many picture squares on the table, and the other players ask questions in order to guess under which square the counter is hidden, progressively eliminating and removing squares until one square remains, and the counter is discovered. For the final five minutes of the session, I invited Sari to join us. We played her the Puppet Pals video we had previously recorded and then played a game of Chinese whispers, in which Sari whispered to Rona, and Rona whispered to Naomi. We played once more, but this time Rona whispered to Sari. The aim of this session was joyfully completed—Rona had whispered to Sari in the kindergarten!

175

Session 19 proceeded much as session 18, except that after the Chinese whispers with Sari at the end, we played Secret Square, with Rona asking Sari questions such as, "Is the counter under the square with the fish?" Rona asked the questions, shyly but surely! This week's talking task was a chart in which the girls were to play a shortened version of Secret Square with Sari once a day. Rona was going to speak to Sari as part of the regular school day.

Sessions 21 and 22: In the kindergarten common space with Rona and several friends and the teacher, Ellie. Here we replicated session 19, during which Rona first talked with an adult in kindergarten—the teacher's aide. This time the aim was to talk to the main teacher, Ellie, a dominant, loud, and somewhat unpredictable character, who was unapproachable in Rona's eyes. Again we prepared a recording—this time Doodlecast Junior—about our favorite foods.

In this session our group was made up of Rona, Tali, and Hayley, with whom Rona was by now speaking freely in our group and occasionally outside the therapy sessions as well. We followed the sequence of games as in the previous few sessions, starting with games calling for minimal speech and progressing to activities requiring spontaneous speech; for the final ten minutes, Ellie was invited to join us. First I played the Doodlecast recording to her, and this seemed to be well within Rona's comfort zone—no discomfort was apparent. Then we progressed to Chinese whispers, in which Rona whispered to me and her friends but not to Ellie. We moved on to Secret Square, but Rona refused to take her turn. It seemed that talking to Ellie was just too daunting a step. By session 22, Rona did manage to whisper words within the category game in Ellie's presence, but it was labored, painful, and reticent.

Meanwhile, the talking tasks were being carried out beyond the requirements set out in the chart—the children happily played lengthy games of Secret Square with Sari, and beautiful parallel progress was taking place, as Sari engaged Rona in conversation several times a day, and Rona happily complied. Similarly Rona was becoming increasingly verbal with peers throughout the school day, even with children who had not been included in the therapy sessions.

Not so with Ellie; this seemed to be one of the two bastions of SM within the kindergarten, the other one being speaking in front of the whole kindergarten during circle time.

By the time 22 sessions had been completed, the summer vacation was imminent. Rona's progress at the end of the school year was as follows: Rona was talking to everyone in the kindergarten except for Ellie and not in circle time. She fully participated in the activities, freely (if shyly) expressed happiness and sadness, voiced laughter and crying, and went contentedly to kindergarten every morning.

There was so much more consistency between her home and school personas—in both settings she was bubbly and communicative, although shyer and more cautious in kindergarten, particularly with adults.

At home too Rona's parents saw her far less frustrated, more contented, and less withdrawn when nonfamily members visited.

The final breakthrough came after the summer vacation, as Rona began first grade. Transitioning to a new class or new school is a window of opportunity for children with SM. When beginning a new school, teachers and peers have no preconceived ideas about whether or not you speak, and this often enables a child to talk with *staff from the outset—although it can also be daunting and challenging adjusting to a new setting, staff, and children.*

During the summer, we continued to meet intermittently at Rona's home, recording ourselves, talking about first grade, inviting family members with whom Rona had previously not spoken, and carrying out interventions similar to those we had implemented in kindergarten. Rona had found a way of speaking freely with family members: she would read a book together with one of her siblings, each in turn reading a sentence. (Rona was an almost self-taught fluent reader, a brilliant little girl.) When people came to her house with whom she had previously been unable to talk, such as one neighbor and a kindergarten teacher from a previous year who was also a friend of her mother, she would read a book to them together with her sister, after which the neighbor would ask a few questions, and she would answer. After that she was able to answer them when they addressed her. We adopted this as our strategy for talking to the first-grade teacher before school started.

I explained to Rona's teacher about her SM, and she agreed to visit her at home during the last week of vacation and then meet her once in school the day before term began. All went as planned in the home visit—Rona read a book alternating with her sister and answered questions the teacher asked her. She even asked the teacher something herself—whether she could eat the candy that the teacher had given her! This was successfully repeated in the classroom the day before school began, and I built a behavior-shaping schedule with the teacher, in which she would be sure to talk to Rona every day and ensure that she was answering her, thus speaking in school at least once a day. Rona outdid all our expectations on the first day of school by speaking freely with all the children and staff, like any other child. She was thrilled with herself; one year earlier she had been frozen, expressionless, and voiceless in kindergarten. Now she could answer teachers and put in requests, build relationships with classmates, and see herself to be a competent, communicative child who had overcome her SM, enabling her to express who she is both at home and in school. Her everyday experiences were so much more enjoyable and less fraught, now that she had put her selective mutism behind her.

Therapy in the Clinic, without Home and/or School Sessions

I am a deep believer in therapy in the child's natural settings whenever possible; if the child suffers from SM in the school setting, then that is where treatment will be most effective. However, sometimes, for a host of reasons, school or home sessions are not viable, and the only treatment option is within the clinic setting. In such cases, this treatment method can be adapted to be implemented in the clinic. This can be done in two ways.

The first is for the therapist to meet regularly with parents and an assigned keyworker who in effect is the therapist carrying out the intervention outlined in chapter 6, in this way overseeing the application of the therapeutic interventions.

A second way is for the therapist to meet with the child regularly in the clinic, enabling him to talk to the therapist by fading him in;this will be explained shortly. Once the child talks to the therapist,generalization can follow in two ways:either by bringing the child's world into the clinic setting by inviting fellow students and staff to the clinic and helping the child to talk and communicate with them there, or by setting exposure talking tasks to be carried out with peers and staff in the school or kindergarten setting. Usually a combination of both components is employed. Let me briefly explain how one may adapt the therapy described in chapter 6 to be implemented either in a school or in a clinic setting, without the home sessions.

Guidelines for Treatment without Home Sessions

Again, while it is highly preferable to hold initial treatment sessions at the child's home, as this usually significantly shortens the length of the therapy, it is not always feasible. In such cases, sessions take place at the school or clinic alone.

Whenever possible, effort should be made to maintain fluid and open contact and collaboration with parents, because even when treatment occurs exclusively at the school or clinic, parents potentially remain an important contributing factor to successful treatment. They should be consulted with in the assessment stage,given the Parents' Manual to read, and guided regarding the implementation of their interventions as well as their management of their child's selective mutism. When parents are willing and able to assist in taping their child at home for use in the school sessions and can hold playing-talking sessions with their child in school or kindergarten as described in the manuals, this may greatly assist the course of therapy. So prior to beginning treatment with the child at the school or clinic, meetings should be held with the parents in order to consult with them, guide them, and ensure that they will carry out their part in the treatment triangle of parents-school-therapist as much as possible.

Starting treatment in the school or clinic

When treatment begins at school or the clinic, the beneficial jump start of initial home sessions is lost. The aim of the home sessions is to enable the child to talk to the therapist with relative ease and speed by slotting in inconspicuously at home. When starting directly in school or the clinic, establishing initial speech between the therapist and the child is often a challenging task. All the principles regarding sessions and the behavioral tools for shaping speech described in chapter 6 are still relevant; the starting point of the school or clinic sessions is usually non-speech to adults.

When introducing yourself to the child for the first time in school or the clinic, the principle described in chapter 6 regarding the playfulness and light character of therapy should be borne in mind. This helps to ensure the enjoyable, relaxed nature of the sessions, which in turn allows anxiety levels to remain low. The therapist can be introduced as someone who has play sessions with children, sometimes alone and sometimes with friends. The level and nature of further explanations—the cognitive component of therapy—depends on the age and developmental stage of the child and whether he initiates further discussion of the aims of the sessions, as outlined in chapters 6 and 8.

Therapy will proceed according to the stages outlined in chapter 6, starting from stage 2-ii. In the original program, which begins with home-based sessions, this is the stage at which the child fails to speak to the therapist once the sessions are moved to the school.

If at all possible, **initial school or clinic-based sessions should be set up to resemble the home sessions as closely as possible**. If the parents are active partners in the therapy, they may be invited to the initial sessions so that the child will speak to them, initially alone, freely in the therapy room. The therapist will gradually and as inconspicuously as possible join in the sessions.

All sessions including a parent must be carefully planned with the parent beforehand, including which activities and games will be played in the session, how the parent will explain the sessions to the child, and having a playful attitude to the sessions. All this is elaborated on in chapter 6.

Parent-child sessions

In the first session, a parent (or sibling or other family member) may come to the therapy room and play with the child, as previously planned by the parent and the therapist, without the therapist being present. The games and activities should be according to the preferences of the child so that it will be a pleasant experience. T**he activities should require at least a minimal amount of speech**, or the parent can engage the child in conversation during the activities. For suggestions of activities, see the session outlines in chapter 6. Recordings of the child from home should be played during these sessions, such as the child interviewing siblings, singing, or reading. The parent-child sessions should take place uninterrupted in **a closed therapy room** in the school or the clinic. The parent should come to sessions until the child is speaking freely with the parent in the closed therapy room.

Once this is achieved, the **therapist will gradually insert herself into the proceedings**, as is described in sessions 2-ii to 2-vii in chapter 6. After that, therapy may continue as outlined in the t-Therapist's Manual if it is taking place in school. For how to continue in a clinic setting, see below.

Initial school or clinic-based sessions without family members

If a family member cannot be present at the initial school- or clinic-based sessions, then the therapist begins sessions in which she utilizes techniques to elicit speech without the parents' presence. Whenever possible, it is important nevertheless to include the parents and family in the therapy in other ways, as described in chapters 4 and 6. This includes consulting with them about preparing the treatment plan, encouraging them to invite friends home and to record or video their child, considering the possibility of talking-playing sessions in school, working with them on possible anxiety issues of their own, and guiding them regarding the implementation of their interventions at home.

If the child speaks to a classmate outside or inside school, it may be possible to include this friend in the initial sessions (with his parents' permission) and then to follow the steps from 2-ii in chapter 6, with the friend substituting for the family member. The sessions would need to be structured in a way in which the friend experiences the meetings as games and activities and, unlike the parents, is in no way involved in planning or carrying out the sessions.

All the therapy guidelines set out in chapter 6 still hold true, including taking gradual steps that are tolerable in terms of the child's anxiety level and ensuring that the sessions are pleasant and, whenever possible, fun for the child.

The therapist in the school or clinic should plan a behavioral program in which the aim is to develop a relationship with the child that is initially nonverbal and that gradually progresses to eliciting sounds and eventually speech in the therapy room.

Below is a postulated exposure program with the following steps:

- **Establishing a relationship in which the child feels at ease with the therapist**
- **Nonverbal communication**
- **Noise production**
- **Eliciting sounds**
- **Speaking real words**

The initial school- or clinic-based sessions have the aim of establishing a relationship in which **the child feels at ease with the therapist**. Activities for these sessions should be according to the child's baseline of social communication and should have no speech requirements if the child doesn't initially speak to the therapist; nonverbal communication requirements must be in the range of the child's current abilities within the therapist-child relationship. Activities could be telling or reading stories, arts and crafts, card or board games, and so on.

Once the child is playing comfortably with the therapist, the steps are structured to include **nonverbal communication**, such as nodding, pointing, and gestures. When the child is ready, full-body gestures such as acting in games like charades can be included.

The following stage incorporates games that include **noise production**—for example, playing musical instruments, clapping, stamping, and the like.

The next stage could be **eliciting sounds** coming from the mouth of the child within the framework of games as described in chapter 6, which may be clicking the tongue or sounds such as "shhh" or "t." For example, a ball may be thrown between the therapist and the child, and each time it is thrown, the thrower makes the sound "shhh," then clicking of the tongue, followed by animal noises.

The hardest transition is often between these nonverbal sounds and **speaking real words**. Sometimes words can be substituted for these nonverbal sounds in the framework of a game such as the ball game described above, so that the child says "boom" instead of "shhh" each time he throws the ball. Similarly, if snap had previously been played with a tongue click each time both players laid down identical cards, now the players might say "snap."

Whenever possible, it can be very helpful to have **recordings of the child speaking** made with his family at home for use in the school or clinic therapy sessions, as this is a pre-direct speech way of having the child's voice present in sessions. Recordings should be incorporated early on in the treatment sessions as a way of breaking the first barrier of hearing the child's voice.

The therapist can include recordings as a tool for relaying messages between herself and the child—the therapist may record questions and leave the room, and the child records the answers. Gradually, the child may progress from sending audio WhatsApp messages or speaking in a recording device to speaking to the therapist when the therapist is standing outside the door, and then inside the room looking away, and, finally, looking toward the child.

Other ways of eliciting speech can be playing games that require whispering such as Chinese whispers, gradually shaping the whisper so that it becomes louder as the therapist moves further away from the child. If the child manages to whisper, the therapist could play games in which the whispering is amplified, such as having the child speak into a microphone.

Great patience is required to move gradually from one stage to the next. Care must be taken not to give in to the urge to rush ahead, as this might not only fail to bring the desired result, but it may also set the child back, as her feelings of competence could diminish, and her anxiety level may rise.

Once the child is saying words in the sessions, the therapist should work toward more spontaneous and complex speech. This often occurs naturally in the course of conversation and activities within a warm,comfortable child-therapist relationship. Sometimes it has to be engendered through games and activities that require increasingly complex levels of speech. Such games include I spy, twenty questions, Guess Who, and Taboo. For additional suggested activities, see Appendix 2.

Once the child is speaking to the therapist in a closed room in the school, therapy can proceed to the generalization stages, as described in stages 3 and 4 in chapter 6. If the therapy is taking place in the clinic, some adaptation is required as outlined below.

Implementation of therapy in the clinic
(When home- and school-based sessions are not possible)
Once speech has been engendered between the therapist and the child, as described above, but the therapist is unable to move the setting of the intervention to the school, therapy may continue in the clinic. As mentioned above, this can be done in one of two ways: First (preferably), the therapist will fade in a keyworker who can carry out the therapy in the school or kindergarten as described in chapters 6 and 8 and can meet for guidance with or without the child on a regular basis. Alternatively, if there is no keyworker, the therapist will continue the intervention in the clinic, pulling the strings from afar to generalize progress into the child's daily life.

Once the child is speaking to the therapist in the clinic, if no keyworker is being employed in school, the therapist can move forward in two parallel and complementary channels:setting talking and communicating tasks for the child to carry out in school, and inviting staff and friends into the clinic to engender communication and speech therein. Either way, much interchange with staff and family is necessary to outline the current school-based talking tasks, to hear how they have been progressing, and to ensure that whatever progress occurs in the therapy room finds its way to the child's real life.

Inviting friends and staff into the room: the child must be informed in advance who will be included in each session—sometimes it is best to tell him only shortly before the actual session so as not to engender simmering anxiety, as the apprehensive child frets about the upcoming session for a number of days! When inserting peers or staff with whom the child has not previously spoken into the clinic setting, the stages and principles are the same as those described in chapter 6: gradual behavior shaping, starting with listening to recordings previously made of the child's voice, followed by whispering games, then rote speech, and eventually spontaneous speech. All this is harder to achieve in the clinic setting because the participants have to come especially, rather than be included while they are in any case located in the school or kindergarten.

Once the child has mastered speaking to a peer or teacher in the clinic, talking tasks must be planned so that this behavior is applied to the child's real life—in school or kindergarten or other settings in the outside world. This involves ongoing contact between the therapist, the teacher, and the child's family to outline the current talking task, to convey how and when to implement it, and to verify how the child responds to the task in school. So there is much logistic work to be done when sessions do not occur in the school itself.

For example, the teacher may come to the clinic for sessions in which the child speaks to her using an exposure ladder of graduated tasks, as described in chapter 6. After this, an exposure schedule has to be constructed with the teacher so that the child will gradually speak to her in school, first listening to recordings of their talk in the sessions, followed by talking in vivo with the teacher in a private room in school, later in a public space, and finally in the classroom. The ways in which speech is engendered, be it through recordings, tasks, or games, must also be included in the exposure ladder. In my experience it is very helpful when the therapist writes a detailed plan, with probable dates and places, including which activities are to be engaged in with the aim of facilitating speech. There should also be a way for the teacher to summarize how each school talking task actually went to be e-mailed intermittently to the therapist and parents. An example of an exposure ladder can be viewed in chapter 5, the Teacher's Manual.

Similarly, once the child starts talking to a select few people, a school or family member must guide her to gradually broaden the circles of friends and teachers with whom she speaks, along the lines of the sessions described in chapter 6. Older children are often able to take this responsibility upon themselves, using a chart in which they document their speech in school. Examples of such charts can be seen in chapter 8.

In summary, this treatment method can be adapted to be implemented either without home sessions, in school sessions alone, or to be carried out in a more conventional clinic setting. It is often a more laborious and lengthy process, because the advantages of starting therapy in the low-anxiety, optimum-functioning setting of the home is lost, and progress gained in the clinic must be subsequently transferred to the school or kindergarten. When possible, it is always recommended for the therapist to carry out at least occasional school-based sessions to ensure that the child is progressing in the setting that counts—that of her day-to-day real life!

Therapist's Manual 2

CBT for Teens and Preteens

still waters run deep

Cognitive-Behavioral Therapy for Teens and Preteens

Overview of Therapy with Older Children

How Anxious Avoidance is Established and Extinguished

Cognitive-Behavioral Tools

1. Assessment
2. Initial home-based sessions
3. School-based sessions
4. Psychoeducation
5. The adaptive value of anxiety
6. Relieving anxiety, relaxation techniques
7. Cognitive restructuring
8. Building a stepladder of goals
9. Homework—talking tasks
10. Medication
11. Social skills, self-esteem, assertiveness
12. Core beliefs
13. Voice projection
14. Parental interventions with teens
15. Teachers' interventions with teens

Putting it all Together—Two Case Studies

Therapy with Joey and Leslie, youngsters overcoming SM

Cognitive-Behavioral Therapy for Teens and Preteens

The treatment of choice for young children with selective mutism is usually behavioral with certain cognitive components. This is the treatment plan outlined so far in the manuals. Behavioral treatments attempt to alter the child's behavior in small, structured steps. In the case of SM, the aim is to guide the child from the inability to speak, toward speech in all settings. With young children, certain cognitive elements may be included in the treatment, including psychoeducation, normalization, and belief in the child's ability to change his behavior. The child could, at the appropriate time in therapy, be given explanations about selective mutism, how many other children suffer from it, and that it can be eased by treatment. The relationship between the adults involved and the young child with SM is not egalitarian; the course of therapy is set by the therapist, parents, and teachers according to their understanding of the needs, anxiety level, and abilities of the child.

With an older child, and certainly with teenagers, the cognitive elements of therapy become more prominent. As the child matures and becomes more introspective, the therapy has to be run along more egalitarian lines in which the child becomes an active partner working with the therapist to understand and treat his condition. Together with the therapist, he will consider and select steps that can be taken to enable speech, will share the responsibility in achieving these goals, and will assess his behavior retrospectively. In addition, there must be fuller disclosure by the therapist regarding his insights and treatment plan.

In this way the therapeutic balance between the behavioral and cognitive elements changes with older children, as greater weight is given to their understanding and ability to implement behavioral steps based on this insight. Thus, for teens and preteens, therapy combines cognitive and behavioral elements, although the backbone of therapy must remain behavioral;the aim is to remove the symptom—the inability to speak in certain settings or to specific people—to enable the teenager to resume a normal path of development and to engage in social communication in an age-appropriate fashion. Sitting in a therapist's office considering how realistic one's thoughts are and learning to twin relaxation with anxious thoughts may be conducive to change, but building a ladder of step-by-step goals, within an operative plan to actually begin speaking, is putting the theory into practice,overcoming selective mutism where it matters—in the young person's life.

Overview of Therapy with Older Children

Treatment of older children has much in common with the treatment for younger children outlined in this book, including two major components:

The importance of the joint work and fluid communication between the triumvirate of parents, teachers, and therapist.

Usually, school is one of the main settings in which the symptom of inability to speak manifests. The teacher is in the eye of the storm, strategically placed to carry out her own interventions that are planned together with the therapist and parents, and are designed to supplement their therapeutic tasks. In this program, after working with a therapist on cognitive restructuring and relaxation, the teen will apply her newfound insight and begin to work her way up a stepladder of tasks that will bring her from silence to speech and social communication. If the symptom occurs in school, then the application of the desensitization ladder must take place there too. Parents also have a therapeutic role—they can oversee the implementation of stepladders of tasks to further speech with friends and family members, in stores, to doctors, and so on. Parents may be pivotal in other ways, such as help with preparing homework in the investigative, cognitive restructuring stage. The parents' attitude to the SM is crucial too; parents should try to project belief in the child and to lower the pressure to speak. More will be said about the parents' and teachers' roles later on in the chapter.

Behavioral implementation of gradual steps toward speech

This remains the backbone of the therapy, which will have been facilitated by the cognitive work. In the protocol outlining therapy with younger children in chapter 6, the therapist builds a series of tasks and games, applying them in diverse settings, building a bridge of small steps guiding the child to speech. With teens, the therapist builds the stepladder together with the youngster, utilizing cognitive tools that have been acquired in therapy to ease his way in overcoming selective mutism. So for older children, the therapy consists of two distinct but interconnected components: work in the clinic or therapy room on understanding thoughts and feelings, attempting to restructure cognitions, and learning to relax; and the implementation of these insights and tools in order to overcome SM in practice, using gradual, small, but sure steps within the child's real life.

How Anxious Avoidance is Established and Extinguished

How does the mechanism of anxiety work to establish the entrenched behavior of not speaking to certain people or in specific settings, and how can that anxiety be extinguished?

Earlier on in the book, we looked at the vicious cycle of how anxiety is reinforced. The child is in a stressful situation; he is asked something requiring a verbal response; he feels threatened and refrains from answering. This brings down his level of anxiety and is henceforth reenacted in stressful situations. The avoidance behavior is reinforced and incrementally becomes more firmly entrenched.

Reinforced Anxiety

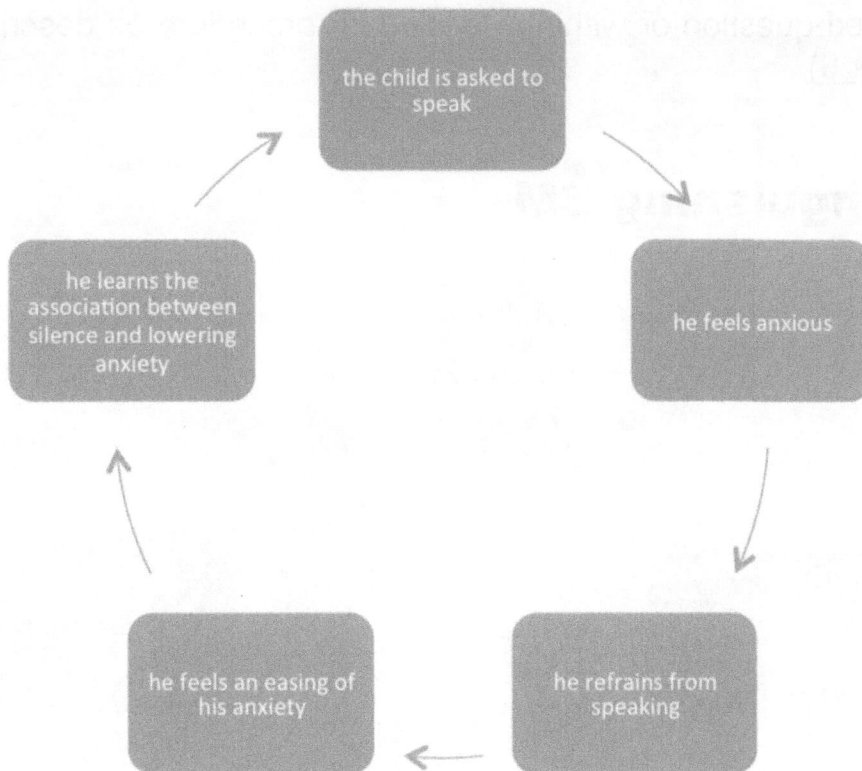

This cycle can be activated in a more adaptive way to overcome SM, as shown in the table below, utilizing that **key player in overcoming anxiety: habituation**. When a child is helped to overcome his anxiety and engage in the feared activity, he may see that nothing catastrophic occurs, and if he persists in this activity for long enough, he will experience a lowering of anxiety as he habituates to this previously avoided task. This cycle too can be repeatedly reinforced.

In the table below, we see a child who has investigated his thoughts and feelings, internalized more adaptive thoughts, and learned how to relax his neck and mouth. Then in a controlled setting, he speaks for the first time to a teacher (say, a one-word answer to a pre-

prepared question or within a "sliding in" procedure as described in chapter 6).

Extinguishing SM

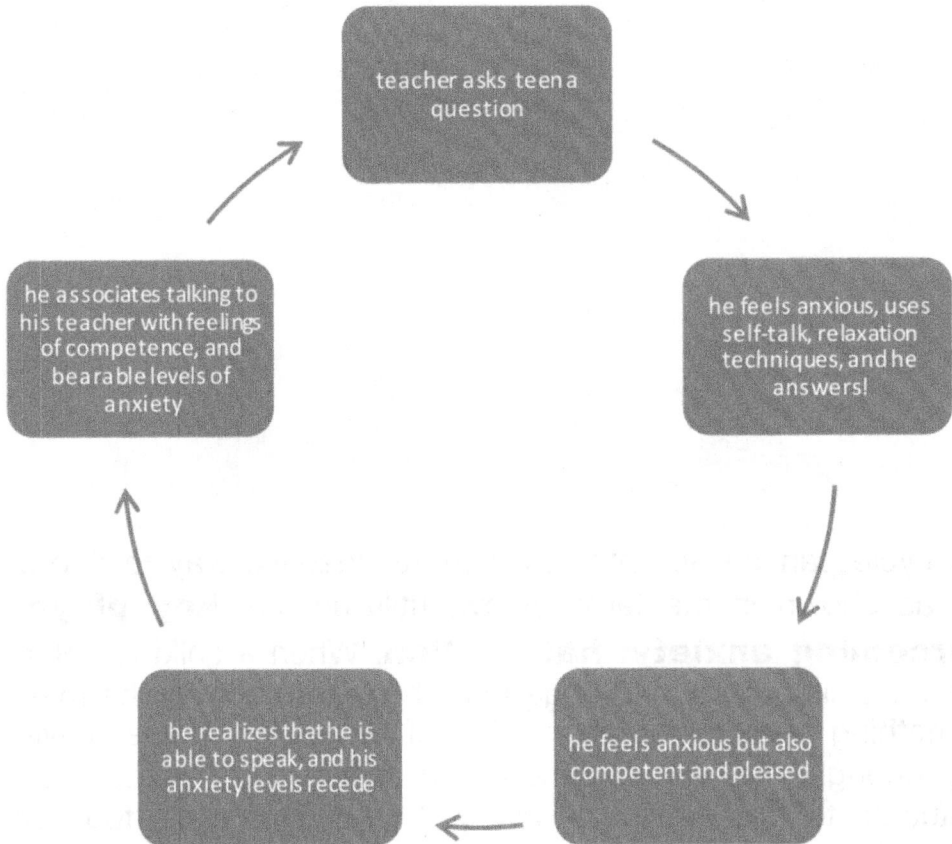

```
        ┌──────────────────┐
        │ teacher asks teen a │
        │     question      │
        └──────────────────┘
```

```
┌──────────────────────┐              ┌──────────────────────┐
│ he associates talking to │            │ he feels anxious, uses │
│ his teacher with feelings │            │  self-talk, relaxation │
│ of competence, and      │            │  techniques, and he    │
│ bearable levels of      │            │     answers!          │
│      anxiety           │            └──────────────────────┘
└──────────────────────┘
```

```
┌──────────────────────┐              ┌──────────────────────┐
│ he realizes that he is  │            │ he feels anxious but also │
│ able to speak, and his  │            │ competent and pleased  │
│ anxiety levels recede   │            └──────────────────────┘
└──────────────────────┘
```

Cognitive-Behavioral Tools

Here we will give an overview of techniques and stages of CBT therapy with teens suffering from SM. While cognitive elements are important, the backbone of SM therapy for all ages is behavioral; the practical goal is to help the young person to speak and to improve her social communication functioning.

1. Assessment

It is important to meet with the parents and teachers and conduct a thorough assessment to ensure an accurate diagnosis. This is outlined in chapter 3. As stated there, it is very useful for the therapist to see a video of the youngster's optimum functioning, taken at home by the parents in a relaxing and playful atmosphere—the teen does not have to be told that this is for use in assessment.

At this initial meeting with parents, they should be asked to do two things that will be helpful later on in therapy: to make ample recordings or videos of the teen speaking at home and to encourage the young person to invite friends home. This will be elaborated on in the section about the parents' role later on in the chapter. Teachers too may be advised to attempt to begin a behavior shaping schedule in school, built together with the therapist and parents. They may be advised how to help the child to lower anxiety levels and feel more comfortable in school (more about that in the section about teachers below).

2. Initial home-based sessions

Whenever possible, I strongly recommend **beginning therapy with home sessions**. This is usually the place where the child is most relaxed and speaks and communicates with the greatest ease. When the therapist initiates therapy in the teen's home, several significant advantages are gained: Firstly, because this is usually the least anxiety-provoking setting in the youngster's life and the place in which she exhibits her optimum speaking and communication, it is likely that the therapist will be able to establish a verbal, warm, and spontaneous relationship with her at home within several sessions, as opposed to a longer, more laborious process in her office or in school. So it is economical in facilitating speech and warm relations between the therapist and teen early on in therapy. The second advantage is the supportive and mutually trusting relationship that can be built between the parents and the therapist when the initial sessions begin in the parents' territory;if the therapist enters into their home in a totally nonjudgmental, appreciative manner, this may assuage much of the mistrust and defensiveness that parents may feel toward therapists. This is conducive to an open and fruitful parent-therapist relationship, which may enhance the outcome of therapy.

Once a communicative verbal relationship has been established between the teen and the therapist during the home sessions, we recommend that whenever possible the sessions continue in the setting in which the SM is manifest—usually in school. This enables a seamless combination of the cognitive, planning, insightful components of therapy and the application of the goals postulated on the exposure stepladder. We outline below how to plan and execute the initial home sessions.

Once the assessment is carried out, the home sessions are due to begin. With older children and teens, a stranger's appearance in the house must be explained. As with the younger children, if the therapist can enter the house for the first couple of sessions and be introduced vaguely—for example, as someone who has come to talk to the mother, not as a therapist—it will probably enable the teen to speak more freely and sooner in his presence. It is important not to lie, but there does not necessarily have to be full disclosure from the start. When it is felt by all that the therapist must be introduced as such, it is advisable to do so in a light and nonthreatening manner; for example," Ruth is coming today at four to meet us; she has helped many young people who find it hard to speak in school, and she will do some artwork, play some computer games, or chat for a while with us" (depending on what the teen enjoys doing).

The first home session must be planned with the parents so that there is an activity that the young person enjoys which is not too bombastic that it will increase the teen's anxiety. If the therapist has been introduced vaguely as someone who has come to talk to the mother, then whenever possible, it is helpful to have at least one or two sessions in which the therapist does not interact with the teen and stays out of the limelight, trying to blend in with the furniture. These structured home sessions are described in detail in chapter 6, the Therapist's Manual. The aim of the first session is to enter the teen's home as inconspicuously as possible and to refrain from any contact with him, including eye contact and speech directed toward him. At the same time as you are melting into the background, the youngster will be engaged by his parents in a desirable activity that involves speech. Hopefully the teen will speak in the therapist's presence and will habituate to doing so with tolerable levels of anxiety. After a couple of sessions in which the teen speaks freely with his parent (or siblings, etc.) in the therapist's presence, the therapist becomes more noticeable by sitting closer to the teen, joining in his activities, and gradually speaking to him.

If the therapist has been introduced more openly as someone who has come to assist the child with his speech, then a different structure for initial sessions may be required. In this case, there is a higher probability that the child will not speak to him, as he is associated with SM. If he doesn't speak in his presence spontaneously, then a continuum of activities should be employed that can bring the child from prerecorded speech to direct speech.

It is advisable that the therapist initially chats with the mother or father, showing no interest in the young person for a period of time, thus enabling the teen to engage in some talking activity with another family member while the therapist is in the background.

The therapist may introduce himself in an unthreatening way, and then the parents could play a recording of the child, engage in activities involving rote speech, and move on to direct speech. An example of a first session in which the child is aware that the visitor is a therapist, could be as follows:The session could begin by playing a prerecorded movie or recording of the teen so that her voice will be present loud and clear from the first moment, which may ease the way to direct speech. After everyone has heard the recording, a game could be played with the child and her parents involving rote speech, such as throwing a ball from one person to the next while counting, so that each person says a consecutive number when it is his or her turn to throw the ball. Then a word game such as twenty questions could be played so that the teen engages in minimal speech with the therapist, through questions requiring yes or no answers asked by the therapist.

Hopefully, using a combination of these methods, the child will be speaking to the therapist within a few sessions. The home sessions should be continued until the teen is talking freely with the therapist. These initial sessions can be carried out in a therapist's office, but frequently in this setting, it may either take much longer for the child to speak or the quality of the speech may be poorer—less spontaneous, quieter, and more hesitant. Often the difference is either free speech after four sessions in the child's home or whispering, hesitant speech after months in a therapist's office!

Once the teen is talking to the therapist at home and before the move to school, if the therapist has not already done so, he must be open regarding the purpose and nature of his meetings with the teen, in a way that will arouse the least anxiety possible. His explanation should include three elements:

1. The sessions will be continued in a private room in school and will be planned together with the youngster;
2. The therapist knows how to help the child—and many teens have been helped in the same way;
3. The therapist aims to make the sessions fun and will not do anything that the teen does not agree to.

3. School-based sessions

Once the young person is speaking freely to the therapist, the location of the therapy is moved to a private room in school. Hopefully, if it is done in a controlled and reassuring enough way, the teen will be able to continue talking to the therapist in school. The structure of these initial school sessions should involve activities that the child enjoyed in the home sessions, as well as the above-described continuum of prerecorded speech, rote speech, and spontaneous speech. An example of an initial school session may look like this: the session may begin by playing a prerecorded movie or saved app so that the young person's voice will be heard in school (see chapter 9 on the use of apps in therapy), followed by a game requiring rote speech, then questions that have a one-word answer, and finally natural conversation. If the youngster doesn't manage to speak in the initial school session, parents can be included, and several techniques can be employed as described in chapter 6, pages 123-127, in order to ease the child into speech with the therapist at school.

Once the teen is speaking freely with the therapist in the school,the therapy can take on a more classic CBT format. Again, this can take place in the therapist's office, but when it occurs in the setting in which the symptom is strongest—usually school—the therapist can juggle that exquisite balance of planning, insight, and implementation all in one session, as opposed to joint planning in the office, followed by implementation by the young person in school, without the support of the therapist in vivo. The two prongs of therapy are CBT techniques, together with structured, planned behavioral steps toward speech. With young people, **it is unusual to employ all of the CBT techniques described here—it is vital to constantly assess what appeals to the teen, what "speaks to her," and what works**. For most of the techniques, a level of introspection, understanding, and maturity is required, and children vary widely in their pace of maturation. So it is up to the therapist, together with the parents, to determine though trial and error and through insight, empathy, and intuition which methods are best employed for each teen.

Below we describe a series of CBT techniques that can be helpful in facilitating speech. These techniques can be powerful tools enabling growth, to be used in many other challenging situations throughout the teen's life. These skills are only helpful when put into practice and must be applied to help the young person ascend the ladder of target behaviors leading her to improved speech and social communication.

4. Psychoeducation

Early on in therapy, one can explore how the young person understands his SM, what his strengths and challenges are, and how he experiences his daily life. This should be done gently and with caution so that the teen does not feel a surge of anxiety while discussing this sensitive issue. It is vital to hear how the young person feels about receiving treatment, what has been attempted in the past, and how he has tried to help himself.

At this stage the youngster should receive an explanation about SM, including how it is usually anxiety based, how it impacts the person, and how it can be overcome in therapy. It is essential to transmit your belief in the ability of the young person to progress and to surmount his SM.

Now it may be time to investigate further with the teen how and where he talks, and on what level he functions socially.

To this end, the teen and therapist can draw a **talking map** (Johnson and Whitgins 2007). This is a diagram put together by the teen and his therapist that illustrates the people and the places in which the child is able or unable to speak. It gives a clear picture of where the difficulty presents and will be helpful in building a ladder of goals. It is also a springboard for discussion with the child about where it is difficult to communicate his needs and where he would most like to be able to talk. Here is an example of a simple talking map. More information can be added, including additional people, places and levels of communication.

Talking Map

Friends on
the block:
Lisa ☺
Julie ☺

Doctor ☺
Dentist ⊗

Stores ⊗

Family:
Mom, Dad ☺
Uri, Davy, Grandma ☺
Grandpa, Aunt Liz ⊗

School:
Teachers⊗
Friends⊗
Lisa, Julie☺

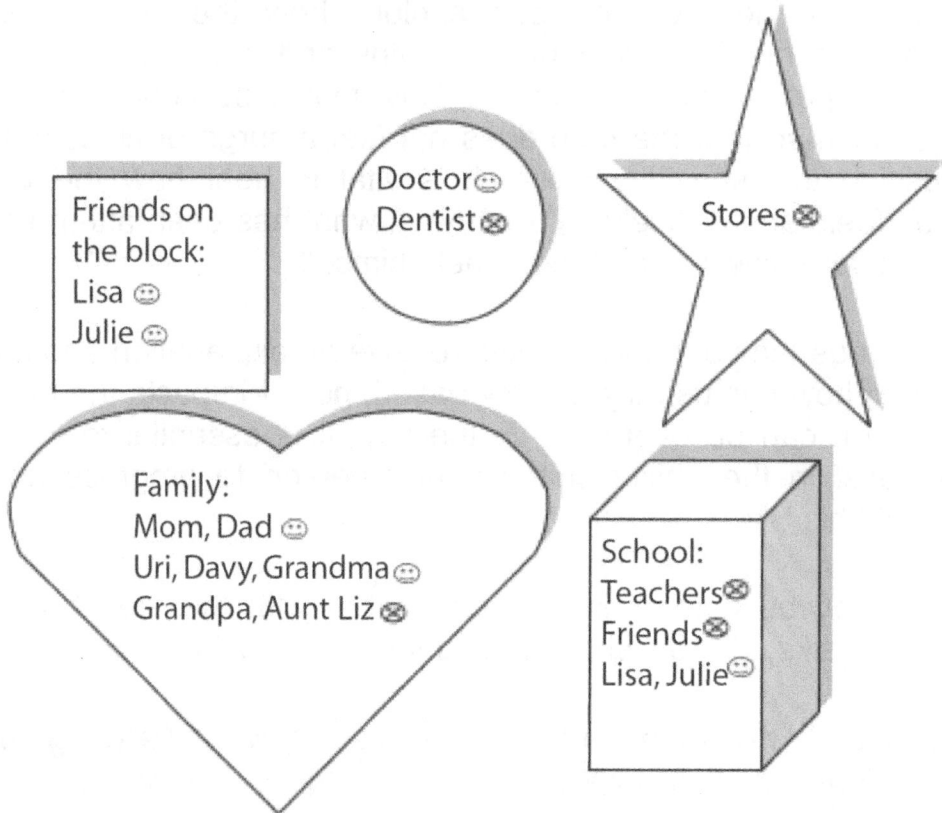

Normalization: Teenagers with SM usually feel different and inadequate—after all, they have not mastered the basic tool of social communication in certain settings. It comes as a huge relief to them (and to their parents) to understand that they are not alone, that many people suffer from SM, and that it has effective treatments. There are often torrents of tears of relief on understanding that the therapist knows how to treat SM and that he believes that the teen will overcome his SM.

5. The adaptive value of anxiety

It is reassuring for teens to learn that anxiety is a vital feeling that safeguards everyone against dangerous situations. Anxiety is our response to our perception of danger, and it readies our bodies for "fight, flight, or freeze" responses—either to confront and combat the danger or to flee from it. The teen could find numerous examples of her own to illustrate the adaptive value of anxiety. When a person suffers from SM, her anxiety thermostat needs adjusting so that its alarm doesn't sound when a desirable, non-dangerous behavior is called for.

How anxiety affects our bodies: When danger is perceived, the body prepares itself for "flight, fight, or freeze." The teen can consider times when she met with real danger that called for each of these three responses.

She may remember a time when she saw a large man running toward her while she walking alone late at night, and she was scared of being attacked. In this situation, what should she do? She may decide to fight. To do this, her heart would pump faster, her breathing would speed up, and her muscles would tense up. Sweating would cool her body. She would be ready to fight! (This physical priming for action is less helpful in the face of the perceived danger of being asked a question by her teacher.)

A second option would be to flee. To escape quickly, she would activate the same body reactions she needed to fight—a speedy heartbeat, rapid breathing, and tense muscles.

A third option is to freeze—maybe the man will not notice her if she stands perfectly still. For this she needs to tense up her muscles, tighten her chest, make her breathing shallow so that it barely moves, and freeze her facial expressions.

While these three responses may serve one well during a physical attack, they are misplaced when they occur in SM; anxiety prevents the child from responding when spoken to. The teen learns that her physical responses to anxiety are usually adaptive and normal, protecting her from harm, but in SM they are applied inappropriately, causing suffering, not safety.

6. Relieving anxiety, relaxation techniques

Once a teenager understands how anxiety affects his body and mind, he can learn to employ relaxation techniques that will ease his anxiety. These include deep breathing, tightening and loosening muscles, and guided imagery. It should be noted that many young people find relaxation techniques unnatural and unappealing, and if this is the case, these tools may be omitted from therapy.

When a teen does learn to relax, he has a powerful tool for combating anxiety, because the body cannot be simultaneously relaxed and anxious. There are two interconnected types of relaxation: physical body relaxation and mental relaxation. The two influence each other—when your body is relaxed,your mind picks up the physiological message and becomes more relaxed. Similarly, when your thoughts are calm, that will affect your body. There are various methods of relaxation, and usually a combination is used; the teen should try several methods and see what most appeals to him.

Relaxed breathing. The first type of relaxation training is controlled breathing. When people become anxious, they tend to breathe either shallowly or irregularly, and this affects the balance of oxygen and carbon dioxide in the body, which can cause physical signs of anxiety. Aim for the breathing exercises to last for four minutes, which is how long it takes for the oxygen levels to stabilize.

The basic technique involves breathing in and out for equal time spans—say, to the count of four—and breathing deep into the belly. You can put your hand on your belly to feel that deep breathing is happening.

Breathing is usually the initial step in the relaxation schedule. At the same time as breathing deeply and evenly, it can be helpful to pay attention to the inhalation and exhalation of the breath and to allow other irksome thoughts to drift out of one's mind. Soft music and lighting (candlelight is atmospheric) can help set the scene.

An example of a deep breathing schedule can be heard on YouTube: Selective Mutism – Ruth Perednik.

Tips for relaxation with children: Sometimes it helps to make the task slightly more concrete with young people so that they stay focused. For example, they can be told to spell out their name, one letter with each breath, so that after eight breaths, a young person will have spelled out the name "Jennifer." They could also put a small stuffed animal on their stomachs to see it moving up and down with the deep breaths.

When young people have mastered the four-minute relaxation technique, they can learn a shortened version lasting a few seconds that may help them to talk when called upon to do so—tensing and relaxing their muscles;then one deep-breath inhalation, which deepens the relaxation;followed by a breath out, at the end of which, a word is spoken. This gives the teen a feeling of control—he can do something to ease his discomfort and facilitate speech when attempting to talk. An example of a shortened relaxation schedule to practice and then use before speech can be heard on YouTube: Selective Mutism – Ruth Perednik.

Muscle relaxation. This technique is often practiced after or before the child has had a few moments of deep breathing. The teen is guided to tense and then relax different areas of muscles that may be taut as a result of anxiety. You can do this from head to toe or vice versa, starting at the feet. Thus the youngster is guided to start, say, at the head and to tense his forehead for five seconds and relax it for five seconds. After this is repeated, the eyes may be tensed and relaxed twice, then the mouth, shoulders, hands, stomach, feet, and toes. Finally the teen can tighten all of these muscle groups together and then relax his entire body. An example of guided muscle relaxation can be heard on YouTube: Selective Mutism – Ruth Perednik.

Each person tenses up in distinct ways, with pressure on unique constellations of muscles. Each teen might consider which areas of her body are prone to be tense, and these areas may be central in her relaxation. Usually a feeling of floppiness and well-being is reported after progressive muscle relaxation.

Guided imagery. After priming the body with deep breathing and muscle relaxation, guided imagery can induce a deep state of relaxation and feeling of comfort. This can be savored and later induced in times of stress to alleviate anxiety. The young person is encouraged to think of a beautiful, peaceful scene and to try and experience it in his imagination as fully as possible, using as many senses as he can—vision, touch, smell, and hearing. He should then bask in this serene scene, in which he feels totally at peace. Later, when he is anxious about moving up on his stepladder of tasks toward speech, he will be able to conjure up the calming, serene picture. An example of guided imagery for teens can be heard on YouTube: Selective Mutism – Ruth Perednik.

Mindfulness. This acquired attention skill involves focusing on the here and now, thus diminishing anxious thoughts. Those who master this tool have a powerful method of not only feeling more at ease but of savoring the moment. In the movie *Kung Fu Panda,the* master sums up mindfulness when he says, "Yesterday's history; tomorrow's a mystery; but today is a gift—that's why it's called 'the present.'"

When you are anxious, you are generally thinking of what came before or what the consequences of what's happening now are going to be. A young person who has not spoken in front of friends for many years tends to have two worries about uttering those first words—that people will laugh at his voice, or they will make such a fuss about his speech that he will be deeply embarrassed. If he is focused on the task at hand—say, answering a simple question—he will be less attentive to his apprehension, and he will have less cognitive fuel to kindle his worry.

The child can practice focusing on the here and now. Many exercises can be used;you can be heard on YouTube:Selective Mutism – Ruth Perednik.

This is a recording that guides the teen as he walks around a garden, concentrating only on what he sees, allowing all other thoughts to float away. Initially he walks around the garden using his vision to perceive the sights, then he concentrates only on smell, and the third time he focuses on sounds. Many young people are bowled over by all they perceive when concentrating on what is actually in front of them at the moment—all that they see and hear and smell when walking around a garden without allowing other thoughts to intrude and conquer.

7. Cognitive restructuring

Adaptive and Automatic Thoughts

A young person can learn to analyze how she thinks in diverse situations and to consider how productive, helpful, or adaptive her thoughts are. Do they make her feel more relaxed or more anxious? Do they help her to deal with situations productively or self-destructively? She can learn to recognize the thoughts floating through her mind and to consider more positive ways of thinking. Thoughts are inexorably linked to feelings. When young people learn to channel their thoughts, softening them and making them more positive, it gives them a heightened sense of control regarding the way they perceive and experience their lives. Once this is understood, the young person practices her newfound insights and considers situations in her life in which her thoughts sabotage her attempts to communicate and speak.

In order to engage in cognitive restructuring, it is necessary to learn to recognize feelings. This can be stimulated by looking at pictures of people in various emotional states and to consider what they may be feeling.

A feelings thermometer may help the young person to discern the strength of her feelings and particularly her anxiety in different situations. Here 0 is as relaxed as can be, and 10 is extreme distress. Young people can then think of different situations and consider and note where along the scale of the feelings thermometer the severity of their feelings would be charted.

Feelings Thermometer

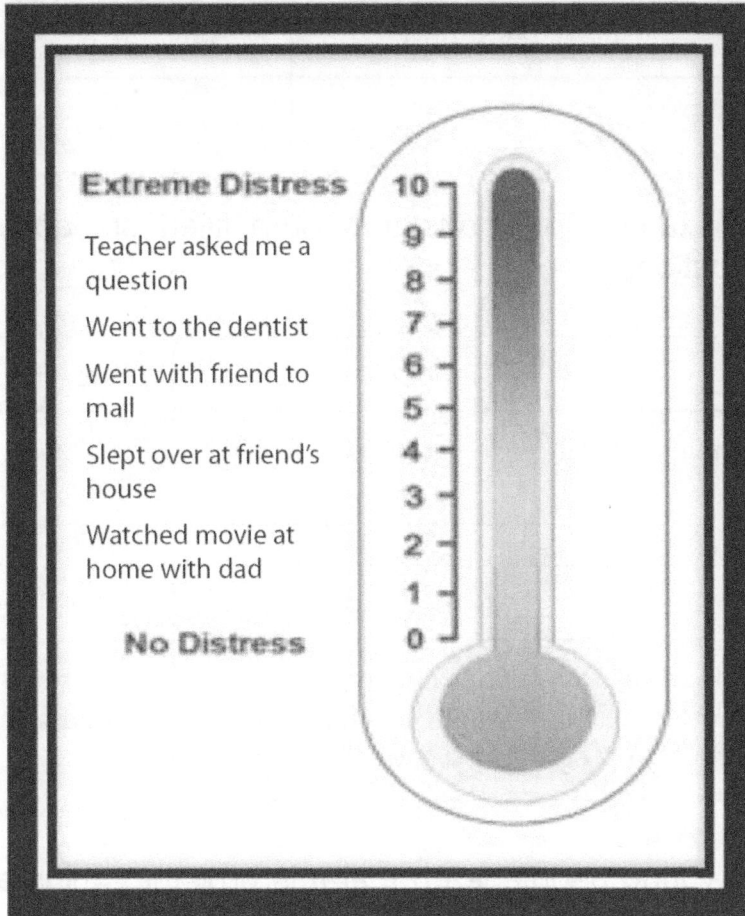

Extreme Distress   10

Teacher asked me a   9
question   8

Went to the dentist   7

Went with friend to   6
mall   5

Slept over at friend's   4
house   3

Watched movie at   2
home with dad   1

No Distress   0

After working on recognizing the variety and strength of emotions, the next stage is looking at different situations and seeing how the young person feels in these settings. This is illustrated in the table below in which children can fill out situations that they have experienced, adding the thoughts that went through their minds and how they felt in the given situation:

Situation, Thoughts, Feelings

Situation	My thoughts	My feelings

Here is an example of charts that Sara filled out about anxiety-arousing situations:

Situation	My thoughts	My feelings
A dog is walking toward me	He might bite me	Terrified

Situation	My thoughts	My Feelings
A teacher asks me a question	She will think I'm stupid; maybe she'll punish me	Embarrassed, scared, sad

In this way, young people learn that it is how they think about their experiences that shapes how they feel. If only they could learn how to modify their thoughts...

Young people can learn that there are **alternative ways of thinking** about any given situation. The two diagrams below require the young person to conjure up two contrasting ways a person could think about a potentially frightening situation. One way would be anxiety provoking and the other calming.

214

1. Teacher asks me to write the answer on the board

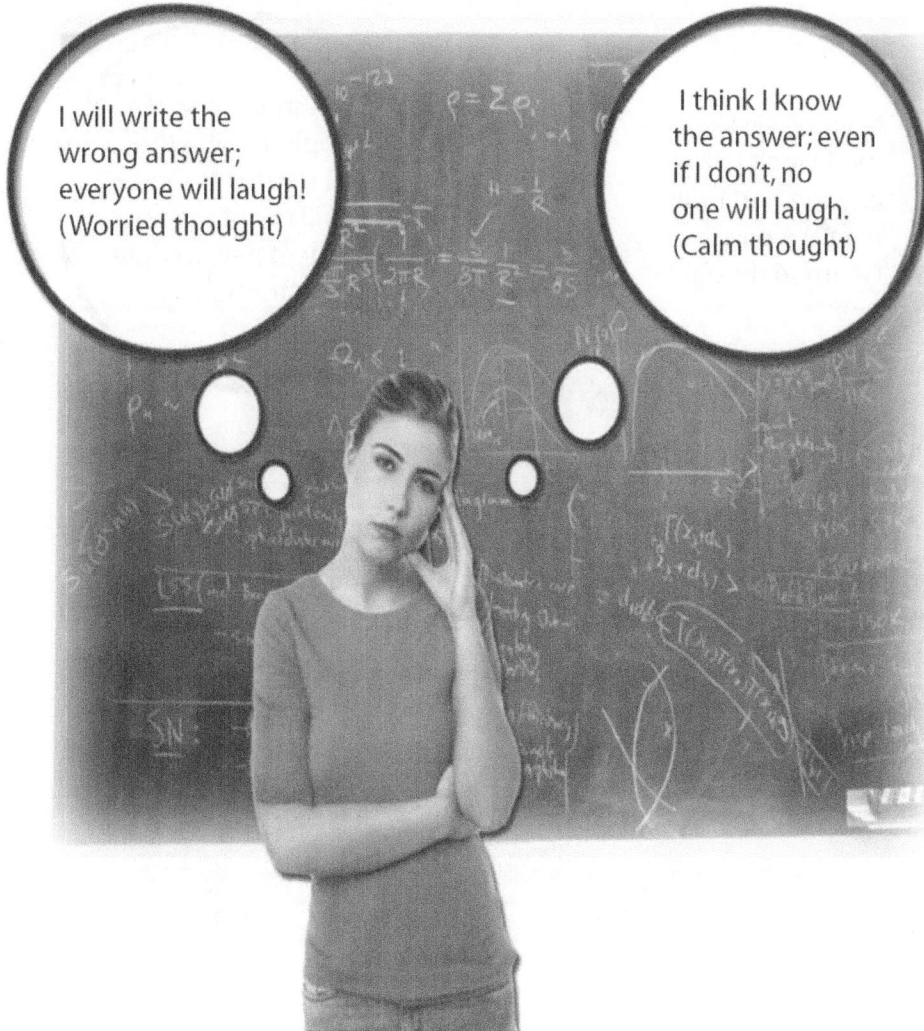

2. I'm invited to a party and won't know many kids there

No one will like me, I won't talk to anyone, and I will hate the party. (Worried thought)

I will smile to some people. Maybe they will talk to me, and it will be interesting to meet new people! (Calm thought)

In the first example, the automatic (scary) thought might be, "I won't know the answer," "Children will laugh at me," or "I'm going to blush; I will be so embarrassed." The calm thought might be," I think I know the answer," "No one will notice if I blush," "Plenty of times kids write on the board, and other kids are not particularly interested and don't laugh at them," "They have no reason to laugh at me," and so on.

In the second example, the scary thought might be," I will hate the party," "No one will talk to me," or "I will feel uncomfortable," and the calm thought might be," My best friend will be there; I can be with her," "I might enjoy it," or "It might be entertaining, even if I don't know many people." It is often liberating to understand that your way of perception and thinking have been limiting your enjoyment and engagement in life and that they can be modified.

Self-talk, self-reward
Teenagers can learn how to talk to themselves in order to feel braver and more competent. Self-praise may help them to progress up the stepladder of tasks and to feel good about their behavior.

Self-talk is powerful in that it can both help the young person to achieve a goal by making him feel more able and brave, and it can reward him by metaphorically patting himself on the shoulder and feeling competent having achieved a goal. Exercises to facilitate positive self-talk include looking at one's negative beliefs about oneself and putting them through a "magic hourglass" that transforms them to positive thoughts. You may throw into the hourglass the thoughts, "I'll never be able to speak to my friends," and they might come out as, "I will overcome this slowly, one step at a time." In another example, the negative thought may be, "Everyone thinks I'm weird," which comes out of the hourglass as," People like me" or" I have a few good friends." A young person can remember a few choice phrases that engender a feeling of capability and optimism and say them to himself in times of stress. An example of a diagram of this "magic hourglass" is shown below.

"Magic Hourglass" Transforms Negative-Positive Thoughts

Understanding the connection between events, thoughts, feelings, and behavior

The cognitive-restructuring components, which include the awareness of a spectrum of feelings, the ability to consider the relative strength of feelings in different situations, and alternative thoughts for any given situation, can be combined in order to comprehend the causal cycle of thoughts, feelings, and behavior—the connection between **thoughts and feelings** that leads to **behavior**. For example:a child is asked to speak in front of the teacher (situation); he thinks, "I don't know the answer; everyone will laugh at me" (thoughts); and he feels scared and self-conscious (feelings). As a result, he lowers his head and doesn't answer (behavior). A child can learn to recognize his scared interpretations of situations and can acquire the vital skill of restructuring his thoughts so that they are calmer, less anxious, and more adaptive.

(They are usually more realistic too.) For every given situation, there are diverse ways of perceiving it, and the anxious, scared way makes life daunting and frightening, while a calmer, more positive way of thinking about situations leads to greater confidence and competence. Learning that one can select or channel thoughts and perceptions so that they will be more positive facilitates overcoming fears. This process is illustrated in the worksheets below.

A Basic Premise of CBT
Thoughts → feelings → behavior

CBT Worksheet 1
1. Situation: A friend invited me to his birthday party

2. Calm thought:
"Maybe it will be entertaining."
"Maybe a friend will be there."

3. Feelings:
"I feel fine."

4. Behavior:
"I'm going to the party."

2. Anxious thought:
"It will be scary"
and "I will be
alone all the time."

3. Feelings:
"I'm terrified."

4. Behavior:
"I wouldn't dream
of going
to the party."

CBT Worksheet 2
1. Situation: The teacher asks me a question

2. Calm thought:
"I know the answer."
"No one will laugh."

3. Feelings:
"Confident."

4. Behavior:
"I answer the question."

2. Anxious thought:
"I have no idea what's
the answer."
"I'll be a laughingstock."

3. Feelings:
"Worried sick."

4. Behavior:
"I can't say
a word."

A young person can learn how his thoughts influence his feelings and behavior, and that there are numerous possible ways to think about any given situation—some more adaptive and others less so. He can learn how to channel his thoughts so that they will be more adaptive, optimistic, and confident and less scared and hopeless. This will affect how he feels and ultimately how he acts. By analyzing his thought patterns in various situations, he can pinpoint maladaptive and unconstructive thoughts, and he may consider more positive ways of thinking. When a teenager acquires these thought-channeling tools, he gains an increased feeling of control over the way he perceives and experiences his life. It is important that the young person practices his newfound understanding by analyzing situations in which he feels threatened as a result of the need to speak.

Here follow two examples of charts that could be used by teens to investigate their thinking about a situation that makes them anxious, to recognize their anxiety-provoking thoughts, and to consider if they are realistic. Finally, the young person is guided to consider more adaptive, more realistic, and less worrying thoughts. First is an example of a blank chart, followed by one filled out by Adele, who is concerned about going on an outing with her aunt.

Investigating Thoughts

The event/situation: What exactly happened?	• *Description of the event* • *What happened?*
What am I thinking? Worrying thoughts	• *What thoughts pass through my mind?* • *Which thoughts are worrying?* • *Underline my most worrying thoughts* **Level of anxiety/worry**
What evidence is there for my worrying thoughts? What are the facts? What else could happen? What has happened in the past when I was so worried? What do I think will happen? What has happened to other people in similar situations?	
Calm thought	**Level of anxiety/worry**

Adele Investigates Her Thoughts

The event/situation: What exactly happened?	*My aunt came to visit and wanted to take me out for an outing*
What am I thinking? Worrying thoughts	*I won't be able to communicate with her, she won't understand me, <u>I will feel uncomfortable all the time.</u>* **Level of anxiety/worry 9**
What evidence is there for my worrying thoughts? What are the facts? What else could happen? What has happened in the past when I was so worried? What do I think will happen? What has happened to other people in similar situations?	*I have never been out with my aunt alone before. I don't know what it will be like.* *She is always kind and warm to me.* *Maybe it will be fine.* *In the summer I really didn't want to go with my grandma to a movie. In the end I went and had a great time.* *Maybe it will be nice.* *Other kids love going to new and fun places.*
Calm thought	*Maybe it will be fun.* **Level of anxiety/worry 4**

Here is a different way of checking thoughts and their connections to feelings. This type of notation may be more fitting for older teens. The second horizontal row contains the questions that can be asked in order to check and document how realistic the thoughts may be and to think of alternative more positive and adaptive thoughts (adapted from Rapee et al. 2006, "The Cool Kids Child and Adolescent Anxiety Program").

Investigating Thoughts

1. Situation /event	2. Feelings	3. Automatic thoughts. Circle the dominant thoughts	4. Evidence supporting the dominant thought	5. Evidence contradicting the dominant thought	6. New realistic or calm thought
Who? What? Where? How?	What did you feel? What mood were you in?	What went through your mind at the time of the event: thoughts, memories, images? Circle the dominant thought.	What evidence supports or contradicts the dominant thought?	What are the facts? What happened in the past? What else could happen? What is the worst thing that could happen?	

1. Situation /event	2. Feelings	3. Automatic thoughts	4. Evidence supporting	5. Evidence contradicting	6. New realistic thought
Saturday morning, we ate at family friend's house. I couldn't answer when they asked me what my name was.	-Sad -Scared -Embarrassed -Angry with myself -Angry with the world -Despair	-I'm stupid -Everyone will laugh at me -I'm different -I will never get over this -I want to die	-I saw Jamie smile -No one stared at me	-No one laughed -Maybe Jamie smiled in friendship -It has happened often in the past, and people didn't laugh -Most of my friends accept me as I am -Even in the worst case, if someone would laugh, I could continue to live with it.	People seem to respect me as I am, even if I don't answer—I have many strong points.
	Anxiety level 1-10: 8				Anxiety level 1-10: 3

It is important for the young person to understand that scary thoughts are not only unproductive, but they are also usually not reasonable.

Realistic thoughts would cause the requisite amount of anxiety to keep oneself safe, not more. For example, if a child is scared when alone in the home and thinks that "something bad will happen when my parents are out," this thought is both anxiety provoking and unrealistic—it is improbable that there will be a disaster because his parents are out. Whether or not the thought is realistic can be discovered by investigating one's thinking, as illustrated by the charts above.

8. Building a stepladder of goals

Overcoming avoidance, desensitization
Now that the young person has acquired relaxation and cognitive-restructuring skills, and she is talking freely with the therapist, it is time to employ these newfound techniques to overcome what is the hallmark symptom of selective mutism—avoidance.

To overcome the avoidance and anxiety, we need to build a hierarchy of situations and people with whom it is hard to talk and then order them from the easiest to the most difficult. The young person can start attempting the tasks, beginning with the easiest ones, using relaxation and cognitive-restructuring techniques to ease anxiety and empower the child. The steps must be small, and lower steps must be mastered before moving up to successive steps.

The teenager and the therapist build the stepladder of goals on the basis of their understanding of the client's difficulty speaking in various places. This and further exposure stepladders will take the young person from a state of non-speech through nonverbal communication to speech with an array of people in a diversity of places.

The theory behind the exposure schedules (stepladders)
The theoretical underpinnings of this method are the three tools of behavioral therapy that are outlined in the Therapist's Manual in

chapter 6. These could be summarized as "fighting fear by facing fear." No amount of cognitive understanding about thoughts and feelings or relaxation training will enable you to overcome a deeply entrenched fear, unless you are exposed to the fear for long enough to habituate to the fear-producing stimulus, causing the anxiety level to recede, establishing a new, more adaptive baseline of behavior. The three basic techniques are summarized as follows:

Desensitization

The young person and the therapist build a scale of steps that guide the client incrementally closer to speech; for example, the initial step could be playing a recording of his voice; then whispering to the therapist; next speaking one word; and so on. The therapist helps the child to approach and achieve the goals by employing techniques described here including relaxation, guided imagery, positive thinking, anxiety lowering activities and games so that the client can speak to an ever-increasing number of people in successively more situations and places.

Behavior shaping

Shaping is approaching a hierarchy of goals, together with operant conditioning—rewards that are either intrinsic (satisfaction at conquering a fear) or external (such as a prize at the end of a stepladder). The hierarchy could be as follows: nonverbal communication, whispering sounds (such as animal noises), gradually incorporating audible sounds, consonants, words, and ultimately sentences.

Stimulus fading

The final technique discussed here is stimulus fading; here the speech of the child is fixed, while the setting or people present changes. "Sliding in" is a variation on this theme, which is described in chapter 6. Older children's ability to cooperate, to contemplate, and to be self-observant may enable sliding in to be a dramatic tool facilitating the rapid inclusion of new people into his circle of speech.

Several examples of stepladders

Here follow some examples of stepladders of tasks I constructed together with several young clients:

The first two are from therapy with eleven-year-old Dan. At the onset of therapy, Dan didn't speak to children or adults in school; he spoke to some children and to most members of his extended family outside school. Therapy began with four home sessions, as described in chapter 6. Dan gradually habituated to speaking in my presence, followed by direct speech with me. After that, our verbal, communicative relationship was successfully transferred to the school in a designated therapy room. We worked for a number of sessions on thoughts and feelings, relaxation, and cognitive restructuring. Dan did not relate to the relaxation techniques, and the cognitive restructuring was understood but not considered by him to be a useful tool.

We began to construct a desensitization schedule to be carried out in the school therapy room; together we analyzed where and to whom he spoke freely and organized a hierarchy of tasks that reflected the relative difficulty he imagined having when attempting these goals. Much discussion and give-and-take went into formulating the stepladder, but once Dan typed each step of the ladder on my laptop, it seemed to be accepted by him as something he would and could master. The first stepladder pertains to speaking to children, and the second involves approaching speech with his teacher.

Dan's Stepladder of Goals with his friend Dave

Stepladder of targets	Outcome
I will record "hot" and "cold" together with Ruth on an MP3, and we will play hot or cold in the therapy room at school.	
I will include my friend Dave; will play with him hot or cold in the therapy room using my recording.	
I will play hot or cold with Ruth and Dave in the room, using my recording; then we'll all play Chinese whispers. I will whisper just to Ruth.	
I will play hot or cold with Ruth and Dave in the room, using my recording; then we'll all play Chinese whispers. I will whisper to Ruth and Dave; we'll play Talking Tom on the iPad.	
I will play hot or cold with Ruth and Dave in the room, saying "hot" and "cold"; then we'll all play Chinese whispers. I will whisper to Ruth and Dave. We'll play Talking Tom on the iPad, and then we'll play throwing a ball, and each person will make an animal noise.	
I will play a Puppet Pals recording I made with Ruth at home; then we'll play Talking Tom on the iPad; then we'll play throwing a ball, and each	

person will say a number counting from one to twenty and then backwards from twenty to one.	
I will play a Puppet Pals recording I made with Ruth at home;then we'll play Talking Tom on the iPad; then we'll play throwing a ball, and each person will say a number counting from one to one hundred and then backward from one hundred to one. We'll play Guess Who.	
I will record a new Puppet Pals with Dave and Ruth; then we'll play throwing a ball, and each person will say a color. We'll play Guess Who. Then we'll invite Josh to hear the Puppet Pals!	

In this way, over the course often sessions in a school-based therapy room, Dan managed to speak to his friend Dave and to play a recording of his voice to a second friend, Josh, both of whom he had not spoken to previously. This paved the way for upcoming sessions in which he would gradually speak to Josh, just as he did to Dave. The pace of progress is usually faster after the young person has succeeded talking to some friends, and understands that he can speak in this way to others too.

These behavioral steps can be paired with the techniques the child has learned during therapy. For example, the teenager may use some relaxation techniques while attempting each new task; he could consider his unrealistic thoughts and investigate them so that he finds more adaptive, calming thoughts. Self-talk is short and sweet and can be effective. In this case, Dan used brief self-talk before attempting each new task. This gave him a sense of mastery—he could approach a daunting task, help himself to stay calm, and think more positively.

A few rules to be followed in the exposure stage of therapy:

1. Attempt only one new task each session.
2. Always repeat previously attained goals before attempting a new goal.
3. If the child fails to manage a task, do not project to him a feeling of failure but analyze with him how to break the goal down to smaller, less daunting sub-goals.
4. Stay alert for types of tasks that the young person finds easier than others—for example, some children (not all!) are tempted and distracted by apps, which enables them to progress faster than with activities that are not electronic. For some young people, recording at home and playing the recording in the session is an important stage in habituating to hearing one's voice in school and facilitates faster speech acquisition. For many teens, activities with some motor activity, such as running or ball games, lower anxiety levels and facilitate attaining goals with greater ease.
5. Before a young person attempts a new and daunting task, role-play and practice it with him. In this way, I played the ball-throwing game with Dan before inviting Dave into the room.
6. Consider with the teen which of the cognitive and relaxation tools could be helpful, and practice them before attempting a goal.
7. The name of the game is generalization; once the teen talks to a given person, another person can be added to the small group, utilizing gradual behavior-shaping steps.

Once Dan was able to speak with Dave, we added more peers into the sessions following a stepladder we constructed together. Dan felt a surge of confidence due to his successes, which enabled him to incorporate more classmates with successively shorter intervention schedules. It is a truly empowering feeling to build your own intervention schedule (with a little help from your friends) and overcome maladaptive behaviors that have been plaguing you for years!

Dan was soon talking to all of his classmates, and the next challenge was to be talking to teachers. Here follows a schedule we built together to facilitate talking to his (beloved) teacher,Jonathan:

Stepladder of Goals: Brave Dan will speak with his teacher

Goal	Result/Date
I'll sit with my teacher Jonathan, and Ruth in the school therapy room; I'll show him the Puppet Pals show I recorded with Dave on the iPad.	
I will show Jonathan the Puppet Pals and then play with him hot or cold using the recording I made with Ruth.	
I will show Jonathan the Puppet Pals and then play with him hot or cold using the recording I made with Ruth. Then I will play Chinese whispers but whisper only to Ruth.	
I will show Jonathan the Puppet Pals and then play with him hot or cold using the recording I made with Ruth. Then I will play Chinese whispers. I will whisper to the teacher.	
I will show Jonathan the Puppet Pals, and then I will play Chinese whispers; I will whisper to the teacher. Then I will play a card game, and when I have to say "war," I will say it aloud.	
I will show Jonathan a new Puppet Pals, and then I will play a card game, and when I have to say "war," I will say it a loud. Then I will play a game throwing a ball, and each thrower says	

a word in a given category, such as food or colors.	
I will invite Dave and Josh to join in and show all of them, including Jonathan, a new Puppet Pals that I prepared at home with Dave. Then I will play a game throwing a ball each time saying a word in a given category, such as food or colors.	

The magic of multi-layered sessions in the school setting including slots with the child, a group of his friends, and the teacher, all in one session! Usually teachers are too busy to participate in lengthy sessions, and I have found it most doable to include teachers for mini-sessions of about five to ten minutes—a lot can be achieved in that time. The session may begin with just the therapist and the teen, in order to assess how the previous session went and to plan and practice for the current session. That may take half an hour. Then a group of friends may join in for half an hour of generalizing toward speech with peers, followed by ten minutes with the teacher and the teen, and finally a summing up analysis with the teacher for ten minutes. In this way, in the space of one (long) session of one hour and twenty minutes, there has been a planning and analyzing chunk with the young person, plus two implementation segments, one with a group of friends, and one with the teacher. The cherry on top is the short session with the teacher alone,in which you can together analyze the current session and fine-tune his solo and joint interventions for the coming days.

A multi-modular planning, applying, teacher and peer therapy session may look like this:
10.00-10.30: planning session with client and therapist
10.30-10.50: application of current goal with client and two friends

235

10.50-11.00: application of current goal with client and his teacher
11.00-11.10: feedback and planning of the therapist with the teacher (without the child)

This process that might have taken one month of weekly meetings in a therapist's clinic can be completed in one (long) session in the school!

Often, once the young person is talking to some friends, it is easier for him to include friends in the sessions with the teacher than being the only child in the teacher–teen-therapist session;there is less intensity of focus on the teen, and it may be less intimidating and more playful.

Young people vary greatly in their resistance to change and in the degree to which they are paralyzed by their anxiety. Sometimes, having embarked on a stepladder of goals, it may become apparent that it is necessary to break down the steps to smaller, more gradual increments, going from nonverbal communication to sounds to words by incorporating recordings, apps, microphones, plays, and so on.

Below follow two more examples of stepladders; the first is a girl called Hayley in fourth grade attempting to talk to her friend Laurie. At this point she was talking to me freely in the room. She was having difficulty moving from whispering to speaking out loud. She required repetitions and small, incremental steps between one rung of the ladder to the next.

Stepladder of Goals for Brave Hayley with Her Friend Laurie

Goal	I did it!!
I play Chinese whispers with Laurie and Ruth, I whisper only to Ruth (psychologist)	

I play Chinese whispers with Laurie and Ruth, I whisper to Ruth and then to Laurie.	
I play Chinese whispers with Laurie and Ruth, I whisper to Ruth and then to Laurie. Then I play "hangman" with Laurie and Ruth, I whisper the letters into a microphone so we hear them out loud.	
I play "hangman" with Laurie and Ruth, I whisper the letters into a microphone so we hear them out loud. Then I play a card game, each time I have to say "War" I say it out loud.	
I play "hangman" with Laurie and Ruth, I say the letters without the microphone so we hear them out loud. Then I play a card game, each time I have to say "War" I say it out loud. We play telling a story in installments – each person adds a new sentence.	

The following stepladder is that of a thirteen-year-old boy attempting to talk to his teacher. Shaun's non-speech was highly entrenched, and a good enabling tool was recording him reading sentences at home and then playing them to his teacher at school. In this way he became accustomed to his voice being heard loud and clear, and this facilitated direct speech with his teacher.

Stepladder of Goals for Shaun and Mr. Brown

Goal	I did it!!
I will record myself reading sentences at home. Then I will play them to Mr. Brown in the therapy room.	
I will record sentences at home, and then I will play them to Mr. Brown in the therapy room. I will also record a request of mine for Mr. Brown and play that to him (I want to ask him to allow me to move my seat next to John).	
I will record sentences at home, and I will play them to Mr. Brown in the therapy room. I will play Chinese whispers and whisper to Ruth.	
I will record sentences at home, and I will play them to Mr. Brown in the therapy room. I will play Chinese whispers and whisper to Ruth and then to Mr. Brown.	
I will record a doodlecast at home about my hobby of making model airplanes, and I will play it to Mr. Brown in the therapy room. I will play Chinese whispers and whisper to Ruth and then to Mr. Brown. I'll play hangman and whisper the letters into a loudspeaker.	
I will play my doodlecast to Mr. Brown in the therapy room. I will play Chinese whispers and whisper to Ruth	

and then to Mr. Brown. I'll play hangman and say the letters out loud.	
I will play my doodlecast to Mr. Brown in the therapy room. I will play Chinese whispers. I'll play hangman and say the letters out loud. We'll play throwing a huge balloon, each time I throw, I say the name of a boy in my class.	

Frequently with older children, together with the gradual exposure to speech, other elements are called for such as social skills training, which is necessary as a result of the ongoing avoidance of social engagement in some of the teens. In addition, language difficulties are frequently an underlying cause of the maintenance of the selective mutism—the young person may not feel proficient in English or may have pronunciation or language-processing issues.

The stepladder below was part of therapy with a twelve-year-old girl who spoke poor English and had very low self-confidence. After a few home sessions, she was speaking freely to me and continued doing so when the therapy moved to a closed room in the school. She then progressed to speaking in Spanish to a group of friends in school in the therapy room, and at this juncture she needed help speaking in English with her friends. She also needed social-skills training in order to be able to initiate conversation and to ask common, frequently used questions and phrases. These three difficulties—language, social skills, and confidence issues—were incorporated in the following stepladder, where Barbara managed for the first time to speak to friends in English in the context of a game, after which she asked them frequently used questions such as, "Can I sit next to you?" or "Could you help me?" (This was structured as a game where the girls paired up and asked each other questions so that she would not feel singled out.) Finally she was filmed in a quiz with friends that was shown to the whole class, so that within ten sessions, she was talking to friends in English in school, and the entire class had heard her speak.

Brave Barbara's Stepladder: Speaking with Friends in English

1	I will say ABC with Ruth and Sue, and June will listen	♫
2	I will say ABC with Ruth; I will count in English with Sue and June while throwing a balloon between us.	♫
3	I will say ABC with Ruth; I will count in English with my friends. I will play "happy families" with Sue and June in English.	♫
4	I will say ABC with Ruth; I will count in English with my friends. I will play "happy families" with Sue and June in English. I will play hangman in English.	♫
5	I will count in English with Sue and June. I will play "happy families" with friends in English. I will ask my friends (and they will ask me) the following questions: Can I sit here? What do we have for homework? Could you help me? What's the time? Where do you live?	♫
6	I will play happy families with Sue and June in English. I will ask my friends (and they will ask me) the following questions: How old are you? How many brothers do you have? Which TV shows do you like? What is your favorite food? Then I will play Taboo with them. Finally we'll prepare a quiz on snow for the class and record the questions, and we'll show it to the class before the winter holidays.	

Estimating Success

The therapist and the teenager should assess her attempts to achieve her most recent goals. Based on the relative success of reaching a specific goal on each rung of the exposure stepladder, they refine the next step on the ladder so that it is a natural continuation of the last session that takes into account her functioning. When the young client doesn't manage to achieve a goal, this is a sign that she needs smaller steps forward and a more accessible goal that utilizes her strengths and takes into account her vulnerabilities. It is vital that a teen doesn't feel demoralized by failing to meet a target behavior; she should understand that occasional steps backwards or treading water are an unavoidable part of growth and overcoming SM.

Rewards

It can be effective to reward a young person on achieving a goal or on his attempt to do so. Caution is advised so that rewards or prizes stay proportional and will not cause the young person to feel pressure or overly mourn any failure to reach set targets. Rewards are more powerful when the therapist and teen choose together what the prize will be for completing a stepladder—in this way the reward is concrete and waiting to be garnered. The therapist and young person could look together for a prize in a store or online so that the teen will know exactly what his reward will be but won't purchase it until the goals are met.

9. Homework—talking tasks

In order to maximize the pace and effect of the therapy, as well as to transmit to the teen the belief that he can progress independently, talking tasks may be set by the therapist for the teen to carry out between sessions, when the therapist is not with him. These must be set by the therapist according to the young person's progress along the stepladder and be complementary to what is happening in therapy at that point.

Examples of charts of talking tasks

Here follow some examples of talking-task charts that were prepared together with teens and their friends at the end of a therapy session.

In Barak's homework chart below, the talking task was aimed at enabling speech with friends when the therapist was not present. At that point in therapy, Barak was talking to a group of peers but only in the presence of the therapist. The task was as follows: Each child had to count together with his friends up to fifty, passing a ball between them as they counted; the person holding the ball would say the number as he threw it. This meant that every day, Barak would count to fifty with seven friends without the therapist being there—impressive achievement! Group talking tasks are powerful because there is peer pressure to comply so that the participants will get a prize (the prize can be minimal—for example a candy or time playing a computer game). Talking tasks also facilitate that most sought-after ripple effect in therapy—spontaneous progress beyond the therapy hour. Having spoken to these boys in the homework task, Barak continued to speak to them in recess.

Barak's Talking Task
Mark X after counting until fifty

	Mon	Tues	Wed	Thurs	Fri
Barak					
Liz					
Paul					
Dory					
Steve					
Saul					
Tom					
Jane					
George					

Everyone who fills in the chart gets a prize!

Here is an example of a talking task given to fourteen-year-old Deena who was talking to friends in the therapy sessions but could not speak to them outside the room in either the corridor or yard. This talking task was aimed at having her pronounce sounds outside the therapy room—which for Deena was a huge leap forward and paved the way toward speech in school.

Deena's Homework
Each girl says to the others once a day: "SHHHHHHHHH!"

	M	T	W	T	F	M
Sandra						
Deena						
Talia						
Sharon						
Tami						
Hannah						

A different type of homework can be designed to give the young person practice in guided imagery or relaxation by downloading a recording onto an MP3 or iPod and listening to it before sleeping each night. Here is an example of homework given to Barbara, who was having difficulty speaking in English to friends. She had practiced guided imagery in therapy and liked it, so she was given homework to prepare her mentally to play "happy families" with two friends and the therapist in the upcoming session.

Brave Barbara's Imagining Homework Chart
Homework: Every night in bed, practice the short deep-breathing relaxation on your iPod, and then imagine playing "happy families" with Karin, Ruth, and Julie and asking "Have you got a red card"? After you imagine it, say it out loud.

Saturday	
Sunday	
Monday	

Tuesday	
Wednesday	
Thursday	
Friday	

Recording, Filming

It can be helpful to record or film the young person at home and then play it in the place in which speech is challenging. With some teenagers, breaking the barrier of having their voices heard loud and clear in school can enable subsequent speech with relative ease. This is discussed in chapter 6; various devices may be used including an office recorder, cell phone (WhatsApp voice messages), camera, or iPad. When a child records herself at home at night and plays it to the teacher the next day in school on a daily basis, the child's voice is heard, and this can be a powerful step toward speaking directly to the teacher. This must be done with the teen's agreement and in a controlled setting that is arranged with the youngster before the teacher hears the recording. For example, the teacher may use WhatsApp to send a question to the teen every evening, and the child sends her answer back as an audio WhatsApp message. The teacher may hear the recording every day in a small room where she is alone with the young person. Later on she may listen to it in the classroom before school begins and finally at her desk when there are other children in the room. Occasionally, once the teen has heard her own prerecorded voice in the class regularly, speech follows spontaneously. Here too, it is helpful to construct a ladder of goals for the teacher in which the successive steps are mapped out so that the current goal is clear and progress can be easily documented. This can be reviewed with the therapist on a weekly basis;ongoing guidance is often pivotal in ensuring perseverance and incremental progress.

Self-Modeling

Filming the youngster talking and then editing the film so that it appears that she is talking to a teacher or friend or relative can be a powerful way of seeing the potential she has to overcome SM. Similarly, for young people who speak very quietly, filming the youth and then upping the volume and playing it back can instill confidence in one's ability to speak out loud.

10. Medication

In a series of influential studies, Black and Uhde (1994) looked into the use of medication for SM. More recently, Manassis and Tannock (2008) gave anxiety-reducing medication to children with SM and found significant symptom improvement over six months.

Medication is given in order to lower anxiety sufficiently so that the child will have the courage to develop the coping skills to modify his anxious feelings.

Medication can be used in two basic cases:

- When the youngster is too anxious to acquire strategies and to benefit from therapy. Medication can lower his general anxiety level so that he can become an active partner engaging in therapy.
- When the distress is such that the young person is suffering greatly or his behavior is severely dysfunctional. Often with older children, their behavior and self-image are so entrenched, that their resistance to change seems impermeable. Here medication may enable a weakening of their defenses, which may enable progress.

The most common medication prescribed is within the group of selective serotonin reuptake inhibitors (SSRIs), which have various trade names including Prozac, Zoloft, and Celexa. These should be prescribed by a child and adolescent psychiatrist.

Often low dosages are sufficient to induce a noticeable relaxation in the child. It is highly recommended to have therapy together with medication—the medication may relax the child, but the therapy will take the teen by the hand through graduated steps toward social and verbal communication.

11. Social skills, self-esteem, assertiveness

Among older children, anxiety and the inability to speak during many years may leave its mark and leave the teen with insufficient social skills or low self-esteem, or develop into a wider social anxiety disorder. In these cases, together with the therapy aimed at helping the young person to speak, it may be advisable to work on CBT techniques to increase the teen's self-esteem and assertiveness and to hone his social skills.

Within therapy, the quest for improved self-esteem, assertiveness, and social skills has two elements: the cognitive side, in which core beliefs are challenged and refined, and the behavioral element, in which skills are practiced and implemented.

Self-esteem will almost always be much the worse for wear after many years of suffering from selective mutism. As one teen said, "At some point I realized I was not special; I was deficient." So how can one go about restoring self-image? Clinical experience shows that overcoming SM usually results in a boost of self-confidence and feelings of competence. Overcoming a limitation that has plagued you for years is an empowering experience; all the more so with a disorder such as SM, which influences almost your every minute and consequently affects your ongoing assessment and internal appreciation of yourself.

12. Core beliefs

Usually with older children, social functioning and social self-image has been affected by SM, and this may be alleviated by therapy. Let's start with the cognitive side—how investigating your beliefs about yourself and formulating and internalizing a more adaptive and positive self-image can be worked toward.

When working on thought records as described above,some thoughts may have emerged that were a type of absolute belief about how the teen saw herself or the world: these are core beliefs. They are shaped by our perception of how others have responded to us and our interpretation of our past experiences. Core beliefs are usually persistent, and when they are negative or self-deprecating, they can keep people stuck in anxiety and negativity. Examples of negative core beliefs, which may have been reinforced by reactions to SM, could be, "I am inadequate," "I am less able than others," or "I can't cope in social situations."

You can uncover core beliefs by delving deeper into thoughts that come up in the thought records. For example, when Toni investigated his thoughts regarding his fear of speaking to his classmate in school, his striking thought was, "He will laugh at me." To delve deeper, you can use the downward arrow technique, in which you consider each thought by contemplating: "What does this thought say about who I truly am?"

Here is an example from therapy with fifteen-year-old Toni. The feared situation being considered was talking in front a classmate.

Toni's initial thought was:

"He will laugh at me."
(What does this mean about me?)

"I'm embarrassed in front of other people."
(What does this mean about me?)

"I don't know how to behave socially."
(What does this mean about me?)

"I'll never have friends."
(What does this mean about me?)

"I'm unlikeable."

Toni's core belief was that he was unlikable, which then colored his self-esteem and much of his social functioning. Let's look at one more example of initial beliefs, peeling away at the layers and getting to core beliefs.

The situation was that a friend invited Laurie to a party, and her initial thought was,

"I won't have anyone to talk to."
(What does this mean about me?)

"When I talk to people, they are bored."
(What does this mean about me?)

"I'm boring."

Another way of looking for core beliefs is to consider thoughts that arise frequently when investigating the situation-thoughts-feelings cycle, such as "I'm not good at anything" or "I can never change."

Once core beliefs are revealed, they can be challenged by seeing how much evidence there is supporting or disproving the core belief. For example, if the core belief is "I'm unlikeable," you can look with the teen to find evidence that this belief is not absolute. This is usually most effectively done by searching for clues during sessions and then asking the teen to find evidence as his daily homework task—he should jot down his findings, and go over them subsequently in therapy. For example:

Evidence for and against Toni's Core Belief "I'm Unlikeable"

- My cousins always want to visit me
- I have a best friend who likes me

- Taylor invited me to her party
- I was the third person to be chosen by the team leader in sport
- My little brother copies and admires me
- Daniel asked to sit next to me in class

More realistic and positive core beliefs based on the evidence accumulated can be formulated, which can do wonders for a teen's self-esteem. In this case it may be, "I am a loveable person." Turning around core beliefs—when it really rings true to the adolescent and comes from her—can be a moment of epiphany enabling a profound change in how the youngster views herself. Here's an example of a recent transformation of core beliefs a fifteen-year-old experienced in therapy: her original thought was, "I am too sensitive and get upset too easily," which was reframed as, "I have a heart of gold."

Conveying confidence, role-play

The second element of working on self-esteem and social skills is the **behavioral side**, or how to act in a way that will exude greater self-confidence and assertiveness. Here young people can learn **what conveys confidence within social communication. This** includes eye contact, a clearly audible voice, posture, and expressing your message clearly. All of these skills can be practiced with the therapist; **role-play** of different real-life situations may be the first behavioral step. You might role-play conversations with the young person in which you are a classmate, and the teen has to look at you as you converse. Another example may be a teen who cannot think of what to say when he enters a room full of people, and you could think together of suitable things to say, write them down, and then practice them in a role-play. Homework is vital so that the teen will implement these skills in real situations. It is also helpful here to **consider the automatic thoughts** that may be self-defeating that the teen has associated with these situations and to work on cognitive restructuring as described above to formulate more positive (and realistic) thoughts about the daunting social situation. Then the teen must **practice thinking these new thoughts in role-plays in therapy and in the true-life situation. T**his, together with relaxation techniques, may enable the young person to approach the feared situation with greater equanimity.

13. Voice projection

Often children who have suffered from SM have difficulty projecting their voices or speaking in an audible voice. This can be practiced with the therapist, gradually increasing the volume of their voices until they are shouting at one another. Role-play of social situations can be enacted, in which the aim is that the teen speaks audibly. These role-plays can be filmed and viewed afterward so the teen becomes aware of the way he is speaking. Volume gauges on a computer, iPad, or tape recorder can show the volume at which the teen is speaking; he can learn to self-regulate the volume of his voice as he tries to raise the voice meter by speaking more loudly. You could use the app "Speak up" that is described in chapter 9. Miniature stepladders can be built in therapy for the teen to work on during the week, engaging in progressive situations in which he attempts to speak in a loud, assertive voice. Here is an example of a miniature stepladder working toward louder speech:

Brave Barbara's Talking-Loud Homework Chart

Record myself saying "hello" and "good-bye" in a loud voice, and listen to it every night	🙂
Say "hello" in a loud voice when I see my classmates in school in the morning	
Say "hello" and "good-bye" in a loud voice to my piano teacher	
Ask one question loudly (pre-prepared) to the home room teacher in class	
Ask one question loudly (pre-prepared) to the math teacher in class	

14. Parental interventions with teens

The importance of parents' and teachers' involvement
The family and educational staff should be active partners in the endeavor toward regular speech and social communication. They should be consulted with at every stage of therapy,from the initial assessment through the behavioral aims and their implementation. It is highly desirable for parents and teachers to implement their respective therapeutic interventions, thus enhancing and augmenting therapy. In this way, the selective mutism will be combated on all fronts simultaneously, with the aim being normative speech and social communication in all the settings of the young person's life.

Much that is written in the Parents' and Teacher's Manuals for younger children is appropriate for older children too. It is most important that parents and teachers play their part in ensuring that the therapy has as much impact on the child's daily life as possible. Some interventions that were possible with younger children are less acceptable for teens, such as parents coming to school and having talking/playing sessions. Other parental interventions are tailored for older kids.

The older child may have a strong say as to how much parental intervention is acceptable; much depends on the relationship between the parents and the young person. Here follow a few parental interventions that can be helpful with older children, in addition to those described in the Parents' Manual.

Partial parental participation in therapy sessions
Despite the child's increasing maturity, it is usually necessary for parents to be present either intermittently or for a few minutes at the end of sessions that involve the therapist and the child. This will enable parents to understand what is happening in therapy, what the current aims are, and whether relaxation, cognitive restructuring, or exposure ladders are being utilized. If the parents follow the course of therapy and have a reasonable relationship with the child, they may be able to help ensure that the homework tasks are done, be it cognitive restructuring or behavioral implementation of stages on the stepladder. Often when recordings are used as part of the therapy, parents can help by purchasing the required equipment, recording or filming the child, and thereafter ensuring that the recorded material finds its way into the child's school bag.

Playdates with the youngster's friends at home
These are often an important element in the treatment of SM, as speech is easiest in the place in which the youth feels most relaxed and confident. While parents cannot always play the same active role in facilitating friends' visits with older teens as with young children, more subtle assistance may be helpful in ensuring the success of such visits: making sure that younger siblings will not interfere, having appealing games or art supplies, stocking the fridge with goodies, and so on. Parents can encourage their children in their attempts to invite friends home, perhaps helping with chauffeuring duties if necessary.

As with younger children, **parental modeling of socially outgoing behavior**, as well as using the therapeutic setting as an opportunity for working on any anxiety issues parents may have, is a powerful vicarious learning experience for their child. Therapists should keep their eyes open to assist in pointing the parents in helpful directions for working on parenting issues that may be connected to their child's well-being, such as facilitating independence, boundary setting, and parental authority issues. Sometimes movement toward better mental health of the child encourages families to tackle additional difficulties.

Other issues discussed in the Parents' Manual are relevant here, such as how to talk to children and family members about SM, normalizing it, and being optimistic about overcoming it. Lowering general home anxiety levels is helpful, and particularly lowering the anxiety connected to the teen's SM—as with younger children, if the teen feels that his parents are not overly concerned and are optimistic about his probability of recovery, that will infuse him with hope and courage.

15. Teachers' interventions with teens

The teacher is strategically situated—usually—where the symptom is most prominent and consequently can play a significant role in easing the child out of her SM. The teacher's interventions with older children are similar to those described in the Teacher's Manual, so they will just be briefly mentioned here.

The building blocks of the teacher's intervention are a personal, communicative relationship with the teen. If the teen is only able to communicate nonverbally by nodding, pointing, or other gestures, then these should be milked to the hilt. And it is often surprising to discover what an understanding and warm relationship can be developed without words!

Once this relationship has been established, perhaps with two five-minute-long personal chats a week, then the teacher too may be advised to attempt to begin a behavior modification schedule in school, constructed together with the young person, the therapist, and parents. This is fully described in the Teacher's Manual. The teacher may use the foundation, which is the already-established warm relationship, to understand the child's feelings and needs in class and thus help the child to lower anxiety levels and feel more comfortable in school. For example, he may understand that the teen is distressed sitting in his current seat and may move him next to a friend. The teacher may help normalize the SM by explaining it to the other teenagers in the class, who may be talking about it in front of and behind the youngster's back. Or he may stop ongoing bullying or enable the youth to participate in certain desirable activities or to refrain from participating in others.

There are twofold reasons for treating SM as early as possible: firstly, so that the behavior does not become too entrenched and subsequently hard to uproot, and secondly, to avoid residual damage that will have occurred during the course of the disorder to the child's self-image, confidence, and academic and social skills. The response to intervention is often more drawn out with teens, but it is still good—usually teens will respond well to a structured cognitive-behavioral intervention that encompasses the home and school, and involves parents and teachers under the baton of the therapist. Sometimes medication can be helpful for children who are resistant to therapy or when the suffering is great. Usually growth and change do occur, and the teen emerges with a new sense of competence and social engagement, greater ease in navigating her daily social encounters, and belief in her ability to overcome obstacles.

Here follow two case studies of ten- and fourteen-year-old youngsters, which illustrate the CBT treatment methods described for older children and teens with SM. Again, all names are changed; the identities of the children and their families have been blurred and made composite to protect their privacy.

Therapy with a Fourteen-Year-Old Girl in High School
****Leslie****

Background
Leslie is a tall, slim, gracious brunette, who tends to look at people using peripheral vision, giving her a shy and cautious air. She is the only child of educated, soft-spoken parents, who immigrated to England from France when Leslie was three. Leslie is in her first year of high school; she's a star academically, garnering high grades all around for schoolwork.

Leslie has never spoken in any educational framework from the time she moved to England. For the first four years of her life, her grandmother cared for her, as her mother, an engineer, worked long hours away from home. At the age of four and a half, she started kindergarten for the first time in a group of thirty-six four-year-olds, all of whom chatted away in English—she knew a fair amount of French but little English. She had not been exposed to many other children until then, usually keeping the adult company of her parents and grandparents and their friends. No one in her kindergarten recalls her having uttered a word. She was silent and introverted, seldom played with other children, and kept to herself. She was compliant, participating in the kindergarten activities to the minimal level acceptable, without ever speaking. This pattern continued in elementary school, during which she diligently completed schoolwork and excelled, keeping to herself and remaining absolutely silent throughout. Her only source of peer interaction was her best (and only) friend,Jamie, with whom she would chat on the phone and occasionally invite to her house after school. Now Leslie was embarking on her high school career, no change visible on the horizon. At home she spoke comfortably with members of her immediate family, both in English and in French, but fell silent when friends of her parents or strangers came home. She would retreat into her shell and, whenever possible, into her room, shutting the door firmly behind her.

Her parents were worried sick, having done all they had been told to do to help her but to no avail—years of psychodynamic therapy (which had been highly successful according to the psychologist's summary of the therapy!), horse riding, and most recently, over the preceding year, attending CBT therapy in an outpatient facility in a distant hospital once a week. The result of the latter was that one year after starting therapy, Leslie was whispering to the therapist; no improvement had been noted in her daily affairs.

Leslie's parents were desperate—they could see their beloved only daughter leading a lonely life with little social interaction and felt that the future portended possible deterioration into agoraphobia, depression, or at best, isolation.

Leslie: Therapy

Simultaneous medication

Leslie's situation seemed hopeless to her parents, as her behavior had become so deeply entrenched after years of not speaking to anyone in school and precious few people out of it. The time was ripe for pulling out all the stops: this included medication and CBT, along with parental and teachers' interventions.

Before meeting Leslie, I sat with her parents: thoughtful, wise people, running low on hope. They described Leslie's scholastic and social history and their failed attempts to help her to overcome SM. I explained to them the tenets of therapy, as well as their vital roles as agents of change. I recommended that they consider medication, as her age and lack of progress this far indicated that the boost given by anxiety-reducing medication could be pivotal. They were receptive, saying that they had been keen to medicate her last year but were told by the therapist not to do so. Once medication had begun, therapy was initiated.

Home-based sessions

Despite her age and intelligence, I started with home visits. It is simply so frequently the path of least resistance, which enables jump-starting therapy by attaining speech with the therapist relatively early on in the process. However, her age and the duration of her SM caused her to be resistant to talk to me, and the progress was slow but sure—instead of the usual four home sessions, by which time the child is speaking freely with the therapist at home, it was around ten sessions before we reached that point. I was introduced as someone who had come to talk to her mother, which was not complete disclosure but was not untrue.

The initial four home sessions were spent by me as a "fly on the wall" trying to be as unobtrusive as possible, to enable Leslie to habituate to my presence, and to talk freely with me in the room. These sessions were led by her parents, who engaged in diverse activities which included a verbal element with Leslie while I was sitting in the corner. They played card games and board games, baked, and did homework together.

The first time I came to her house, Leslie ran to her room when she saw me in the living room. After a few minutes, with moderate enticement by her mother, she gave into the temptation to return to the kitchen to bake cookies. To begin with she did not speak but rather whispered in her mother's ear, glancing surreptitiously in my direction. After a few minutes, she understood that I would not interact with her in any way, and the whisper in her mother's ear progressed to quiet talking. Over the next three sessions, her talking became more spontaneous, less hesitant, and louder. By the fourth home session, Leslie was talking to her mother in my presence in much the way she would when she was alone with her mother. She had habituated to my being there; I was passive and had "blended in with the furniture."

The next stage was enabling her to talk to me. In the fifth home session, after sitting in my usual corner for a few minutes, I turned my chair around so that I was facing Leslie and her mother, who were in the throes of a game of monopoly. Leslie looked up and, after some hesitation, returned to her game. After another ten minutes, I moved my chair closer still, so that I was sitting with them at the table, manifestly following the game. Again, she gave a brief hesitation and then went back to the game. In this way, by the end of the fifth session, Leslie was talking freely to her mother while I was sitting next to her at the table.

The final aim for the home sessions was that Leslie would talk freely with me. What characterized Leslie's therapy, which is common in therapy with teenagers where the SM has become deeply rooted, is that each stage had to be labored over, with little of the spontaneous progress that we tend to see with younger children. In the sixth session, I joined in a game with Leslie and her mother, and while Leslie continued to talk to her mother, she did not address me at all. In the seventh session, we played a card game that required speech with me; part of the game was that I asked her questions, and she had to answer. She complied but only offering communication with *me as was called for in the game. All the while she continued chatting freely with her mother. Then we played a game that required more speech—Taboo; she spoke freely and thoroughly enjoyed herself, taking pleasure in the difficulty that her mother had expressing herself in English and pride in her fluent, precise descriptions.*

We had gone through all but one of the requisite home-session stages: initially Leslie habituated to talking to her mother in my presence, after which she gradually became able to talk directly to me within the framework of games and also in asides and social banter as long as her mother was present. The final goal of the home sessions yet to be attained was direct and free speech with me alone, without her mother's presence in the room. This seemed to be an insurmountable challenge; we began the eighth session with Leslie chatting to me and her mom seemingly carefree and spontaneously. Yet when her mother left the room "to make a phone call," Leslie followed her and refused to stay in the room with me. Later her mother attempted to stop playing Taboo while remaining in the room, and Leslie reverted to speaking in a whisper, trimming her talk to the bare minimum. How could we progress through this impasse? We were so near and yet so gridlocked!

It was clear that the time had come to explain to Leslie the purpose of my visits in order that she work together with her parents and myself to enable her to overcome her selective mutism in the longer term and, in the immediate future, to speak to me at home without her mother's presence. This is termed psychoeducation. She had been on the receiving end of these explanations several times in the past—recently during the therapy she had had the previous year and once again before beginning to take anxiety-reducing medication one month prior to the start of our sessions. How did my explanation differ from all previous ones? This explanation followed eight therapy sessions in which Leslie experienced progress that was monumental from her perspective: she had managed to speak to me, a stranger, within her home (albeit in her mother's presence) and enjoy our relaxed and playful verbal interaction! Here was tangible proof that she had the ability to break barriers and to speak freely to strangers—to be herself beyond the confines of her family! What a liberating and empowering realization this was for Leslie; while the upcoming stages were challenging and labored, she knew she could break free from her shackles and fly! In our elucidating session, Leslie, her mother, and I considered what SM is, how it is anxiety based, and how it is often exacerbated by bilingualism. I normalized SM for her, delineating how common it is and how people usually manage to overcome SM with therapy and medication. I explained how our therapy would be made up of pigeon steps; we would plan the sessions in advance together and always decide together what the next goal would be. She was to be an active member of the therapy at all the stages from now on—planning, implementing, and reviewing every session.

Leslie was both shocked and excited by this revelation, which she had had an inkling of sometime earlier. In our subsequent first planning session, I pulled out of my hat one excellent method of breaking through quagmires: recordings. I explained how hearing one's own voice often helps a person feel able to talk. Leslie's homework following the eighth session was to record herself either using one of the apps mentioned in chapter 9 or on a plain office Dictaphone. After much deliberation Leslie chose the latter option: she elected to read a short passage and to play it to me the next session. We began the ninth session playing a game with her mother during which she spoke freely with me and after which her mother went to the side of the room to make a phone call. We then played the paragraph that Leslie had recorded the night before, after which I asked her to read the passage in vivo. She did so and in an *audible voice. Then we played several of the games we had previously enjoyed, and at one point her mother left the room. Leslie was able to continue talking reasonably freely and audibly to me. The tenth session was similar in that it began with hearing a freshly recorded passage read by Leslie, following which she read it to me live, after which we played some games. The difference was that during this whole session, she was alone with me, without the presence of her mother. The time was ripe to move the therapy to school and try to generalize her speech with staff and peers. She was daunted and excited, and I gave her an overview of how and where the sessions were likely to proceed. We then worked out together what the first school session would involve, and I gave Leslie recording homework to be used in the first school session. From now on in therapy, each session would be preplanned by the two of us, and Leslie would type the upcoming goals on my laptop— which was both a manner of planning and keeping track and an implicit agreement that Leslie felt ready to attempt the new step.*

School-based sessions with therapist
The first school-based goal was for Leslie to speak freely with me in the school therapy room. I was to come twice a week to the school; therapy would take place initially in a private room designated for small-group work. Our first session began with the two of us listening to a recording Leslie had made the previous evening at home. This was the first time in her fourteen-year-old life that her voice had been heard in school or anywhere outside the confines of her immediate family and best friend! She was radiant with excitement at this breakthrough. It looked like the transplant of the home therapy to school would be smooth—but no! We played the category game, throwing a ball to one another and saying items within one category, and she barely managed a whisper in such a tiny voice that I found myself lip reading. So I took one step back and played Chinese whispers. Leslie managed to whisper in my ear.

But when I tried several more games involving speech louder than a whisper in my ear, Leslie faltered.

We summarized together the first session: it had been a watershed in that for the first time, her voice was heard in school, and she had managed to whisper to me. We decided to invite Leslie's mother to participate in the next few school sessions, as this might be a way to make her feel more at home in school.

Leslie and I constructed a gradual-exposure schedule in which we would work our way through a continuum of speech-related tasks. The aims of successive sessions would be hearing recordings of herself, whispering in my ear, a loud whisper from a distance, one-word utterances, sentences in a regular voice, and finally spontaneous speech with me in school. In the following session with Leslie's mother and me, we began by hearing a recording of Leslie, which was accompanied by the beaming expression of breaking a barrier! We managed to get through the entire exposure stepladder (which we had built thinking it would take a few sessions to complete) with her mother in that one session. Our activities after hearing the recording were whispering letters in a game of hangman, then throwing a ball to one another and saying an item from a category, which initially was said in a loud whisper and became louder until eventually it was said in a regular voice. We then played a game of Bananagrams in which we had to say the letter we took and the word we spelled out. And by the time we played our final game, Taboo, Leslie was also engaging in some spontaneous banter with me, all in the presence of her mother.

The next stage was to fade out her mother, enabling her to speak freely with me alone in the therapy room in school. This took a number of sessions; every session began with a recording and a mini-continuum leading from whispered to regular speech within several activities. When Leslie's mother went to the side of the room, she shut down and spoke to me in a whisper, constantly looking in her mother's direction. So we decided to break down the steps to be even more gradual, and after the warm-up activities with her mother and myself in the room, her mother would leave the room. So it was over the course of several weeks that we followed this schedule: a warm-up session with recordings and ten minutes together with Leslie's mother, during which she spoke freely with me, and then working our way up the continuum of speech without her mother's presence. Initially when alone with Leslie, I would play the recording again and play games in which Leslie whispered, working on increasing the volume of the whisper until it was audible from across the room. After a number of sessions, the baseline was loud whispers. We then followed a procedure in which I left the room and Leslie repeated a word several times using the Speak Up app, which registered the volume of her speech until it was regular, audible speech. Then I entered the room, and with my back to her, she repeated the Speak Up activity until she reached regular speech volume. In the following session, we repeated this procedure, after which she did the Speak Up activity with me by her side. In the next session, the Speak Up routine was followed by a game in which Leslie had to speak directly to me in an audible voice, without her mother there—her choice was hangman. And she managed.

By this stage, we decided that Leslie could move forward without the initial ten minutes of regular speech with her mother, since she was managing to speak in a regular voice with me—albeit in a circumscribed, constricted way. The focus of the following few sessions in the school, without Leslie's mother, was broadening and naturalizing the way in which Leslie spoke to me, so that it would be free and spontaneous, as it had been in the home. We always began by listening to a recording of Leslie from her home; that set the stage for regular, audible speech. This was followed with a three-minute Speak Up session in which she regulated her voice until it was sufficiently loud. And then we played several games in which there was an incremental amount of speech required. Eventually I used social-skills cards to simulate social settings in which the requirement to talk was general, and Leslie would have to ad lib her part. For example, you come into a room in school with many kids, sit down next to one of them (me), tell her a statement about yourself or the situation, and then ask her a question. For example, "That math lesson was boring" (statement about yourself), "Did we get any homework?" (question to the friend), or "What beautiful weather. Would you like to go with me for a walk after school?" (statement and question). There are also more open-ended social skills cards that could be used, such as, "A young child is crying in the street. Go up to him, and try to make him feel better," or "Your mother is mad at you for coming home late. Explain to her why you were delayed." As we progressed, Leslie's speech became more natural, and she expressed preferences to me that facilitated jointly planning the subsequent session's activities at the end of each session. Her speech was not as free as it had been in the home; it was more cautious and quantified, but she was able to speak as required in any activity and to engage in spontaneous speech. We were ready to move on to two new stages simultaneously: The first would be to include her best friend, Jamie, in the sessions, enabling her to speak to Jamie at school. The second involved one session a week working on relaxation and cognitive-restructuring techniques. I will delineate each prong in this fork separately.

School-based sessions with therapist and one friend
Now that Leslie was speaking to me relatively freely, the aim was to generalize this speech to include a progressively broadening circle of peers. The obvious place to start was with her friend, Jamie, with whom she chatted on the phone and occasionally in her home. This

went surprisingly smoothly. I often find that when a young person manages to speak to strangers using exposure techniques, she learns that she is able, with this tool, to speak to others too and that the process of speaking to successive people within the behavior-shaping schedule becomes progressively faster and easier. We began each session with Leslie, Jamie, and me listening to recordings that they had prepared together at home, and then we went through the verbal scale from whispered to limited audible speech to whole sentences and spontaneous speech, much in the same way as she had done with me. Her new favorite game was Taboo with Jamie, in which Leslie was the champion! But instead of the ten sessions it had taken Leslie to talk to me in school, after two sessions with Jamie, Leslie had met all the goals of spontaneous speech. Again, she was more inhibited than at home but well within the definition of "normal" speech with Jamie.

School-based sessions mastering CBT techniques
Once Leslie was able to talk to me relatively freely without her mother's presence, I decided to try to utilize CBT techniques to facilitate lowering her anxiety, increasing her self-confidence, and viewing the world in a less threatening way. This would in turn affect her behavior and enable her to open up socially and verbally. So over a period of two months, one of the twice-weekly school therapy sessions was focused on CBT and relaxation tools, with the hope that this would augment the therapy and ease her social anxiety in general. These and more CBT techniques are described in chapter 8.

*She enjoyed the **relaxation** and **guided imagery**, with which we opened each of these CBT sessions. Examples of these activities can be heard on: https://www.youtube.com/watch?v=KgqL_8JTjNo.*

During our eight CBT sessions, we lit candles and dimmed lights, played relaxing music or sounds from nature (waves breaking was her favorite), and practiced various muscle tightening and relaxing exercises, followed by deep breathing and relaxation schedules, along with guided imagery. Leslie received homework to listen to the exercise we were currently using every night before sleeping. She loved the feeling of being able to relieve some of the tension that had been so pivotal in her life and to self-soothe. We then practiced a shortened relaxation schedule lasting under a minute, to be employed when attempting to talk to someone for the first time (see https://www.youtube.com/watch?v=p9jLojOTNIs). She used this technique in the school exposure sessions when talking to friends for the first time, and reported that she felt it gave her a tool to help her contend with challenging situations.

*We practiced optimistic, empowering **self-talk**. We examined how she thought about diverse social situations and how her automatic thoughts often were self-fulfilling prophecies. For example, "I am going to hate the school social activity" gave her a doomed attitude before the event had begun, whereas "I enjoy being with Jamie and Tanya—true friends," would give her a positive take on the event. Her homework was to employ these techniques in concurrent social events. She felt the powerful effect that her thoughts had on her feelings.*

*We explored the way that **thoughts affect feelings** and how many of our thoughts are not only unproductive in that they generate unpleasant feelings, but they are actually unrealistic, and that usually the more realistic thoughts are less anxiety producing. We learned together how to do **cognitive restructuring**—that is, to look at an event and our corresponding thought processes, analyzing whether our thoughts are realistic and productive; then we practiced*

266

generating realistic and calming thoughts for the same events. For more information on these techniques, see <u>chapter 8</u>.

And of course, we reviewed the desensitization schedules that were taking place once a week, enabling her to talk to friends and teachers. We considered past sessions, planned for the upcoming session, and chatted about feelings and aspirations.

School-based sessions with therapist and friends
Back to the school sessions, in which Leslie was speaking fairly naturally with Jamie. Leslie had never spoken to any friend other than Jamie. So the next huge challenge was to include other friends in our circle. I had suggested to Leslie and her mother that she should invite other friends to her home, so that she may perhaps speak to them there, and if not, at least she might feel more connected and relaxed with them. But Leslie refused to do so, and so it was we invited a friend with whom she had never spoken before, to join our therapy group. Within four sessions, Leslie was speaking to Tanya almost as freely as to Jamie —with whom she had spoken for many years! We started each session listening to a joint recording of Jamie and Leslie, followed by whispering games in the first session; in the second session, the whispering games included loud whispering that approximated regular speech; in the third session, we added a game of blind man's bluff, in which the person who is caught by the blindfolded chaser had to say a rote sentence in a strange voice and see if it was recognizable. Leslie managed to accomplish these aims, and by the fourth session, she was able to move on to playing Taboo speaking in a regular voice. We had several more sessions to increase the ease of Leslie's speech with Tanya, after which we added another girl. Leslie followed a similar series of goals; Leslie had learned that she could indeed talk to any girl in her class using an exposure stepladder program.

School-based sessions with therapist and teacher

These same strategies were now put to the test with her teacher, Paula. Leslie loved her teacher, who was accepting and warm and did not push her to speak. We decided together that Paula would visit Leslie at home and hear the recordings there for the first time and also have a whispering activity with her and her mother. Leslie was happy to receive her, and she listened to recordings together with her mother and me. We had decided to follow this with a game of Chinese whispers, but Leslie could not whisper to Paula. However, she did whisper to me and to her mother in the same game, and we whispered to her teacher. This was partial success in terms of meeting our goals for the session but total success in Leslie's feeling that she could change her long-maintained status quo.

Bolstered by this feeling of empowerment, we began mini-sessions with the teacher twice a week in school. Leslie's therapy sessions with me were as follows: the first forty-five minutes were with friends, and the following fifteen minutes with the teacher. The first few sessions were painstakingly slow, so that after four school-based sessions with the teacher, we had barely progressed along the exposure stepladder we had constructed: Leslie was managing to whisper to the teacher in a barely audible voice. Then Leslie had an epiphany: she had been feeling childish and inappropriate playing games with her teacher. Instead, she would record herself reading, play it to the teacher, and then read live, progressively larger chunks of the text that they had just heard. This really worked for her. (I learned so much from Leslie, as I do from all my other young clients, which I have since implemented with other teens.) In this way we progressed within a few sessions to Leslie reading several paragraphs to the teacher during each session, and we included questions that Leslie would ask the teacher, and she would answer questions the teacher asked her. Within a couple of months, Leslie

268

was speaking to the teacher, answering her questions, and reading to her with ease in the therapy room.

School-based sessions outside the therapy room

Leslie's progress this far was little short of spectacular; although it had taken her six months to reach this point, with little spontaneous progress beyond the painstakingly gradual desensitization steps outlined above, when we made an appraisal of her progress, we saw that she had achieved remarkable goals. After fourteen years of speaking to almost no one outside her nuclear family, she was now speaking to the many friends included in the therapy group, as well as to her teacher. Deeply entrenched behavior patterns had been successfully uprooted, and Leslie was about to embark on her next great challenge: to speak to friends and teachers outside the therapy room so that the headway made would improve her real life on a daily basis.

Leslie was painfully sensitive to people's reactions on hearing her for the first time, and that is why she had resisted carrying out homework tasks that involved speaking with her little therapy group in the yard or to the teacher at her desk. We decided that one way to combat this would be to make a PowerPoint with three friends with whom she spoke, regarding a subject relevant to what was being studied in class, and in that way the whole class would hear her voice in one fell swoop. Leslie was terrified at the thought of everyone hearing her voice but bravely decided to go through with the plan. She met her friends at home (without me) and prepared a PowerPoint presentation on healthy nutrition and lifestyle choices for teenagers. We played it in the therapy room with her friends and the teacher, and it was good. Leslie was unnerved about playing it to her class and used her relaxation skills and guided imagery, together with her self-talk and cognitive restructuring tools, to help her through the experience. She survived the PowerPoint presentation;

all her classmates heard her loud and clear, and barely a comment was made about her speech. That paved the way for speech outside the therapy room.

The following sessions transplanted the procedures we had followed in the therapy room to more public sites. Initially we sat in the yard where few people passed by, yet it was not closed off, and it was never clear if others were within hearing range of Leslie. Once she was comfortable talking in the yard, we sat with three friends in the corridor and played Taboo and other word games, and within several sessions she was comfortable speaking there too. Our next location was inside the classroom during recess. This was daunting because all her classmates were potentially in range. However, this too she managed after a few sessions, during which the verbal requirements gradually increased. While she managed to accomplish set goals for most of the sessions, there was very little spontaneous speech; mostly she spoke within the requirements of any given game or activity.

The icing on the cake came when I joined the teacher in a class activity that required limited speech with the whole class. We started with a game where all the students sat in a circle and counted in increments of fifteen, with each successive youngster counting in turn as a ball was passed around the circle. We moved on to a quiz in which the students worked in small groups; Leslie was with her friends, and she read out her group's answers to the entire class. We finished with a group activity—storytelling—with each participant contributing a word or phrase. Leslie managed beautifully and felt that this was the harbinger of her ability to talk in class on a daily basis. The teacher rose to the challenge and ensured that from then on in her lessons, Leslie would be approached by her to answer a question and whenever possible would be part of a small group in which her verbal participation was mandatory.

Other areas of work with Leslie

In addition to what has been described here, Leslie's parents were working simultaneously to help her speak to people who were not connected to school. One tool useful for her parents' friends was a talking album, described in chapter 9, which she prepared with Jamie on household pets. This could be shown and played to friends or distant relatives and allowed Leslie's voice to be heard for the first time, which made her less inhibited about talking thereafter. As she progressed in school, she felt more able to talk to salespeople and other strangers, initially with the support of her mother.

In school there was more work than that described here, which included helping her to speak to staff other than her homeroom teacher. The formula that worked for her was to play them a recording of her reading at home, after which she would read a short passage herself. The next stage would be reading followed by reciprocal questions. This was followed up by the staff member asking her a question in class (not in front of the whole class; the teacher approached her personally).

Leslie remained shy and cautious by nature, but over the period of one year, with medication and a finely tuned therapy program involving Leslie and her therapist, teacher, and parents, she tackled and overcame her selective mutism. She altered the course of her life, opening social and academic options, and most importantly granting her the feeling of competence and normalcy. During our year of therapy, she did not engage in much spontaneous talk beyond her three best friends, but over the years since then, her mother reports continued growth and social openness. She is due to complete high school next year and is considering diverse options for continued studies or work, most of which would have been unthinkable had she remained in the grip of selective mutism.

Therapy with a Ten-Year-Old Boy in Fourth Grade
****Joey****

Background

Joey was tall and blond with chiseled features and a shy but mischievous grin. He was the second oldest of four boys, son of devoted and successful parents—his father worked in high tech, and his mother was a part time librarian—who always made it home on time to put a hot lunch on the table when her boys returned home after school. Joey was smart and funny with a sharp sense of humor; he loved science and technology but hated school.

Joey had never spoken in school or kindergarten and had developed a de facto way of functioning: he went unwillingly to school most mornings, arriving late as a rule and frequently being absent. Once there, he spoke to no one—neither children nor staff—but communicated with them through gestures: yes, no, and pointing. His abstention from talking had generalized into a general disengagement from school activities and learning. As class began, he halfheartedly took his books from his locker, plonked them on his desk, and opened to a random page.

Because of his selective mutism, his teachers accepted this lack of involvement and compliance with study requirements and tolerated his semi-attendance and lack of schoolwork. They neither chastised him nor attempted to help, and so Joey went through his school day in a twilight zone—almost invisible to staff and peers. He rarely played with friends and mostly sat at his desk alone or wandered around the school during recess. The exception was table tennis— he was an outstanding player, and when it was his class's turn to play during recess, he would rush to the tables and wait for his turn to demolish some unsuspecting victim!

At home, he was a totally different child—joking and fighting with his brothers, riding his bike, playing on the computer, chatting with his mother, and helping his grandfather with building projects in the garage. At home, he had a short fuse—he was extremely sensitive and easily insulted and frustrated. Only during long summer vacations, he relaxed into a more contented and less volatile mood, which evaporated as the first of September approached.

Joey was anxious at home too—he was scared when his parents went out and would not sleep alone in a bedroom. With his extended family—grandparents, aunts, and cousins—he was talkative and social, yet he was silent when strangers came to visit.

His parents were caring and concerned yet unaware that Joey needed help—the school seemed to accept his level of functioning, and at home he usually talked. But when he started fourth grade, the school held a meeting about him and suggested to his parents that he be placed in special education, mainly because they felt that he had irremediably fallen behind in his studies. At this point, Joey's parents sprang into action, researched and read, and eventually were referred to me.

I attended a school meeting in which Joey's teacher was very interested in learning about SM and taking an active part in the therapy, while the principle felt that it was too late for him to overcome SM in this school, but they would allow this attempt to help him. If unsuccessful, Joey would have to move on to a small special-education framework.

Joey: Therapy

Home-based sessions

Despite Joey's age and cognitive level, I preferred to begin therapy in a totally behavioral way, not announcing myself to be a therapist but rather to naturally build a communicative relationship with him in his home; once he would begin talking to me, I would explain the process to him and move over to a more cognitive-behavioral track. This is because children with SM are often very resistant to speaking to new people, and many parents ha ve reported to me that they took their child to a therapist for months or years, by the end of which the child was barely whispering to the therapist. There is great value in taking a behavioral track initially, which will enable the child to speak to the therapist, usually after a few sessions, in the place in which the child expresses himself most freely—generally in his home. Once he is talking freely to the therapist, the sessions can be moved to his school or kindergarten.

I met with Joey's parents and outlined the probable therapy schedule, including home and school sessions, and they understood that the home sessions were designed to enable Joey to speak to me. They would have to be the ones leading the home sessions so that I could start off inconspicuously and gradually make my presence felt.

Altogether, it took six home sessions for Joey to talk comfortably to me. The first session I stayed in the shadows, sitting with my back to him, with no eye contact or speech. He got used to speaking in my presence, and in the second session I was slightly more noticeable, although I didn't talk to him. I watched the game he was playing with his brother, while chatting minimally with his mother. By the third session I joined in a game that he was playing with his brother, and in the fourth session I was playing alone with him. He enjoyed playing with me; he talked as much as was required by the game but did not say much beyond what was required. It took another two sessions for more spontaneous speech to emerge. We rode bikes *together and baked cookies with his mother, by which time he had become chatty and quite open. It was now time to explain to him who I was. I told him that I met with many children at various schools, and from now on I would be coming to school to play with him there. I did not tell him yet that my aim was to help him to speak, because I wanted him to speak freely to me in the school setting before I filled him in on my purpose, which would indeed prove to be very anxiety provoking.*

School-based sessions with therapist

I had found in Joey's teacher, Alan, a true collaborator in the attempt to help Joey to overcome SM—he saw the sparks of intelligence and sociability in Joey and was keen to be a partner in this therapeutic alliance. He couldn't wait to implement interventions in the classroom; we met for a few minutes once a week after my sessions with Joey to think how he could help him speak and be a part of the learning environment. His interventions were immediately effective. He held daily short chats with Joey in which he built up a warm, trusting, and communicative relationship—Joey answered with gestures and pointing, as well as smiles and frowns, and this affected Joey in two main ways. Firstly, he realized his teacher cared—if he felt mistreated by a child or was excited about a project, Alan was interested in him and eager to help him. Joey's invisibility cloak was being lifted. Secondly, his greater engagement with his teacher meant a greater obligation to school—to schoolwork, arriving on time, and being part of the class. Alan's commitment to the cause made my work pleasant. I could come regularly, I had a suitable room available, and I could always take Joey out of class for his sessions, as well as other children when the time came.

The initial school-based sessions with Joey were very structured and were aimed at replicating the warm talking relationship we had established at home in the school therapy room. We started by listening to jokes Joey had recorded at home with me, continued by playing hot or cold, taking turns to hide a candy and guiding one another to the place it was hidden by chanting "hot" or "cold." We played card, board, and ball games in which some speech was required. It took a good few sessions before he talked with me reliably, and we failed to replicate the level of spontaneous speech previously achieved at home. After consulting with his parents, I decided to invite his brother, Johnny, to join in the sessions, thinking that this may facilitate spontaneous speech with him, which could generalize to me. It worked perfectly, as Johnny was thrilled to be taken out of class to play games, and much fun was had by them both. As I was part of the games, I was included in the discussions and banter. After three sessions with Johnny, Joey was talking to me freely, both initiating and answering without hesitation.

Now it was time to include some friends in the sessions. Joey's mother had been working hard to persuade Joey to invite friends home, but Joey would only agree to have Tom come to a playdate. I had explained to Joey's mother how to facilitate speech during the playdates, playing with apps and games that require some level of speech. Gradually Joey spoke to Tom at home quite freely.

School-based sessions with therapist and friend
Once Joey was speaking to Tom at his house, I included him in the sessions and tried to ease Joey into speech with him, but to no avail —Joey refused to show him the Puppet Pals we had recorded and would neither play Chinese whispers with him nor hot or cold. He simply could not do it. This was a clear sign for me that the time had come to explain to Joey the aim of the sessions and build a structured intervention with him in which we would plan a stepladder of tasks leading to speech to be implemented with each new person whom we were to include in the sessions. In this way, Joey's intervention was different from that of Rona;hers was mainly

behavioral—it consisted of games, and she was not privy to the explanations and planning of the sessions. Rona was led by the hand through the stages that took her to speech. Because of Joey's more advanced age and understanding, he would, at this point, become my partner in planning and evaluating the steps and assume some of the responsibility for carrying them out.

Although it was clear to me that this more cognitive track was necessary for progress to continue, the following session was heartbreaking. Joey skipped happily into the school therapy room and chatted with me about a new building project he was working on with his grandfather—a tree house! Such excitement and happiness! And then his mood changed radically as I rationalized to him our change of track, explained to him what SM was and how together we could overcome it, how I have helped other children, and how I was sure that together we would beat this too. It was all very positive and upbeat, but as Joey sat opposite me in rapt attention, silent tears ran down his face. Occasionally he said, "I know" or nodded his head in agreement—he wanted to continue therapy, but floating the bare facts of his SM and how we could overcome it to the surface of his awareness was unsettling. We constructed our first stepladder of tasks that same session, which became a double session, because I wanted him to see in black and white how we would build small steps to conquer SM. His first stepladder was "Talking to Tom with Ruth in the therapy room at school." It consisted of ten steps that would take him from playing a prerecorded Puppet Pals that he had made with Tom at home, through whispered speech, on to a loud whisper standing at some distance from Tom while playing hangman, and answering twenty questions out loud to Tom when he was outside the room and could hear through a closed door. Finally the last step of this ladder was one-word answers while playing twenty questions when he would be inside the same room as Tom. He was keen to write out the steps himself on my laptop, *and each rung was negotiated with suggestions from me and counter-suggestions from Joey until each stage was crystallized. We also negotiated what his prize would be on completing the stepladder: he would get a candy after each session and binoculars after the whole stepladder was completed.*

It was clear to Joey that we would review each step after he had attempted it, and whatever proved to be too hard would be further dissected into smaller, more manageable steps. By the time Joey left the session, he was hopeful and totally exhausted, and I arranged with him that I would come the following day to begin attempting the first step so that he would not be in suspense for too long as to whether he would manage to put these steps into practice.

The next session began with a short relaxation breathing exercise, which Joey liked, and I gave him an MP3 with some longer relaxation exercises to practice with his parents before going to sleep at night. Then we slipped into a format that would stay with us for the following few months, until Joey would be talking to his whole class and his teacher. Each session began with chatting about his life and feelings, a nonstop train of thoughts. He needed and loved to be heard and understood. After this, we would look at the stepladder and think how the previous step had gone and consider if he was ready for the next step. Sometimes he would feel comfortable with the upcoming step, and sometimes we would practice it together, including a short relaxation before Joey had to speak. About half an hour into the session, I would call the child whom we were including—in this case Tom—and we would put into practice the step that we had planned. Today the aim was to play to Tom the Puppet Pals show, which Joey did unhesitatingly, and all of us listened and laughed. We repeated it a couple of times and then played a game together that did not require speech. Tom and Joey both received a candy at the end and left happily to recess. I then sat for about ten minutes with Alan, his teacher, to review the past week's intervention that he had done and to plan for the forthcoming week.

Something wondrous happened with Joey as we worked on successive exposure stepladders. Once Joey agreed to and wrote down a step on my laptop, it somehow entered his consciousness that he had thought it through, agreed to it, written it down, and that consequently, he could do it! This process prepared and empowered Joey to carry out the planned steps. I loved seeing him tap the keys of my laptop because I knew that as he typed the step, it was going to jump out of the computer screen and translate itself into deeds.

Joey learned that through these gradual steps, he could speak to friends, and through the laborious process of building the stepladders, inviting one friend after another, he began speaking in the therapy room to ten friends. The stepladders became shorter as he felt more confident and competent.

It was almost the end of the school year, and in order to generalize his speech so that the entire class would hear him speak inside the classroom, Joey and three friends with whom he was by now speaking freely made a movie together. It was based on a fable with witches and wizards, we practiced it, and finally I filmed the boys performing the funny tale. We used a green screen and added special effects so that it looked like it was taking place in a castle and a haunted forest. It was heavily edited to increase the volume of Joey's voice, who spoke softly during the filming. On the last Sunday of the school year, we screened the movie to the class, who were most taken by the special effects and, along the way, heard Joey speak loud and clear for the first time in four years!

School-based sessions with therapist and teacher

Alan, Joey's teacher, was involved in the therapy from the word go—he spent a few minutes most days building a warm, communicative relationship with Joey, using gestures and facial expressions, and they had become very close. He had visited Joey at home, heard his recordings on a talking album, and played football with him. Toward the end of the year, Joey agreed to bring in a recording of him reading at home three times a week, and Alan heard the recording in a corner of the class. This was groundwork toward speech, but there was no breakthrough of direct speech. So at the start of fifth grade, I sat with Joey and built with him a stepladder leading to speech with his teacher.

I had upped the frequency of my sessions with him to twice weekly, and this is what the sessions looked like: initially chatting and touching base, followed by a review of the two stepladders that were simultaneously being implemented—one with peers and one with the teacher—relaxation, and practicing the current task. Then began the implementation of the exposure ladders—first inviting a group of friends to the session for twenty minutes to attempt to achieve the goal set in the friends' stepladder, and then ten minutes with Alan to implement the current step with the teacher. It sounded complicated, but in reality it flowed comfortably, and progress was rapid.

The stepladder with Alan went from listening to recordings, to playing whispering games, to playing one-word games when we were all blindfolded, to playing one-word games without blindfolds, and then moving on to games that required sentences or more. The steps Joey agreed to were small, but he consistently managed the step that had been decided on and was accumulating a nice stash of prizes and an even nicer stash of self-confidence. He had a beautiful relationship with Alan with reciprocal warmth and respect, and both left the ten-minute sessions beaming. After a couple of months, Joey was talking comfortably with Alan in the therapy room but was notable to do so in the class, so that was our final challenge: helping Joey to talk to friends and teachers outside the therapy room and inside the classroom.

School-based sessions with therapist, teacher, and friends in the classroom

Up until this point, Joey was resistant to homework talking tasks involving talking to friends outside the therapy room when I wasn't with him, and our attempts were abject failures—he lost the homework chart, or he simply couldn't do it. Joey's SM was so entrenched that he needed to be taken by the hand through each and every step—no shortcuts or parallel progress!

His parents had been inviting friends home frequently, and by now he was speaking freely with them there. Our final set of stepladders was talking to friends and teachers in the classroom. Our sessions now looked like this:just the two of us for the first twenty minutes in the therapy room to chat, review past steps, and plan upcoming steps, followed by about ten minutes of relaxation and practicing the task at hand. Then we moved on to the classroom for about twenty minutes to interact with the children according to the current step on the exposure ladder with peers, and at the end, we spent ten minutes with the teacher to implement the latest step on the stepladder of tasks with him.

The implementation of the steps took place in the classroom during recess, sitting in a corner with Joey and two friends of his choice. We utilized recordings, played iPad games that required speech including Talking Tom, and enjoyed games requiring speech— initially minimal and later building up to high-speech requisites, such as Taboo, Guess Who, and Puppet Pals. At the end of each session Alan joined us, and we played games requiring speech with him.

Joey complied with all the steps, and after a couple of months, he was talking quite freely to the group in the corner of the classroom as well as to his teacher. We moved the location of the activities to his desk in the classroom and continued to play in recess sitting around his desk. Finally our small group sat around his desk during lesson time and played games requiring speech. The composition of the group changed so that eventually most of the children in the class had been part of the therapy group. (We always asked permission from their parents before including children.)

Finally Joey agreed to talking tasks to enable him to speak to other children when I was not with him. We started by constructing a chart in which he had to speak to his neighbor at least once a lesson, after which the task was to speak to a group of boys in recess by playing a ball game and saying words according to categories.

The teacher was reporting that finally, Joey was spotted talking to friends spontaneously and not as a part of the therapy tasks. We all decided that therapy was coming to a close, as Joey was speaking to his teacher and friends, but we wanted to end with an exclamation mark—so we planned that I would lead a class in school together with Alan, playing social games that required Joey to speak in front of the class. Joey was ready for the challenge and raring to go! He believed in his ability to overcome. We sat in a circle and played a huge game of categories—throwing the ball and saying a word connected to sport. Joey's turn came, and he said "table tennis" for all to hear. Next we played group Taboo, with Joey as his team's spokesperson, and finally we played green light, red light, and when it was Joey's turn, he veritably screamed out the words! What a way to go!

Although we ceremoniously and victoriously terminated therapy, pockets of SM remained, which I left in Alan's capable hands to surmount: Joey did not speak to other teachers, but Alan felt he had learned how to build a structured stepladder, which would involve meeting for a few minutes twice a week with each successive teacher, until Joey could answer their questions and ask them basic requests. I remained in touch intermittently with Alan to guide him in the implementation of this final lap of overcoming SM. After a few months, Joey's longstanding SM had been relegated to memory, and Joey was now a somewhat shy, chatty, mischievous, regular fifth grader.

Technology and Apps in the Treatment of SM

Kids love technology, and often a cool app or gadget will be so tempting that the child will overcome her SM and speak. There are many excellent apps that slot in perfectly to treatment. Two efficacious factors are the strong visual element, which is distracting and helps lower anxiety, and the recording functions intrinsic to many apps, which enable recording the child's voice and then replaying it in settings in which the child is usually silent.

There are three main ways in which electronic devices can be useful: to record the child's voice so that it can be played later in the presence of people who have not previously heard it; to encourage the child to talk; and to enable the child to control and raise the volume of his voice.

Here follows a list of some of the apps and gadgets that we have come across and used effectively in therapy. Undoubtedly this is a partial list; cyberspace is punctuated with innovative and potentially useful apps.

1. **Apps that record the child's voice, which can then be played, enabling exposure of the child's voice to people who had not**

previously heard him talk. Recording a child and playing the recording to a teacher, relative, or friend with whom the child does not speak is an excellent way of overcoming the hurdle of having others hear his voice. This takes the child a big step closer to being able to speak to others directly. Many children with SM dread the moment that they will utter their first word because they imagine that they will be derided or laughed at or that a huge fuss will be made, which will put them in the spotlight. Repeated exposure to the prerecorded voice assuages that fear, and sometimes repeated playing of recordings to a teacher will be sufficient to enable the child to begin to speak directly to his teacher. When the leap to spontaneous speech is not made, recordings can be very useful as part of a structured behavioral therapy plan.

- Puppet Pals:This is a beautifully made puppet show app that appeals to the dramatic instinct in children (and adults) and can incorporate pictures of the narrators so that it looks as if the child himself is talking in the movie. This app enables one to create puppet shows, choosing backgrounds, music, animals, vehicles, and characters. When recording the puppet show, you put your finger on the character and narrate the show; the app records your voice, and the character you are touching moves its lips in sync with your voice so that it appears to be talking in your voice.

- Toontastic: Another app for cartoon and puppet shows; it's a longer and more complex version of the above app.

- Doodlecast Junior:This app enables the child to draw a picture and narrate at the same time;the drawing and narration are simultaneously recorded and can be played back afterward. It can be done freestyle, or it offers many templates with starting questions. For example," What is your favorite food?" with a template of a plate in which you draw with your finger foods that you like, narrating all the while.

- Doodlecast Pro:This is a more advanced version of the above for older children and adults. This app enables the creation of quite sophisticated presentations, which you draw and narrate simultaneously. It includes comics that can be composed of photos or drawings, as well as tables, graphs, pictures, and movies.

- Super Duper Story Maker:This is designed for younger children, up to around eight years old. It enables you to create a storybook utilizing hundreds of drawings, on which you can draw or add photos. Then you narrate the story, which can be saved and replayed.

- Sparklefish:You create a funny story by filling in missing words that are recorded.

- Story Wheel:Spin the wheel, and tell a story based on the picture that you see. Then the next participant spins the wheel and continues the story narrating about the picture shown when the wheel stops spinning. After several turns, a story is created, with accompanying pictures, which can be replayed to others.

- Voice Recorder HD:there are myriad voice recorders in the app store; these can be used to record the child's voice, alone or with family or friends, which can then be played to a teacher or other people with whom the child does not speak.

- Office recorders: Miniature tape recorders can be used to tape and replay the child's voice. The advantage of an office recorder is that its designated use can be for therapy only, and then it is possible to send it to school regularly to be played to the teacher or peers or as part of therapy.

- Talking albums:These are photos albums in which you can stick pictures or drawings. On each page there is a button that you press to record between ten and forty seconds of narration describing the picture on that page. For example, next to a picture of a child on a horse, the child may record, "This is me in the summer riding a horse. I wasn't at all scared!" Once recorded, when you open the page, the caption is automatically played. This is great fun to prepare, and it can be re-recorded until the child is satisfied with the end result. Like office recorders, this can be used exclusively for enabling the child's voice to be heard and can be sent to school or to relatives so that they will hear the child speak for the first time.

- WhatsApp: Audio messages can be sent to teachers or family members, the messages having been recorded by the child in the low-anxiety setting of child's home. They can enable a conversation between the child and teacher wherein the child is not present when his voice is heard, but he knows that it is being heard by the teacher. As part of a structured behavior-shaping intervention, this can be used as a significant step toward direct speech with the teacher. For example, the first stage could be a week of daily WhatsApp questions sent by the teacher, which the child answers in a WhatsApp message of his own sent back to the teacher, and listened to by the teacher without the child being present. After one week of daily to and fro messages, the teacher may listen to the child's prerecorded WhatsApp responses in his presence; after that has occurred daily for a week, the teacher may ask the child to repeat a WhatsApp message they have just heard together in the teacher's ear.

2. Apps that encourage a child to speak

- Talking Tom and Talking Angela:These games may appear to be inane, but they seem to appeal to the juvenile soul! These are male and female cats, who, when spoken to, repeat what was said in a distorted voice. The child's voice must be sufficiently loud to be repeated by the cat, which is a value-added feature for the treatment of SM. Many children have been tempted by this game to utter their first word, breaking their long-held silence with peers. One can start in therapy by uttering sounds, such as "shh" or "boom" or animal noises, and gradually progress to words.

- Magic voice:This is designed for preschool children. Here animations are activated by the child's voice, with ascending levels of difficulty that correspond to the length of utterance required to activate the animation. For example, in order to cause a rabbit to jump out of a hat, on the easy level, one word must be spoken, such as "rabbit" or "jump."On the harder levels, a few words are required to get the rabbit to appear.

- Cinevox:This psychedelic app is for older children. Here voice or sound activates a selection of designs. These can stand alone or be a frame around an image of your face.

- Garage Band:This is one of the classic apps,on which you can play many instruments, as well as record your voice. It requires some (minimal) musical understanding to work. Teens who love music will probably love this app.

- Free Candle or Blow Balloon Pop: For a child who is having difficulty emitting sounds from his mouth, these are apps that require blowing to put out a candle or to blow up a balloon.

- Dubsmash:This app films the child dubbing famous or funny phrases. Users can choose an audio recording or sound bite from movies, shows, or music, and film a video of themselves dubbing over that piece of audio. It is a self-modeling exercise—the child appears to be speaking although it is not his voice that is heard.

3. **Apps that encourage the child to speak louder:**There are several apps that give children a visual indication of how loudly they are speaking; children with SM often think they are speaking louder than they are, and this visual element can help them learn both to project their voices and give them an objective gauge of how loudly they are talking.

   - Speak up: Here, a selection of animations are voice activated, and the extent of their activation depends on the volume of the child's voice. For example, a tiny star initially appears in the center of the screen, and as you speak more loudly, it grows until it fills the entire screen.

Appendix 1

Speaking Checklist: Where and to Whom the Child Speaks

Key: F=freely, M=minimally, W=whispering

Location: To Whom:	Unfamiliar place	Friend's or relative's house	School inside public areas	School classroom	School yard	Park	Home	Store
Mother								
Father								
Brothers								
Sisters								
Grandmother								
Grandfather								
Uncles								
Aunts								
Cousins								
Child's teacher								
Other teachers								

Family friends: adults								
Family friends: children								
Neighbors: adults								
Neighbors: children								
School friends								
Strangers: children								
Strangers: adults								
Store assistants								
Doctor								

Appendix 2

Games and Activities Conducive to Speech

Physical Movement Games

- Blind man's bluff
- Red light, green light
- Duck, duck, goose
- Color tag

Ball Games

- Throwing a ball and counting forward or backward or saying words according to categories.
- Maintaining huge confetti balloons afloat; each time a participant pushes the balloon, a word must be spoken.
- Throwing a ball between participants; each thrower says the name of the person to whom the recipient must throw the ball.
- Throwing a ball between participants; each thrower says the name of the person from whom he received the ball.
- Throwing a ball between participants; each thrower says a sentence or word in a story told sequentially by participants.

Board Games

- Guess Who
- Perpetual motion
- Kids on Stage
- Pictureka
- Secret Square
- Headbanz
- Taboo
- Bingo
- Lotto
- Submarines
- Story squares

Word Games, Card Games, and Quizzes

- I spy
- Twenty questions
- True or false
- Hangman
- Hot or cold
- Chinese whispers
- Country, city
- Sequentially making up a story by taking turns, adding one word or one sentence at a time
- "I went to the store and bought..." with therapist and child adding bought items in turn and recalling previously mentioned items
- What's missing: look at tray with several objects, then remove one object, and the player guesses what's missing
- Telling jokes
- Story sequence cards
- "What's wrong" cards
- Rat-a-Tat Cat
- Cheat
- Go fish

Acting Games

- Charades
- Puppet shows
- Shows
- Making a movie, and showing it to others

Other Activities That Can Include Chatting and/or Simultaneous Word Games

- Cooking or baking
- Arts and crafts
- Sports
- Dancing
- Competitions

Miscellaneous

Sticker games

Requires a small notebook and stickers. Each page in the notebook is divided into a number of squares, and the therapist displays on the table before her an array of tempting stickers, such as animals, flowers, cars, and so on. The child must ask which sticker he would like. For example, "Please, can I have the red flower or big elephant or yellow smiley..." after which he gets that sticker and adheres it onto one of the squares on his paper. Once all the squares on one page have stickers, he gets a small candy or prize.

Appendix 3

SM Handout for Teachers

Selective mutism is a childhood anxiety disorder in which children cannot speak to certain people or in specific places. Usually, children are most comfortable speaking at home to their nuclear family and find it hardest to speak in school or kindergarten. Each child has his unique pattern of with whom he speaks and where; for example, some children will speak only to children and not to staff, others may find it easier to speak to adults than to children, and some may not utter a word to anyone at all in school.

In severe cases, children may refrain from participating in school activities even when no speech is required; these children may have frozen expressions; barely smile, nod, or use gestures; and be close to invisible in school. Others may participate in all activities and be outgoing and social to the degree that it is hard to notice that they do not speak.

The good news is that selective mutism usually responds well to treatment, and most children with SM will take a normal developmental track after the SM is overcome. On the other hand, children with SM suffer, as they cannot express who they truly are in school, must invest great energy in refraining from speaking, and miss out both on social and academic experience. Early intervention to circumvent both the suffering and the missed opportunities is strongly advised.

It should be noted that SM has no bearing on intelligence and social skills: most children with SM are intelligent and socially able, and for most of them, a regular school framework is appropriate, albeit with the help required to overcome their SM.

How Can I Help?

You, as a teacher, are in the eye of the storm, placed where the selective mutism is occurring, and you can do so much to help the child. Here are a few guidelines on how to help—both what you can do and what you should try to avoid doing.

Do establish a warm, supportive, communicative relationship with the child. It is possible to communicate with every child, using whatever tools she currently has in her communication repertoire: these may be gestures, nodding, smiling, pointing, and so on. In this way you can show the child that communicating with a teacher is pleasant and beneficial and that you see her and care about her. If you can, set aside a couple of minutes a few times a week to meet with her; in this time you can find out more about her, her likes and dislikes and hobbies, and see if you can help her in school. For example, you might ask if she would prefer to be sitting next to someone she likes or participate in a specific activity.

Do not ignore the child. Children with SM can become almost invisible in class; show him he is important to you. Try to see other strengths of the child, and show him you appreciate them—for example, music, drawing, kindness to others, sports, and the like. Children with SM sometimes become seen by staff as solely owning one trait: the failure to speak. Every child has a broad constellation of abilities and traits.

Do not try to force him to talk when it is clear he is currently unable to do so. Most children with SM are repeatedly put in the position in which they are required to give a verbal response, but they fail to do so, and thus they experience failure numerous times a day.

Do engage the child and milk to the hilt any communicative abilities the child currently has with you—gestures, pointing, whispering, and so on.

Do try to gradually broaden the child's communication with you. Perhaps after a couple of weeks of building a communicative relationship a few times a week, you could ask the child to whisper something to you or to send you an audio WhatsApp in answer to a question you might pose. Using recordings in a sensitive, structured way is often a manner of bringing the child's voice into the class.

Do remember that overcoming SM occurs usually as a gradual process, with small steps toward speech. It is tempting to think that after a small improvement—for example, that the child whispers to you—she will be able to speak freely very soon. In practice, SM is usually overcome with small, gradual steps.

Do not punish the child for not speaking—it is like punishing a person with broken legs for not jumping. She cannot do it at this point. Accept her, and appreciate her as she is, all the while looking for ways to increase the quality and quantity of her communication. SM is rarely oppositional behavior; it is usually the child's response to anxiety.

Do consider what could help her to feel socially more at ease: where to seat her, in which groups she might participate, and how to best highlight her abilities in these settings.

Do not make a huge commotion when you first hear him talk: children with SM are usually shy and dread being in the spotlight.

Understated praise usually works best with these children.

Do not enable the child to gradually increase his refraining from engaging in school activities. Be sure that you don't become lax on demands that he is able to meet, such as schoolwork, participation in activities that do not require speech, and social activities.

Do be in touch with his family and think together with them how to help him. Have them show you videos of the child at home in his element so that you know who he really is when not in the grip of SM.

Do consider how the child could get behavioral or cognitive behavioral therapy for SM within the school framework. If you think you may be able to carry out a stepladder exposure intervention, you could read this book to see what it involves.

Do consider, together with her parents, other issues that may be bothering the child and contributing to the maintenance of the SM. For example, many children with SM have language difficulties, and if this is the case, appropriate help outside school may make the SM easier to overcome.

Remember, you can be instrumental in helping your student overcome his SM and making his life so much better!

Made in the USA
Las Vegas, NV
29 January 2025

17212947R00175